The Hip-hop Feminism Pedagogy Reader

EDITED BY
RUTH NICOLE BROWN
& CHAMARA JEWEL KWAKYE

PETER LANG
New York • Washington, D.C./Baltimore • Bern
Frankfurt • Berlin • Brussels • Vienna • Oxford

Library of Congress Cataloging-in-Publication Data

Wish to Live: The Hip-hop Feminism Pedagogy Reader /
Edited by Ruth Nicole Brown, Chamara Jewel Kwakye.
pages cm. — (Educational Psychology: Critical Pedagogical Perspectives; Vol. 3)
Includes bibliographical references.
1. Hip-hop feminism. 2. Second-wave feminism. I. Brown, Ruth Nicole,
editor of compilation. II. Kwakye, Chamara Jewel, editor of compilation.
HQ1111.W57   305.4—dc23   2012029430
ISBN 978-1-4331-0646-0 (paperback)
ISBN 978-1-4539-0899-0 (e-book)
ISSN 1943-8109

Bibliographic information published by **Die Deutsche Nationalbibliothek**.
Die Deutsche Nationalbibliothek lists this publication in the "Deutsche
Nationalbibliografie"; detailed bibliographic data is available
on the Internet at http://dnb.d-nb.de/.

Cover design by John Jennings

The paper in this book meets the guidelines for permanence and durability
of the Committee on Production Guidelines for Book Longevity
of the Council of Library Resources.

© 2012 Peter Lang Publishing, Inc., New York
29 Broadway, 18th floor, New York, NY 10006
www.peterlang.com

All rights reserved.
Reprint or reproduction, even partially, in all forms such as microfilm,
xerography, microfiche, microcard, and offset strictly prohibited.

Printed in the United States of America

WISH to LIVE

Educational
PSYCHOLOGY

Critical Pedagogical Perspectives

Greg S. Goodman, *General Editor*

Vol. 3

_____

The Educational Psychology series is part of the Peter Lang Education list.
Every volume is peer reviewed and meets
the highest quality standards for content and production.

_____

PETER LANG
New York • Washington, D.C./Baltimore • Bern
Frankfurt • Berlin • Brussels • Vienna • Oxford

For Kwesi Adu M'fum

For Lawrence and Evelyn Brown

I wish to live because life has within it that which is good, that which is beautiful, and that which is love. Therefore, since I have known all of these things, I have found them to be reason enough and—I wish to live. Moreover, because this is so, I wish for others to live for generations and generations and generations and generations.

— Lorraine Hansberry
To Be Young, Gifted, and Black (1969)

CONTENTS

PART 4
People: "We can never forget to love."   173

PART 5
SOLHOT: "I wish to live."   207

Contributors   267

FOREWORD

Truly Professin' Hip-Hop and Black Girl 'Hood.

Selling hip-hop studies and gender analysis in a world where girls' and women's bodies do the grunt work on the video screen is a tough product to pitch to students and academics alike. That is, until I throw new jack pedagogy at 'em.

And it is so completely divine that I am not alone. My fellow sista professors Ruth Nicole Brown and Chamara Jewel Kwakye have delivered their contribution with ***Wish to Live: The Hip-Hop Feminist Pedagogy Reader*** exemplifying the diverse, inter-generational, and multi-dimensional pedagogies that are helping to reshape the ecology of academic spaces. It feeds those of us for whom the Western-dominant paradigm of study and thought is often a denial of who we are and who we all can be—women and men. This book is an offering for creating a space of belonging. To paraphrase Paulo Freire, we are not "marginals" living outside of hip-hop. We have always been inside. Inside the structure that made us "beings for others" in hip-hop (*Pedagogy of the Oppressed*, p. 74).

I remember the first weeks I taught my own course on hip-hop as music in 1996. My debut as a teaching-scholar was at the University of Virginia which was one of the top public universities in the country where 12% of the student population was of African descent. UVa graduated black students at nearly the same rate as white students over a five-year period. That golden era is gone at most public universities around the country unless we're talking about HBCs and HBCUs. I wrote a poem for my first day of class planting my pedagogical intentions firmly in the environment of Thomas Jefferson's central campus often referred to as "The Lawn":

> *Hip-hop's come to The Lawn, kn'a mean??!?*
> *No more margins to front or center*
> *Black Popular Music is the name of this record.*
> *I'm Professor G, with my P-H-and-D, tryin' to tell you that this…ain't…no…*
>   *joke!*
> *I'm truly professin' hip-hop.*
> *I'm truly a professor of hip-hop*
>   *(that don't mean I know e'ry'thang, jus' means I got a jawb— to represent.)*

I've always loved double entendres and the power of signifyin' in African American orature. When hired, my senior colleagues allowed me to teach whatever I liked at T.J.'s university (I often referred to him off-record as my "Uncle Tom" with a hat-tip to Sallie Hemmings).

Once given permission to *do the thing my own way,* I knew I had a *job* to represent not only hip-hop as music and as a complex culture with an intergenerational, multi-gendered focus where students and teachers were authorities. I also knew I had a job to *represent* black musical culture <u>well</u> (no foolishness from me or students). For my sake, and the sake of the students and others who might follow my pedagogical footprints, I needed to represent myself as a scholar and a hip-hop head and represent ethnographic truths of people making meaning of their lives through and from music and dance past and present. I needed to create an environment where intergenerational, gendered, oral and kinetic perspectives of the songs and dances of African Americans and those who identify with the music of black folk in order to lead students to a richer appreciation of the social positionalities and inequalities surrounding and within hip-hop. The diverse hip-hop elements of rapping, grafitti writing, breaking, and cutting were a given for many students even back then. But the forgotten double-dutch girls of early hip-hop tours along with other embodied "musicking" (the act of taking part in music practice or performance) like cheers, handclapping game-songs, and the dances through which many of us learned the vernacular identity of musical blackness in urban and rural soundscapes were not. All of this would become a new and divergent academic requirement and outcome for hip-hop as music. This was something that could not be represented merely by reading the right books and formal exams with a sidebar of dialogue.

Girls were to be written back into, taken up from their down-low status. Their stories would help us dance ourselves back into the grooves of the hip-hop record and memory. The eighty black students out of ninety from that first semester of my professing were truly my co-collaborators.

One of the first orders of business was an in-class dance party. I had to have a Soul Train line, of course. I'd tell frightened white, male and non-black students who resisted this piece of intellectual learning, "You must go down the life-giving womb of the Soul Train line! Do what you can, but you must go down!" Those early days of teaching hip-hop as a former women's studies T.A. and also a former classically trained vocalist searching for her diverse chops in musical academic pursuits beyond black art songs by William Grant Still or Margaret Bonds would be the foundation and the departure point of my new jack pedagogy.

The emerging adults—the students—who stepped into the innovative environment of my fall 1996 classroom were mourning Tupac, lauding Wu-Tang, arguing who was better—Nas or Biggie, and they were leaning toward the cusp of what some later referred to as impending death of hip-hop. None of that was "no joke" for me. But I must confess, in hindsight, I was learning on the job, which is why my style of teaching was so…hip-hop. It was codified yet. It wasn't known and familiar to them or me. And most of all, it wasn't some hyper-masculine or sanitized Western-packaged classroom act.

I was interested in being a mediator of the past that young adults often cannot see through sampling. I saw how easily many of them took the aesthetic for granted which had roots in the blues, field hollers and black girls' musical game-songs. They rarely, like good DJs and dancers, mined their sources so they might hide them from others' view. Their ignorance often masked the power of hip-hop's virtuosity in word and sonic force. That needed to be tested on midterm and it needed to be live, fun, joyous.

At the same time I didn't want steal the wheels of their generational thunder. As a trained ethnomusicologist who grew up learning to do music with dance not without it, I was invested in empowering students to know hip-hop's history *and* its misogyny from a black and female perspective. I thought all those young adults who came from France and Turkey as well as D.C. (my home), and Brooklyn, I thought they all should be allowed to speak their multiple and divergent truths in class dedicated to a genre most of them were born into as well as learning from a black, female ethnomusicologist about its African and Latino antecedents and ancestors including the 12 bar blues, the clavé, and jazz scatting. You need both—a background check and a mic check—to make a African diasporic and gendered hip-hop studies work in my gradebook. To highlight these powers, I would, for example, introduce my students to the blues and folk like Bessie Smith singing the last verse of "Mama's Got the Blues."

Here in her 1923 verbal articulation of a feminine gendered positionality of power in the industry of recorded music, with her signified rhymed assonance where identifications with black localities and the implications of the policies of

Segregation still resound from a world of the first "race" records lead by women. This is an similarly gendered sphere like hip-hop where women thrived. I doubt anyone would call Smith's songs and the music of other blues empresses "the hyper-femininization of the city blues" because that's way too threatening in hindsight. Hell, it might even cast a conspicuous shadow silhouetting the contemporary gender socialization of hip-hop and offer new readings of artists from Millie Jackson to Prince or Lil' Kim to Lady Gaga and Beyonce.

Bessie sang:

I got a man in Atlanta
Two in Alabama
Three in Chattanigga
Four in Cincinatta
Five in Mississippi
Six in Memphis, Tennessee.
If you don't like my peaches,
Please let me orchard be.

Just an aside (that isn't so tangential): If you Google this song you'll find that the southern cities whose names are transformed to signify negro linguistics are sanitized, devoid of any signs of the situational social identity politics of a black woman singing about her "niggas," aka her lovers, in various cities. "Chattanigga" is just plain Chattanooga, Tennessee. And what gets lost is the setting up of the final metaphor telling men to stop beating around a woman's bush, if you can't take her own created notions of freedom, her own possibilities of movement and release.

Growing up as a book-smart, big-foreheaded, pretty-for-a-dark-girl, lonely-only child, who joined the black student alliance in high school because it seemed a good thing to do since slavery was rarely talked about in my history book; who noticed the segregated tracking of black and white 8th graders in my public school and got sent to the principal's office for it; whose mama's live-in boyfriend was a upscale drug-dealer in a little black neighborhood over 100 years old in Rockville, Maryland—growing up I never imagined, not even once, of becoming a teacher, and even less so a professor of hip-hop, gender or even black music. I wanted to be Chaka Khan or Minnie Riperton, no joke. While I might be my own Chaka or Minnie now, being a professor of hip-hop feminism wasn't an option when I graduated high school in 1979 choosing to major in classical voice at the local community college. We new jack (or Jalene) scholars are providing a new track of learning.

Ruth Nicole's invitation to write a prelude to launch, or kiss-bless-and-send-off, this remarkable collection of essays, poetry, and songs of the head and heart dancing as a text, revealed the divine pleasure of many hip-hop feminists like me. Writing this was a joy and an honor.

Sometimes I don't like to call myself a "feminist." I know you might have heard that one before, but I have a little different take on it, or maybe not. You be the judge.

I prefer to call myself a hip-hop scholar with a specialty in gender studies, or I tell folk I specialize in teaching hip-hop from the perspective of race, gender and the body. As Audre Lorde once wrote, "I am not one piece of myself. I cannot simply be a Black person and not be a woman, too, nor can I be a woman and not a lesbian, too" (*Sister Outsider*, 1984, p. 262). Similar to her sharp POV, I despise separating the discussion of women from men or music and sensuality. Because listeners and readers still slip way too easily into thinking "feminism" means women only or music means sound not gendered interactions. Thus, I prefer to speak of working in gender studies.

With that in mind, I invite you to consider listening and reading these pages from "what if." What if this were written by the women in my discipline? What if these words or this poem were spoken by the men I know in hip-hop? What if our sons got this? Our mothers taught this?

What I am trying to say here is better exemplified in the design of an assignment I give my students on gender and hip-hop. I assign 15 off-the-beaten-path tracks primarily recorded by underground artists like Jean Grae and Bahamadia. All are women except two: Gil Scott Heron's "The Revolution Will Not Be Televised" is included for comparison to Sarah Jones' banned, fined, and politicized rap remix "Your Revolution (Will Not Happen Between These Thighs)" with DJ Vadim. The other is Talib Kweli's "Four Women" featuring singer-songwriter Imani Uzuri, added to compare and contrast from a gender POV with Nina Simone's original classic text offering a defiant display of colored womanhood like only a High Priestess of Soul can. Students of diverse backgrounds are rarely exposed to such a gendered array from hip-hop on the radio.

While women often need to create spaces, often exclusive environments, where our bodies and minds can be seen and heard without the demoralizing masculinized public gaze of black or white male producers or the un-productive Western processes of academic discourse, I invite readers to explore more than whatever your past thinking and reading allows you to think black women's voices read like. Try on listening as if the words on the page where a dominant voice, dare I say, like a male voice with a big difference. Controversial as that may sound, it is the discourse of learning to "read" texts, read the discourse within it, that I like to play with in my style of hip-hop feminism.

In completing this assignment, one of my black male students, born and raised in the South Bronx in the mid-80s, discovered something indispensable that was then shared with the rest of the class. After learning to transcribe the rap lyrics of Jean Grae through rogue repetitive rewinding rather than the rote cut-and-paste from a Google search, and then wrapping up the assignment, each student was asked to perform the text for at least three people, without acknowledging Grae's female gender identity. After each remixed performance of self and source into their slice of life, each student was to ask the listener to guess the sex of the original rap artist and to share their reactions. In the end, they were to analyze their own experience in the process.

This young brother came back to class and ultimately proclaimed: "As a guy, I've never had to say 'pussy' so many times [from whole of the 15 tracks]. I did Jean Grae's "Block Party." And I wasn't just in her shoes. I was in her underwear." This track never says "pussy," so his response is pretty profound. In response, I recall retorting, "Now you know what it's like for women to have to sing along with Wu-Tang or Biggie all the time." He had never thought of that. Experience is not analysis.

Nothing can replace standing in another's underwear. A critical scholar named Ranajit Guha used to say to his graduate students, "Theory is like underwear. Everyone should have some but it doesn't need to show." I argue that relative to gender and feminist studies in hip-hop, we gotta start showing the under garments of gender exploitation and socialization for both women and men, girls and boys or we'll never got past the institutionalized oppression of all people—female and male, black and all the others.

The struggle comes at us from all sides, too. After one of the first days of my hip-hop class at UVa. A young sister, prim and proper, stayed behind after class to offer a correction to the newbie professor I was back in '96. She wanted me to stay—black faculty are rarely at home and often move about institutions seeking a place to call their own. She thought she better point out a faux pas she thought I had made after speaking in black English for much of the first class. I remember it plain as if it were yesterday. Her hair was pressed and pulled back in a ponytail with a bow. She was caramel-complexioned and her books were tightly held in her arms in front of her body.

"Professor Gaunt? … It's syllabi. You said syllabuses."

I said something Ph.D.-brand-smart cuz I couldn't let her one-up me. "Well, if you look in the dictionary, you'll see that either is correct. One is Latinate and the other is Anglicized." I had to run to my office and check later cuz I made that –ish up really. And it's true.

"Oh." She said. I thanked her for sharing and let her leave as gracefully as I could muster having being challenged by her and many other things my first days on the job, which was a sign of *my* fears, not my humility, in hindsight. But it was all good.

My point here: by reading this collection, I invite you to embrace your fears and your humility relative to whatever you think about hip-hop feminism. From it we may discover the play that is often lost in academic discourse. The love that we hide from each other in intellectual engagement that often occurs like drive-by shootings. We may discover a corner of truth that we've never seen or witnessed from our vantage point whether we too are black and female or not.

Be open. Be curious and most of all, allow yourself to upgrade you, as Ruth Nicole and Chamara and the sisterhood known as *SolHot* says in their performative displays. (I was personally moved and delighted by one at the Black Womenhood Conference at the University of Kentucky sponsored by another sista prof, Law professor Melynda Price in March of 2012.)

Each of the contributors you encounter here is not far from what Lucille Clifton offered in one of her poems. It takes something to be a hip-hop feminist.

won't you celebrate with me
what i have shaped into
a kind of life? i had no model.
born in babylon
both nonwhite and woman
what did i see to be except myself?
i made it up
here on this bridge between
starshine and clay,
my one hand holding tight
my other hand; come celebrate
with me that everyday
something has tried to kill me
and has failed.

Hip-hop, you could stop the misogyny and exploitation…and listen… to what we women and many men desire of you. Listen to what we have given this culture. We won't ask "please" as James Baldwin reminded us in the *Fire Next Time*. We are here to teach and learn lessons. We are doing double-dutch duty, Step up. Don't wait your turn, ladies. Our time has come.

Professor G aka Kyra D. Gaunt, Ph.D.
New York, NY

ACKNOWLEDGMENTS

This book is a reminder that we are more powerful together than we are alone. Thank you to Saving Our Lives, Hear Our Truths for bringing many of us close together and forever inspired to reimagine ourselves and black girlhood anew. We must also thank Incite! Women of Color Against Violence and the Sangtin Writers for providing an inspiring model of collective activist scholarship. To each of the contributing authors, your hard work, critical analyses, and passion are much appreciated.

Thank you, Ebonie Tillmon, for providing much needed organizational skills to the project. Thank you, Dave Stovall and Antwi Akom, for your generous collegiality. To our very enthusiastic editor, Greg Goodman, we so very much appreciate you. John Jennings, thank you for the devastating artwork. Without the support of Dianne Pinderhughes, Todd Shaw, Greg Markus, Aisha Durham, Robin Hayes, Mimi Nguyen, Fiona Ngo, Tiffany Y. Davis, Regina Crider, Karen Flynn, Soo Ah Kwon, Melynda Price, Christina DeNicolo, Tricia Lin, James Anderson, and Margareth Etienne we would not be fly at all. Also, we want to thank everyone involved in Hip-Hop culture, studies, activism, and feminism.

I, Ruth Nicole Brown, want to acknowledge my family, whose love and support guide my steps. Thank you, Getu, ewadehalaheu! Maya Sanaa and Addis, I am so proud to be your mother. I am thankful for the lessons you teach me and the dance breaks you oblige. To everyone who has given SOLHOT life, I am honored and humbled.

I, Chamara Jewel Kwakye, want to especially thank my ancestors Kwesi Adu M'fum, Gertrude Pippins, and Christine Moore, for the gifts of storytelling, the practice of creating theory, and indispensable lessons on feminism. I am thankful to my sisters, Hershini Bhana Young and Lindsey Renee Bever, for being reflections of God's and the Orisha's perfect love and always reminding me to shine. Finally, I am thankful to my parents, Jeweldine Moore and Timothy Kwakye, for being unyielding in their support and love. I am because you are.

INTRODUCTION

By Ruth Nicole Brown and Chamara Jewel Kwakye

This collection of poems, essays, scholarly papers, and performances is primarily concerned with the ways Hip-Hop feminism can be of use in the reading of our everyday lives, articulating the questions we have about the world, and in listening to the narratives young people create and present to us. Hip-Hop feminism as movement work accounts both for the spectacular and the mundane. Collectives of friends, haters, crews, posses, homegirls, bffs, homies, or just a couple of people who know each other often contribute to Hip-Hop feminist thought and practice by giving weekend workshops, intentionally making time for their nieces and nephews to have those very important conversations, and publishing in independent media outlets in the neighborhood. Hip-Hop feminists write rhymes that inspire. Hip-Hop feminism occurs in underground basement spaces where childhood dance routines are created and remembered well into adulthood.

Hip-Hop feminism is the messy work of negotiating generational tensions and ideas about leadership. It is work that requires the right combination of humility and skill; the cleaning up of the room after the juke party, the taking out of the trash after the videos were discussed, debated, and remixed, and it is providing transportation to ensure everyone arrives home safely after the poem was written, recited, and the cipher dissolved. Small in scale, extralocal, a kitchen table throwback, Hip-Hop feminism lives in specificity as much as the celebrity.

This reader uncovers the challenging tasks in the everyday practice of Hip-Hop feminism.

Our Hip-Hop feminism is determined on the dance floor, constructed as we walk down streets, and designed against structures beyond our immediate control that we sometimes and somehow manage to manipulate into something poetic. We practice Hip-Hop feminism every day and every night. It permeates our speech as we quote our favorite rhyme in conversation with friends and cite our favorite artists and emcees as expert witnesses in our scholarship. Hip-Hop's coloring on life is as bold and smart as our feminist commitment to Joan Morgan's ever-inspirational shades of gray. Although our youthful energies are constructed as always in need of control like many of our loved ones locked in cages, we find in a rhythm and a rhyme another reason to live. Though they may not identify as feminists, we draw strength from the ways extra local icons, including our family members, resist systemic and structural inequalities and patriarchal illusions.

As a collection, the essays in this book remind readers that not only have women been there since Hip-Hop's beginning, in many ways we also birthed it, it came through us. Not the misogyny and capitalist greed that annihilate our spirits but the space we created for ourselves and our communities by playing games on the block, to the space we create with choreography in the name of healing like Urban Bush Women. The space we created when posing for pictures with our hands on our hips, to the space we create when behind the camera like Julie Dash (*Daughters of the Dust*, 1991), Rachel Raimist (*Nobody Knows My Name*, 1999), Dee Rees (*Pariah*, 2011), and Robin Hayes (Black and Cuba, 2012). The space created when Salt-N-Pepa asked us to be *Hot, Cool and Vicious* (1986) or demanded that we talk about sex, to the space we create when Gwendolyn Pough (*Check It While I Wreck It*, 2004)[1] asks us to intentionally think about black women, Hip-Hop, and feminism. We continue to play a vital and pivotal role in Hip-Hop's growth, development, and transformation. Our disappearance from Hip-Hop's phallocentric history is not by happenstance but by the heteropatriarchy and the heteronormativity that insidiously surround Hip-Hop and structure our society.

In *Total Chaos*, Jeff Chang (2006) wrote,

> Hip-Hop is one of the big ideas of this generation, a grand expression of our collective creative powers. But when recognized at all, the Hip-Hop arts have often been divided into subcategorical themes—"spoken word poetry," "street literature," "postmulticultural theatre," "post-Black art," "urban outsider art,"—by critics trained to classify trees while lost in the forest. (p. ix)

---

1 Each of these women artists-scholars have created more than the work pointed out here; however, we have named the works we have found most relevant and inspiring in the process of assembling this book.

This sentiment of critics lost in the forest, whether actively participating in one of the aforementioned forms or by being sideline consumers and spectators, also applies to the way women and girls are seen or not seen in Hip-Hop. We, too, are relegated to subcategories and often, when recognized at all, we are "the video model/ho," "the overtly sexy/hard female emcee in the male dominated clique," "the lone b-girl in a b-boy crew," "the background rump shaker," "the subject to be conquered in lyrics"—flat, dimensionless objects who, when believed to be out of sight and often within sight, do not exist. We do. We are here. We exist with various dimensions, live fully, and we continue to exist even when we cannot be readily seen, heard, or touched. We are permanent.

Aisha Durham believes Hip-Hop feminism is necessary and sufficient. In "Using [Living Hip-Hop] Feminism: Redefining an Answer (to) Rap," Durham (2007) wrote,

> I define Hip-Hop feminism as a socio-cultural, intellectual and political moment grounded in the situated knowledge of women of color for the post–Civil Rights generation who recognize culture as a pivotal site for political intervention to challenge, resist, and mobilize collectives to dismantle systems of exploitation. (p. 306)

This essay, as well as the others included in Home Girls Make Some Noise! Hip-Hop Feminism Anthology (Pough, Richardson, Durham, & Raimist, 2007), was incredibly useful and inspirational to the formation of this reader. We take seriously the authors' call to continue the conversations they initiated. By foregrounding the lived experiences and embodied knowledge of women of color who do Hip-Hop feminism, write from a regular folk position, and are growing up on the 1s and 2s of Empire, we share what we know to help make sense of our daily lives and to name the particularities of our struggle and joy. This reader is fundamentally concerned with the ways we rely on Hip-Hop feminism in theory and in practice to build bridges with those even younger than us, for the purpose of personal and political transformation. It is equally informed by what young people know, believe, and contribute to Hip-Hop feminist theory and practice.

Highlighting a version of Hip-Hop feminism is our involvement in building communities of accountability, leading to important questions:

- In what ways do young people articulate Hip-Hop feminism that eludes current scholarly analysis?
- What is the future of Hip-Hop feminism?
- How is Hip-Hop feminism in conversation with previous articulations of black feminism, transnational feminism, and womanism? How is it different from those articulations?

- How are Hip-Hop feminism and Hip-Hop feminist pedagogy useful for those most marginalized by capitalism, nation, and disability?
- What is the relevance of Hip-Hop feminist pedagogy in the context of globalization?
- What is the relationship between Hip-Hop feminism and girls and women who want no part of either a Western, Eurocentric, or colonized feminism, or a part of Hip-Hop?

This book is our public redress to that history, and more specifically our redress to pedagogy, because much like Hip-Hop, pedagogy has relegated the voices of women, particularly women of color, to be only on the receiving end of instruction. However, we teach and learn simultaneously. While we acknowledge the big ideas of Hip-Hop and the bigger movement work it takes to do Hip-Hop feminism, we also assert that the small-scale contributions of everyday women and girls is an equally valid contribution not to be overlooked. If you let it, the reader may prove cause to assemble a collective of your own and do something to improve on what we have stated. Our dream is that this book will inspire people to have the conversations that we still need to have.

Hip-Hop Feminist Pedagogy Redefined

Our use of the term *pedagogy*, in particular Hip-Hop feminist pedagogy, is directly tied to the articles presented in this reader. In general, Hip-Hop feminist pedagogy is one that: (1) appreciates creative production expressed through language, art, or activism, (2) privileges the in-betweenness of a black girl epistemology or a black feminist standpoint, (3) values and cares about the shared knowledge produced by black women's and girls' presence, (4) interrogates the limitations and possibilities of Hip-Hop, feminism, and pedagogy and is, therefore, self-adjusting, (5) stages the political through performance-based cultural criticism, (6) and is located and interpreted through the community (or communities) in which it is immersed (Brown, 2008; Durham, 2011). We use the word *pedagogy* because the chapters in this book are offerings on how to teach and create a more inclusive community. Beyond K–12 and higher education classrooms, we want this reader to be of practical use in diverse learning and teaching spaces. This book is for those who want to have multi- and intergenerational conversations about music, love, and life. This book and its authors see pedagogy as practical wisdom about what we do and how we can continue to make our communities—including the classroom—life-sustaining, mind-expanding, and places of mutual liberation (hooks, 2003).

Wish to Live: The Hip-Hop Feminist Pedagogy Reader offers a diverse and varied approach to the pedagogical implications of Hip-Hop feminism. Each contribution offers a unique perspective for how Hip-Hop feminism may be productively engaged in teaching, learning, and organizing. With this in mind we have included a range of writing styles with the hope that the diversity of form will inspire a varied readership. We also intend for this collection of scholarship to contribute to Hip-Hop feminist studies. Our hope is that the ideas presented in this collection will be considered in ongoing discussions and tensions within the field and incite new ideas, topics, and arguments. In some of the essays, articles, and creative works it is extremely clear how Hip-Hop feminism has informed a particular issue and may be applied in various educational sites, including and extending beyond the traditional classroom. In other cases, it may not be as clear how Hip-Hop feminism is taken up, but we argue that creative formats, forms, and activities are representative of the very kind of active and experimental engagements that Hip-Hop feminism advances. Without attempting to argue for or articulate a "Hip-Hop feminist agenda," we understand each contribution in the reader as a sufficient platform from which to create important conversations, add significant insights to, and build strong bridges with other theories, affiliations, belongings, and revolutionary actions.

The reader aims to inspire dialogue. Dialogue is an essential part of teaching and learning. Many contributions in this reader emerged from conversations about doing the work. The contributions that are most controversial or inspire conversation, we hope, present something new, and if not new, have addressed old topics in new ways so that others may find a way into conversations that may have previously seemed irrelevant or too academic.

Important, in as much as possible, we would like you to participate. Read and perform out loud and in community the creative works in this book (we trust that you can make that take place) and then tell us what happened. Many of the issues addressed in this book are related to activist conversations and organizing elsewhere so we expect you to do your own research, look up the issues represented in this collection, and get involved.

Our definition of Hip-Hop feminist pedagogy rests on a way of asking questions about and speaking to the discrepancies and the contradictions that exist in the material lives of young people. Hip-Hop feminism seeks to examine the multiple, contested, and complex ways women of color—particularly black women and girls—negotiate decision making, employ rhetoric of self-esteem, and oppose punitive social policies in the contexts of their everyday lives (Brown, 2008). Our use of Hip-Hop feminism is less waxing nostalgic of a "Hip-Hop golden era" where women were included and lyrics were less derogatory, or about how traditional modes of feminism consistently forget about race, class, and sexuality as inextricably linked to feminism. Our use of Hip-Hop feminist pedagogy is more about hearing us and seeing us simultaneously; seeing us as human beings ever complex and listening to the embodied knowledge from which we make ourselves known, the two things that rarely happen in traditional conversations and discourse on Hip-Hop, feminism, and education. We operate from the standpoint that feminists must continually question the narratives in which they are embedded, including but not limiting ourselves to the master narratives of mainstream feminism (Grewal & Kaplan, 1994) and that Hip-Hop at its essence is the voice of people and a generation who have not had access to institutional forms of power and voice. Too often, Hip-Hop and feminism are positioned in diametric opposition to each other, though multiple points of cooperation, articulation, contestation, and convergence is much more of the stuff that gives meaning to its style, aesthetic, and commitments.

How This Book Came About

Originally, I (Ruth Nicole brown) was approached by Antwi Akom by a referral from friend and colleague David Stovall to participate as a coeditor on a Hip-Hop reader. Antwi and I had several intense and beautiful conversations about how to fulfill this purpose. Our conversations shifted back and forth from our kids, to our personal well-being, to our travels, to our visions of the dopest book about Hip-Hop we could make possible. Those conversations were invigorating but the book we talked about is not the book that would be produced. For a few reasons, both personal and professional, Dr. Akom invited me to take the lead on the project and withdrew his participation. Although I enjoyed our partnership and would very much come to miss our weekly dialogue, I decided that I could and would stay with the project. I am gratefully indebted to Antwi for his generosity, collegiality, and friendship.

However, it was extremely disappointing to me to restart work on this project alone. I wanted to save the ideas Antwi and I shared, just in case the opportunity once again presented itself to work on the book we imagined. Charged with the task to come up with something else, I gave myself time to rethink the project in its entirety. The more I thought about the kind of reader I wanted to see on bookshelves and to use in the classroom, I began to rethink intensively the book's content. With editor Greg Goodman's grace I proposed not a reader on Hip-Hop but on Hip-Hop feminist pedagogy. As a topic it was more exciting to me and also more possible. I was and am privileged to be at the center of so many conversations spurred by Hip-Hop feminism that not only could I confidently organize a reader that was relevant, inspiring, and doable, I could also invite the students with whom I labor to be a critical part of the process and production.

Collaboration and community must be a key feature of Hip-Hop feminism because, while working on the reader that would become this book, I found working alone and as the primary authority lonely and just not right. I invited Chamara Jewel Kwakye to coedit the project with me. We had worked on several (this is an understatement) projects together and I knew that her intellect and our friendship would make this reader especially different in a positive direction. However, in spite of our close bond, I was initially hesitant. Chamara was not, as

I knew her, down with Hip-Hop feminism. I knew her much more as a womanist, a community worker, a dancer, a storyteller, and a historian even, but never had I heard her identify as a Hip-Hop feminist. Even as we worked together in the name and deed of black girlhood celebration and with all the Hip-Hop feminist musings I brought to the work, Chamara never seemed thrilled to signify a sista girl amen when I explicitly invoked Hip-Hop feminism. This behavior was extremely noticeable to me because, if you know Chamara, then you also know that she is not the quiet type. But I asked her anyway. With fingers crossed and prayers lifted to the powers of hoop earrings loved by us all, I hoped that she would say yes. And she did.

Once she joined, it was time to put the finishing touches on each of the pieces and write this introduction. For the sake of time, there was no open call for submissions. As Barbara Smith (2000) wrote in the introduction of *Home Girls: A Black Feminist Anthology*, I, too, echo the desire that others will consider organizing other collections as there is so much good writing being done with a Hip-Hop feminist inflection that deserves publication.

Overview

The reader is divided into five parts, "Miseducation," "Justice," "Performance," "People," and "SOLHOT." While we make the case that all of the works included in this reader have pedagogical implications, "Miseducation" specifically focuses on how Hip-Hop feminist pedagogy is enacted in the classroom. With more than a handful of university courses across the United States specifically dedicated to Hip-Hop feminism, this part highlights the productive uses and tensions in its institutionalization. With contributions from both students and instructors, we ask, "What does it mean to become introduced to Hip-Hop feminism in such a formal setting as the university classroom? Moreover, how does Hip-Hop feminism transform teaching and learning?" "Miseducation" provides a humble glimpse into the ways elements of Hip-Hop feminism are coded to the benefit of students and instructors who come to claim themselves as artists, mutually dependent on one another.

"Justice" features sharp analytical perspectives on contemporary issues deemed important to us. Giving particular attention to gender, race, class, and sexuality, the writers advance theories and explanations of sexual violence, queer subjectivity, women in higher education, and Hip-Hop media analysis. Each of these contributors explores black women's and girls' bodies as a site of politics, making possible a remapping of the political and theories of politicization. Previous scholarship has noted the more misogynistic elements of Hip-Hop culture, and part 2 thinks through the ways Hip-Hop, as a part of larger society, constrains and enables violence and visions of liberation.

"Performance" as a way of living and as a form of making art is central to all things Hip-Hop feminism. Whatever is expressed is done so with emphasis, style, meaning, and drama. Hip-Hop feminist pedagogy is particularly concerned about how the word, once uttered, operates as a communicative call to action. Whether the performance is improvised, freestyle, communal, personal, created for the people or because of the people, Hip-Hop feminist pedagogy takes seriously the performative possibilities of words and actions. In part 3, poetry, music, dance, and theatrical performance entertain themes such as everyday black girl circumstances, reclaiming identity and representations, healing and wholeness, and generational affirmations.

"People" features interviews and first-person narratives of the Hip-Hop and post–Hip-Hop generations. As it turns out, family members, friends, and favorite teachers take up much more space than celebrities in our daily lives. Each piece offers a fresh perspective on Hip-Hop feminist pedagogy through personal stories that also do not let systems of oppression, racialization, and nationhood off the hook.

Part 5, "SOLHOT," includes contributions by those actively engaged in doing community and cultural work with young people, black girls in particular. All authors use Hip-Hop feminist pedagogy as a critical lens through which theory informs their practice, and vice-versa. Important, each author has been or continues to be involved with Saving Our Lives, Hear Our Truths (SOLHOT), a space dedicated to the celebration of black girlhood in all of its complexity. The formulation of ideas in this part emerge from daily practice and have significant value for enhancing the personal politics of those involved as well as challenging current assumptions about working with youth. It is impossible to do SOLHOT and not think through all the ways processes of racialization, gender, class, religion, and age, mediated through Hip-Hop culture in neoliberal times, matter for feminist praxis, Hip-Hop, and beyond. Each contribution illuminates how and why Hip-Hop feminist pedagogy matters as a means of activism and youth organizing.

Conclusion

What you will not find in this reader is "women and girls" relegated to a subsection or invoked as a subtheme. The presences of black women and girls in this reader are not intended to convey something or anything "authentic." In this book, the silences are intended to be as instructive as what is included. This collection privileges relationships as an inherently Hip-Hop feminist thing to do. Yes, the majority of the authors in this collection know each other. We have worked and organized together. We are fanatical about each other's ideas even if we disagree with them. Because we know and are concerned about each other's well-being, this should make the work presented in this book stronger.

As dissidents of sorts, we wanted to create a book where the most stereotypical Hip-Hop head and scholar might ponder, "What's so Hip-Hop about this?" Likewise, the most stereotypical feminist would respond, "I don't get it," and mean it. Our intention is that this collection of scholarship is first and foremost for those who created it. Others, including those we are writing against, will ask the questions that need to be asked of this collection and that, too, is well worth the time and effort of everyone who contributed. We want this reader to decenter the popular narrative of Hip-Hop and feminism (whatever that is but you know what I'm talking about) and inspire more complex narratives, arguments, and actions that are important to the everyday people who do the work of Hip-Hop feminism in their respective communities.

At this particular historical moment, the rhetoric of occupation is being appropriated worldwide as a means to protest corporate economic greed and the privatization of everything. In solidarity with movements and individuals interested in the material realities of working people, this reader highlights the on-the-ground labor of Hip-Hop feminists. This text is made possible because many of us saw and challenged the limitations of words written about us without our consent. So we center our collective ideas, the work, and ourselves because the revolution can only be as progressive as our personal growth. We wish to live.

REFERENCES

Brown, R. N. (2008). *Black girlhood celebration: Toward a Hip-Hop feminist pedagogy.* New York: Peter Lang.

Chang, J. (Ed.). (2006). *Total chaos: The art and aesthetics of Hip-Hop.* Cambridge, MA: Basic Civitas.

Durham, A. (2011, Spring/Summer). Hip Hop feminist media studies. *International Journal of Africana Studies, 16*(1), 117-140.

Durham, A. (2007). Using [living Hip Hop feminism]: Redefining an answer (to) rap. In G. D. Pough, R. Raimist, A. Durham, & E. Richardson (Eds.), *Home girls make some noise! Hip Hop feminism anthology* (pp. 304-312). Mira Loma, CA: Parker.

Grewal, I., & Kaplan, C. (Eds.). (1994). *Scattered hegemonies: Postmodernity and transnational feminist practices.* Minneapolis: University of Minnesota Press.

hooks, b. (2003). *Teaching community: A pedagogy of hope.* New York: Routledge.

Pough, G. D., Richardson E., Durham A., & Raimist, R. (Eds.). (2007). *Home girls make some noise! Hip-Hop feminism anthology.* Mira Loma, CA: Parker.

Smith, B. (2000). *Home girls: A black feminist anthology.* New Brunswick, NJ: Rutgers University Press.

Part 1

Miseducation

This is not an apology.

Introduction

Part 1 focuses on using elements of Hip-Hop in the classroom featuring reflections (student experiences), process (syllabus), and possibilities (student productions). It gives concrete examples of how conceptions of Hip-Hop's utility in traditional higher education has been limited and, in return, pushes educators to have more comprehensive dialogues, pedagogies, and spaces.

"An Unapologetic Lyric: A Warrior's Battle for Space in Education," by Dominique C. Hill, shares the feelings evoked from her experiences as a black girl in K–12 schooling. By using herself as an example, she discusses how black girls' bodies and minds are equally disciplined through word and action in schools.

"Who Wants 2 b Hard? A Lesbian of Color Critiques the Phrase 'No Homo' in Hip-Hop," by Tanya Kozlowski, is a reflection and critical response to "No Homo." In her paper she creates a conversation about the necessity to engage Hip-Hop feminists in conversation with critical theorists for the important task of creating interstices.

"(Progressive) Hip-Hop Cartography," by Darlene Vinicky, highlights four imperative questions of Hip-Hop and its future: (1) What does it mean to be progressive? (2) What does the past tell us about being progressive? (3) Who makes Hip-Hop progressive? (4) How do we know when we get there? It then answers that each question is necessary to Hip-Hop's continued existence in the academic classroom.

"Lighting the Fire: Hip-Hop Feminism in a Midwestern Classroom," by Zenzele Isoke, is a reflection on three years of teaching a 3000-level course in Visual and Popular Culture. She discusses how she has come to "know" and "be" Hip-Hop and how she uses this knowledge to educate a new generation of learners about the interconnected nature of race, gender, sexuality, and political economy.

The last essay, "For Oya: I Love Myself Dancing . . . and Then Again When I Am Boxed in and Overwhelmed," by Ruth Nicole Brown, traces her Hip-Hop feminist genealogy and discusses its impact on her as a mother, daughter, niece, researcher, dancer, educator, and student of life.

CHAPTER ONE

An Unapologetic Lyric: A Warrior's Battle for Space in Education

Dominique C. Hill

This is NOT an Apology: Declarations of Self, Creating Space and Body as knowledge

> What I say
> and share here,

is just as much about those *feelings* evoked from the words written as the words themselves. These words, and the feelings they hoard, emerge out of responses to my body and the stories it tells. As such, my writing is not intended to prove a point.

> I am writing to speak
> To be heard
> To write myself
> and others like me into space

To claim ownership of myself, see my voice, and change the world around me. I write to tell the story of my body as presence, identity performance, and knowledge. To speak from "the erotic" demands a power, an honesty, and a compassion that reimagines the subject, in this case the black female body. Further, the erotic offers the power needed to re/place myself and thus female of color collective within the universe, society, and the academy—to rewrite history, the present, and future. For, you see,

> *my knee is so badly wounded no one will look at it.*
> *The pus of the past oozes from every pore.*
> *The infection has gone on for at least 300 years.*

My voice blooms out of a need to feel, to be, to explore, and come to know myself and my value in the face of descriptions, accurate and faulty, dictated to me about me. Seen as undeserving of individuality and representative of all female-black-working class—disrespectful, inappropriate, servant, deviant, hypersexual, being grown (before my time, of course), and simply too firm. Too certain of myself. Though I once shied away from puttin' folks on blast, afraid of the consequences, I quickly grew weary. Today, as yesterday, yesteryear, and years before, I am requiring myself to speak from a deep, honest, painful place—to offer, from my perspective, a glimpse into the interrelationship between the body, place, and educational experience.

Criticism came and continues on many fronts, but formal education via schools is the place in which criticisms in the form of judgments of being inappropriate, "at risk," too assertive, aggressive, confrontational, a troublemaker when posing questions to authority are reiterated and rationalized by a culture of poverty, innate nature, and brokenness. Being too certain equated to a need to be "fixed" when really I was set up for the okey-doke that resulted in a breaking of my spirit and confidence. In school my curious and lively spirit read as controversial—though an accurate assessment at times—had to be shattered, at least in the eyes of those running the schoolhouse and investing in reproducing social realities. Through a series of stares, gawking, passive aggressive treatment, and subtle isolation now recognized as microaggressions, internalized racism and sexism, hegemonic theory, and systemic subjugation, I was put in place. Again, what I have to say here, what I am going to say here, is just as much about those feelings that created the words on these pages as the words themselves because I cannot—will not—separate my feelings and body from my educational journey. The body is essential to feeling, knowing, and speaking—essential ingredients of working from the erotic and critical to education.

I am not trying to prove the point that schooling and the formal education process is steeped in heteropatriarchy, sexism, and racism. Nor am I am trying to prove that these ideologies, systemic interlocking systems create varied deleterious effects for different students based on their identities held. I am, however, insisting that my need to share—to demand my voice be heard in the manner I so choose—stems from, is birthed out of, and in dialectical relationship with my formal education process. Such a formal process that was and remains steeped in heteropatriarchy, sexism, and racism resulting in a low blue book appraisal of my worth and the worth of others critical, quiet, curious, female, black, assertive, passive, working class, wild, middle class, eager to learn, queer, heterosexual, in between—people like me.

To share, I offer a pastiche representation of the relationship between body, place, and educational experience by beginning in the present in the form of a mystory that talks back to education and society and speaks me and others like me into place. Then, I use feminist geography to discuss three conceptualizations of the body that help understand the role of the body to educational process. I use body as knowledge as a site for reimagining body as it relates to enhancing life experiences, specifically educational journeys of females of color.

A counternarrative: Went to tha schoolhouse and they tried to play me Mizundastood1:

> Who am I?? You really asking me that? I am your former student. I am here with you. You may try to dictate the physical space in which I can feel comfortable, but you cannot prevent me from going there—especially in my mind, in my thoughts, in my imagination. In fact, I venture to those "forbidden" places every day because to simply accept the places you carve out for me would be to accept and agree with the worth or worthlessness assigned to my body. Besides, those places are everywhere. Hell, you haven't given me much room. You may think you own me, but you do not. You may think you can control me, but without my mind, you have nothing. I stopped reading your books thinking I'd find myself long ago.

> Sureeeee [sarcastically], you have indicated before that I belong here and not there. That I should say this, instead of that. Be this, not that. And that I should behave this way as opposed to another. I have taken your demands into consideration, [smirk] and only consideration.

> Ohhhhh, I get it. I know what you want me to do. Crawl into a corner!? Ball up! Feel afraid! Too unsure of myself to fight! Beg to be part of you and your domination. Accept the place carved out by you for me. I know what you expect me to do, but I ain't! I'm not a lay down, as you please sir, yes ma'am kind of—[snarling with raised voice] PLEASE! I'm a damn warrior. [angrily laughing] Why you backing up? I'm not 'bout to smack, hit, stab, or even spit on you like others have done to me. I am saying my fight, my battle, and my struggle. I am saying and interjecting myself into your line of vision, into space, into history, into present day, into a society that only sees me when I can be of benefit or when, again, I am saying my battle, my struggle and also my response to them. I am saying my demands.

Why do you look so perplexed? [sarcastically] I thought you knew of my disenchantment, positivity, and disgust with the spaces you and others insist on claiming for me. I don't need your help and I don't wish to be looked down upon. You and your colleagues make too many assumptions about me—the same assumptions you made about others like me years, decades, even centuries ago. Your decisions to mark my ancestors as incapable, unintelligible, and objects to be bought and sold have not disappeared.

My accomplishments are deemed significant only for people like me. People like me who have created the ideas that now reside on your vita. We are ever present and nonexistent at the same time. Don't give me the "you cannot be held accountable for your ancestors' decisions" line because I am being held accountable for your ancestors' decisions. My life, my scars—mentally and physically—are representations and reminders of you and the decisions made in the past. You are inseparable. I will not give you the satisfaction of separating you from them because everything we experience now is living history. Every time I look at you, I see both your ancestors and mine. And every time you see me, well I am not sure what you see, but I doubt you see just me. How could you?

My mere presence disrupts your world, upsets your equilibrium, and threatens your ego. Your face is red, your ears are blue, and hands flush. Why? Is it because I have the audacity, yes the audacity, to stand before you and express my unhappiness, my anger, and even more so my strategy to make you see me? Or could your rainbow appearance be a result of your insistence on trying your hardest to see but not say me? I am here, in your face, and I am not going anywhere, especially not until you say me.

Now I know some people have gone easy on you, stayed quiet, in order that you could forget their existence. Some have even changed their appearances for reasons unknown, resultin' in you completely dis-acknowledging their presence. But you see, I am both not them and am them simultaneously. I am not them because I continue to claim spaces you have deemed solely yours while they have not. But I am them because we share common space in that you have labeled us space to be occupied, controlled, and forever regulated. Bravo for your sinister, debilitating, and strategic plan. It worked! We live in a system where my body is always regulated, monitored, and evaluated at higher stakes than others, including yourself. And sometimes I don't have the energy to physically resist that monitoring. Other times, I give in to it. And most times, whether you recognize my fight, I am ALWAYS struggling and contesting this unfair systematic treatment.

So you see, your understandings of my actions are inaccurate. Your read of me is irrelevant and your view of me is a mere (re)presentation of what you want to see when you look at me. I fault you for the impact of your destructive and erroneous views of my predecessors and me. These farce (re)representations have cost me and will cost others a great deal in the future.

But I am not in despair, hopeless, or unfaithful to my spirit and my community. I still believe in us, in me, in the future and its possibilities. But I worry that those after me will become fatigued as I am because I know their bodies will not let them forget what you work so hard to erase—the memory and mapping of racism, sexism, heteropatriarchy, onto our bodies.

I am sure you are baffled by my confidence, my candidness, and ability to articulate my position, because you may presume an inability or simply the behavior of a haughty nigger gurl on my behalf. This is not the first nor last time I will cause someone to do a double take or become uncomfortable. Nor is it the last time I will feel the need to assert myself in a space, in a moment, and say.

I have hesitated too many times and decided against saying my presence in this space, this place, this world. I am done hesitating, retreating, dismissing my importance. Dammit, I helped build this place. My silent resistance has assisted me in being where and who I am at this very moment. So I am not concerned about the lashings I may receive after this discussion. Not concerned that you, like the other teachers, will deem me academically stifled by my attitude, my anger, my self-affirmed speech. I am not worried about the ridicule I will undoubtedly face for actin' less than "ladylike." And I am not in the least bit apologetic for any guilt, pain, or insecurities you may feel now and afterward.

Though society has evolved and progressed enough that I do not have to stand on a materially physical auction block to be sold, it has been appraised since I entered school. My first price tag was assigned in pre-kindergarten and again in my first reading group. What I do with my body is of everyone's concern, especially if my behavior results in a decrease in the profit to be made from it. You must know that.

Didn't you place a bid on me? Weren't you configuring the maximum rate I could go for? And haven't you thought about my mannish-like demeanor and overly sexual features? Aren't I more than enough to spread across a few men and maybe even women? [smirking] Ohhhh, I apologize if any of this is inaccurate. If the assumptions I have made about you and mapped onto you have never been true for you or anyone like you. Thus, I am unapologetic.

A line has been drawn around my body, distinguishing it from "true womanhood." That same line has deemed my body empty or irrelevant space "up for grabs" and possession. The knowledge and information I have created and attained has been taken from me and appropriated as something I am incapable of understanding—something you "made." I have been aware of this thievery and trickery. I reflect deeply on how best to respond and decided that the best thing to do is LIVE—not survive within the spaces assigned to me, but to live within, beyond, and outside of them.

The mystory above joins my articulation of the impact—the shaping, sculpting, and struggle—ensued on my body and in my mind during the educational process. It melds my experiences with other women, scholars, artists, and social justice workers seeking annihilation of interlocking systems of oppression. Rather than focusing on particular educational experiences or in-school experiences, it intends to tell the story of curricula, perceptions, and limitations assumed in light of my subjectivities. Moreover, the mystory bonds history—because it is alive—my experiences, and the experiences of others like me to offer a montage of educational processes and their unholy union to heteropatriarchy, racism, and sexism. While I want my fight to be voiced and seen, I must acknowledge the legacy of warriors before me. These people, not simply soldiers but warriors because they do not act based on orders—they demand change. Created above is a montage of articulations, ideas, and declarations, and it screams back at formal education and its father society. As a collective, the mystory illuminates labor surrounding the creation of space, the body as place, and the lack of value assigned to space and place occupied by blackness. Arising out of my lived experiences and those discussed in writings by many feminists of color, women of color, and the sparse qualitative studies in education on black girls and girls of color, is a need to insert the body into education. Yet, the body is and should be understood as more than corporeality but also as identity performance and knowledge because it is integral to students', especially black girls', educational experiences.

CHAPTER TWO

Who Wants 2 b Hard?
A Lesbian of Color Critiques
the Phrase "No Homo"
in Hip Hop

Tanya Kozlowski

My early adolescent encounters and gradual love and appreciation for Hip-Hop in all its complexities has been and probably will always be complicated; and that is okay with me. All the relationships throughout the course of my life that have mattered to me the most and continued to develop over the years have been complex. Therefore, the multifarious relationship I have developed with Hip-Hop continues to ebb and flow; and the tension within this poem is a part of that developing complexity.

> this is a dis-identification/call it a quare proclamation
> recycle the wrapper/go green if ur long n so lean
> but if by chance ur like me n don't fit into them GAP jeans/
> u can play on my team/it's free
> be all that u can be/just don't ask/'n i won't tell/ shhhhhhhhhhhhhh it's a secret/
> imperialism still sells
> like hard candy to kids on Halloween/recycle the wrapper/u feel me?

don't be so mean/i don't wanna lick the fuckin' wrapper 'n maybe
neither does she
see this is my country 2/'tis of thee/see it's not that easy as the GAZE decrees
you don't have to adhere to that static fucked up immutable form of
black masculinity/
they been stressing on us
by not callin' it what it is/rather than beatin' around the bush/'n all this
homoerotic discussions centering on the tush
pshhhhhhhhhhh/plz don't act like womyns' behinds haven't become numero
uno item commodified over centuries
imperialist nostalgia kills the soul/as well as the trees/just ask al/
but it's more than global warmin'
recycle the wrapper/may i have ur attention plzzzzzzz?
Don't b rude 'n act like u don't remember the trajectory of racialized 'n
sexualized bodies that are imbricated in our histories
mysteries to the untrained Eye/or maybe groups of pale-skinned folks that
always got them Northface jackets on/talking 'bout
"I just wanna get by?"
try to recycle the wrapper/'n kick it to her outside the club/
put all those damn bottles down/
u might just like it/hey it cld b fun
one-don't keep disrespectin' mine 'n me 'n actin' like i don't know/but no i won't
retaliate with a colonial violence that has already permeated
and continues to pass
'n WHEN U SAY NO HOMO IT'S LIKE BEING FORCE FED
BROKEN GLASS
two-don't get it twisted/i won't go out like no punk/but i can't even
fake the funk/
the junk in our trunks been used as the lame ass lines in ur hooks
it's long been whack/step back
reconfigure the stories u tellin'/cuz the kids pay attention 'n mimic what u say/
without the same context of ur adult word play
stayin' true to my first lines/recycle the wrapper/'n when u say no homo in your
rhythms/it's like i keep gettin' tested time after time . . . after time. . . .
i don't really think ur homophobic/but i do think ur afraid/how would ur lyrics
change if heteropatriarchy didn't have its way?/with you
remember this is a dis-identification/a quare fuckin proclamation/GLBTQ ppl
of color exist/race 'n sexuality done up wit a rainbow twist
so it's been time for u to stop sayin' no homo/'n everybody else too/
yeah they know

had to tell it like it is/say it with some conviction/no stutterin'/
no this is not fiction
diction is clear/like my mouth is to God's ear
adhere to my DIS-IDENTIFICATION/my quare proclamation/
recycle the wrapper lil wayne
we deserve respect, luv, 'n celebration . . . not some kinda homonormative
toleration/'n we can't get it when u dis on us
like we ain't nuthin'
so truly understand this communication/it's not a test/no capitalist promo
STOP   SAYIN   NO HOMO!

CHAPTER THREE

(Progressive) Hip-Hop Cartography

Darlene Vinicky

And come this time around, you choose to walk a different path, you'll embrace what you turned away and cry at what you laughed

—Saul Williams (2004)

Armed with the coordinates of her past, Hip-Hop has the beginning of an outline, constellations in a pink urban sky, but to connect the dots, to find her palace at the end of the rainbow, our heroine must unscramble the mist that takes the form of questions. Such as, what does it mean to be progressive? What does the past tell us about being progressive? Who makes Hip-Hop progressive? How do we know when we get there?

Legend
How to read this social map

Maps are projections of space. These projections are completely subjective to the perspective and intent of the mapmaker. Both physical and conceptual spaces can be mapped, meaning maps are not limited to globes, vacation planning, or colonialist attempts to claim the world. Rather, maps guide our pursuits, informing us of where we have been (those places that have been marked and measured) and helping us to find where we need to go, physically, mentally, spiritually, rhythmically, or creatively depending on the purpose of the map. Any state or space, figurative or literal, that denotes a location can be mapped either through images, words, rhythms, textures, or some combination of forms. Therefore, interpreting space and location becomes an exercise in recordkeeping and observation, as well as form making and calculation of the explored and the mysterious. Cartography is the science or art of making maps. By cartographically documenting Hip-Hop, we can form a clearer prediction of where "progressive" has been and should strive to go.

Hip-Hop as a state of mind and a state of action is located in the past, present, and future. The bodies of Hip-Hop take on the role of both landscape and traveler. The landscape is formed by the products of Hip-Hop culture (i.e., beats, style, language); it is the space where exploration becomes material. The Hip-Hop traveler is the producer: the individual, community, or institution that forges new paths, inevitably changing the shape of her location with every movement. Neither the landscape nor the traveler is located completely in only one space at one time, rather both draw on elements of history while simultaneously forging forward into the future. The progression of the journey depends entirely on the shape of the space, which changes constantly in reaction to the traveler, so that the past, present, and future of both bodies (land and traveler) are perpetually influenced by one another.

In order to chart where Hip-Hop is heading we will need to meet the traveler—learn her dreams and fears, what makes her sway or her heart race—and we must gain a better understanding of her surroundings. To do this we need to look back at where she has been and what she has accomplished so that we can orient the terrains of time and experience into a single cohesive environment. From here we can plot the points of interest, determine our scale, calculate the landscape's rate of change, and hopefully plan a path for Hip-Hop that allows her to transform her landscape into one that is even more accessible and fertile than it is now. Our construction of this map will help guide us toward a Hip-Hop that experiments with change and addresses its silences.

Step 1

What does the past tell us? Recognizing important coordinates for mapping the future

At times built on just a beat, Hip-Hop's bare bones quality points to a history of creativity, directness, and minimalism. Some people have disregarded this simplicity as unintelligent or uncreative, while others mount all Hip-Hop on a pedestal and accept anything shaped in a familiar light as worthy of praise (Rose, 2008). Hip-Hop feminist Tricia Rose points out that both extremes (pro- and anti-Hip-Hop) reduce the creative value of Hip-Hop by not fully participating with it as an art form. Rose writes, "The marginality of serious engagement over the creative value of Hip-Hop has reduced the literacy about Hip-Hop even among its most ardent fans and has thus lowered the standards for creative embrace of the music" (p. 218). By ignoring the arches and curls that make each piece sculptural, or just failing to recognize that Hip-Hop is art and more than a controversial issue or a truncated tales from the hood, the mainstream product is destined to end up a spectrum of coloring contest melodies, each trying to replicate some predetermined standard of good Hip-Hop. Rose also points out that while Hip-Hop may have been the byproduct of black creativity, the necessity to make something great out of scraps is born out of having only scraps available. Hip-Hop should strive for grade A ingredients and not accept unforgiving conditions and societal devaluation as "a black badge of honor" (Rose, p. 266). Rose's argument makes tremendous sense; artists and audiences alike should expect nothing less than fair and just social environments from which to create Hip-Hop, freedom from -isms, and should not feel inclined to accept mistreatment as a sign of strength. However, I would complicate this argument a bit in order to better participate with Hip-Hop as art; because Hip-Hop is often pioneering new techniques, the incorporation of cutting in turntablism, for example, the tools to produce new art may not yet have been created. In these absences, the experimental processes of Hip-Hop become almost scientific as artists engineer new equipment or sounds, transforming a void into a creative product. Therefore, I suggest an alternative definition to scraps, one that signifies the deconstruction and reformation of existing materials, grade A or grade F, into something more fruitful. Scraps in this context would suggest exploration and innovation with found media, crediting artists with their creativity but also recognizing their agency, instead of just framing Hip-Hop as the creative transformation of waste. If Hip-Hop heads, critics, and critiques reconsidered Hip-Hop as an art, think of all the movement that would allow? Think, what if more emcees put a full orchestra behind their rhymes, or more producers used a chorus of percussion instruments to make a beat, or even just had the freedom to experiment with new tools or topics rarely discussed, and still got widespread mainstream airtime, how cool could that sound? How would that change our images and imaginations of Hip-Hop art?

Step 2
What does it mean to be "progressive"; what are we expecting to see beyond the fog?

But this music, when suitably used, is meant to enrich your existence/By providing sight of purpose, worthy of your choice to listen./Willingness to see will give you vision,/Conscious acts preserve self-permission.

— Solillaquists of Sound

The definition of *progressive Hip-Hop* tends to be pretty fluid. To some, *progressive* means "conscious" or suggesting a social and political critique of society; to others it means "experimental," indicating experimentation with instruments, sounds, and vocal delivery; and to still others it means anything that pushes against mainstream Hip-Hop. There are multiple other definitions of Hip-Hop that aren't included in these three understandings but that still firmly categorize certain forms of Hip-Hop as progressive. Often, conscious Hip-Hop is determined by the artist's socially and politically conscious rhymes. However, the label *conscious* can be extended to include the incorporation of socially and politically conscious samples, the artist(s)'s (substantial) political extracurricular projects, a conscious exclusion of negative, stereotypical content, or the inclusion of perspectives that are typically not included in mainstream Hip-Hop (women's or queer voices for instance). Political themes are one form of progressive Hip-Hop but not the only route to breaking mass media's plastic mold. In fact, as Rose points out, the "socially conscious" label can be "almost a commercial death sentence for artist visibility and everyday casual fan appreciation" (2008, p. 243).

Additionally, stuffing Hip-Hop in an either/or "gangsta"–"fight the power" binary greatly limits the avenues of expression that artists have to offer (Rose, 2008, p. 243). In both cases, the angsty (at times) formulaic Hip-Hop that reaches most audiences is viewed as an expression of authentic blackness, reproducing negative stereotypes that define black individuals and communities as Others that are either violent, or insensitive, or uncreative, or materialistic, or all of the above. Lupe Fiasco's decision to talk about robots and skateboards in his music instead of reproducing the authentic black lifestyle usually paraded on the radio, speaks to a progressive effort that is not necessarily overtly political (Rose).

Some definitions of progressive Hip-Hop center on the experimental qualities of the sound, movement, and expression of Hip-Hop. In musical forms of Hip-Hop culture, the blending of multiple genres and the use of unconventional sounds are one form of transformation that questions the existing boundaries of Hip-Hop. Similarly with dance, experimentation can mean the incorporation of other styles and movements. Genre blending, including sound and movement experimentation, queers the definitions of Hip-Hop, giving artists more space to explore the possibilities of the terrain and challenge how Hip-Hop is defined.

Some people may interpret progressive Hip-Hop as any form of Hip-Hop that resists the boundaries that have defined Hip-Hop so far. A willingness to step outside the predetermined borders of Hip-Hop offers a vast array of new directions, but this shift would also demand new answers to questions such as: Which voices fit on the progressive Hip-Hop map? What central elements should stay the same? How does consumerism fill this space, if at all? Or, could these changes dilute Hip-Hop into a muddled interpretation of another genre?

Participation is another huge question in the mapping of progressive, boundary resisting Hip-Hop; who is the traveler? Currently, persons identifying as women are less recognized for their role in Hip-Hop; instead male voices are traditionally considered the main path of Hip-Hop, with female voices sprinkled occasionally along the way. However, Hip-Hop feminism—and potentially progressive Hip-Hop—offers a new approach toward the black female body, one that reassesses how female movement and bodies are valued and treated. In the conclusion of *Black Girlhood Celebration* (2008), scholar Ruth Nicole Brown relays her observation of a young woman's enthusiastic lap dance for her man at a restaurant. The young woman's ability to be seen as beautiful in that performance is encouraging but the fractional agency she receives from the dance is troublesome. What Hip-Hop feminism offers is a space that recognizes a woman's dance as beautiful and respects her desire to dance for her own pleasure (Brown). On the journey toward a more progressive Hip-Hop, attention to female space becomes important for transforming the shape of Hip-Hop into something more inclusive. By redesigning how the female body is conceived, we expand the landscape of Hip-Hop to construct more empowering avenues for expression. This change also repositions the identity of the traveler to include female and feminine bodies so that Hip-Hop does not equate masculinity, but is open to a multitude of unique forms.

Step 3
Who makes Hip-Hop progressive? Bridging the border between consumer and producer
This ain't for the underground, this here is for the sun. A seed a stranger gave to me and planted on my tongue.

—Saul Williams (2004)

Almost every critique of Hip-Hop emphasizes the media's negative influence on the music, and there's a reason for this: a mass-produced culture of consumption and violence only speaks for and to a capitalist agenda. Black music has a history of communal participation. Blues, soul, and jazz, for example, were performed within communal venues (like a rent party or jook) and evolved through a tactile, shared participation with the music. All musical genres grew from some kind of folk roots, but collective, physical participation with the production of music was more common when the world was less hi-tech. Now the Internet, transnational corporations, television, and iPods influence and shape our collective and physical participation with music. Information may travel faster and we may have more tools and gadgets to hold and access music with greater ease, but our attention is drawn from personal interactions to the bright lights and chirps of our devices. In some ways, the ease of click, click, right click, drag lulls us into complacency and isolation. Who needs to play music with friends when you can play computer solitaire? Why write poetry when you can watch a cat play the piano on YouTube? While the advancement of technology allows farther regions of the world to connect with one another, it is often at the expense of direct personal connections, even with those closest to us. When technology becomes the go-between for our every interaction, we are more susceptible to the authority of those who control and distribute media.

While technology itself is not a problem, a greater awareness of both how technology changes the ways we interact with our communities (plural, because most people participate in multiple communities, especially with social-networking technology) and an awareness of who controls the technology with which we interact (i.e., considering the interests of those who make or advance certain forms of technological media, such as the construction of listening blogs and Internet music review sites) must be examined carefully.

Technology has had a tremendous (positive) impact on Hip-Hop and music in general; it has changed the way music sounds, how we listen to it, increased the reach of even self-promoting artists, and made production and reproduction more affordable. The sounds and production of Hip-Hop has been greatly impacted by the incorporation of more advanced technologies; advances in production equipment gives artists more control when they are sampling beats, layering, and editing their work. Plus, the inclusion of more technological sounds has enabled further genre blending and queering.

In addition to the production of the sound itself, technology has had a dramatic effect on the accessibility of Hip-Hop and music in general. With free audio-recording programs available for download or already present on some computers, artists have more options for independent recording. The Internet also provides a fertile space to share independent music freely and rapidly. Digital media, while grotesque to some purists, removes need for distribution and in between companies, which removes one layer of industry influence. Digital music releases also allow artists to make their music available for free, legal downloads; a political act that sticks its tongue out at the corporatization of music.

Reclaiming Hip-Hop through community participation and new media reconstructs Hip-Hop so that there is space for individuals to express, create, and define Hip-Hop. Returning Hip-Hop to a do-it-yourself (DIY) process (not that there are not already DIY Hip-Hop spaces) means reinventing what Hip-Hop means and how we listen to it because if it's really communal, as a listener you are also a producer. Ruth Nicole Brown writes that a Hip-Hop feminist pedagogy "creates the space for insight to be collectively shared and distributed, for new (other) knowledge to be produced, valuing and caring for each person who shows up" (2008, p. 140). Relocating Hip-Hop from the unreachable corporate platform means placing it back within the community—not as a second-rate version of the corporate product but as a hearty, more relevant medium for expression. Bringing Hip-Hop back into the community does not mean idle philanthropic projects, those are like candy and pop; they give energy and hope for a second but once the buzz is over you are hungrier than you were before. DIY Hip-Hop means creating something that nourishes people, it means having control over how the community is represented, and what message the music sends. DIY or grassroots Hip-Hop should be like rice, beans, and a heap of mixed vegetables; it should satisfy the hunger for creative expression without the empty gestures. This means recognizing the already present female, queer, and gender-variant voices in Hip-Hop, while also fostering spaces where new nondominate voices can develop. Feeling connected to the music that surrounds you blurs the lines among producer, consumer, and product making it so everyone is a little of each.

Step 4

How do we know when we get there; is Hip-Hop the castle or the rainbow?

After all these directions and carefully considered longitudes and latitudes, it seems necessary to stop and consider the project itself. Is progressive Hip-Hop about reaching a utopian paradise, creating a perfect community, or about recognizing positive change on the way to, and part of, a grand idea? Can the progressive ever be reached? By definition, *progress* is rooted in the term *progressive*, meaning a stagnant utopia is contradictory. Still, the advantage of a goal or product approach is that there is always an objective—an end to reach. If Hip-Hop is the journey, the rainbow, what steps are truly progressive? Tricia Rose recognizes that "sometimes [popular music] involves politically conscious content, but it surely cannot nor should not always do so" (2008, p. 244). Resisting negative stereotypes, even in an apolitical way, is counterhegemonic and itself an act of progressive defiance. Therefore, expectations of progressive Hip-Hop must be examined and scaled to the established Hip-Hop geography in order to determine how and where to proceed. We must proportion our expectations of Hip-Hop to the actual weight that Hip-Hop culture carries within various communities. In other words, we should not expect Hip-Hop to change the world all by itself nor should we ignore its potential power; instead Hip-Hop should be recognized as both a tool for change and a restructuring of social participation. If Hip-Hop is a journey, action is required. Creating spaces for creativity and change mean participating in the artistic work. It would require an openness to change (not a blanket acceptance) and a rapid fluidity that can become very uncomfortable. Hip-Hop feminism— or more generally, progressive Hip-Hop—means rejecting silence.

REFERENCES

Lorde, A. (1984). The transformation of silence into language and action. *Sister/Outsider: Essays and speeches* (pp. 40-44). Trumansburg, NY: Crossing.

Brown, R. N.. (2008). Little Sally Walker. *Black girlhood celebration: Toward a Hip-Hop feminist pedagogy* (pp. 87-110). New York: Peter Lang.

Rose, T. (2008). *Hip Hop wars*. New York: Basic Civitas.

Solillaquists of Sound. (2006). Ask Me If I Care. *As If We Existed*. Anti. Digital file.

Williams, S. (2004). Talk to Strangers. *Saul Williams*. Fader. Digital file.

CHAPTER FOUR

Lighting the Fire: Hip-Hop Feminism in a Midwestern Classroom

Zenzele Isoke

Introduction

On the first day of class after assigning the opening chapters of Jeff Chang's *Total Chaos* (2006), my Sex, Politics, and Hip Hop class erupted in a fierce debate about what the Hip-Hop generation is and what it could be. Toward the end of the debate a quietly charismatic young man vocalized his frustration about my ambivalence to settle the debate by declaring what the *real* Hip-Hop generation is. As the *instructor*, he advised me, it was my *job* to silence the multiracial collective of students who had miraculously enrolled in my usually 99.5% white, nineteen- and twenty-year-old populated, University of Minnesota classroom. He boldly declared, "Well, we all know that Hip-Hop is rooted in black American culture. Why aren't you saying it? Hip-Hop isn't everything to everybody, and everybody can't claim it as they're own. It *is* rooted in *black* experience."

After a few moments, I asked the class if they really wanted me to preach the *his*-story of Hip-Hop. Did they want me to deliver the familiar eulogy of black oppression in struggle in U.S. cities? The class was silent. I added, "I could preach about Hip-Hop—embody the phallocentric role of the Hip-Hop griot who knows best through hood experience the ins and outs of Hip-Hop and Hip-Hop culture. However," I said, as I shifted my gaze to the entire classroom, "I am not a zealot or a Hip-Hop-tologist, whose stakes are grounded in getting the modernist history of Hip-Hop right. I am a thirty-something-year-old black woman whose subjectivity is grounded in the Hip-Hop that I was exposed to as a child, and beyond." I suppose I could have shut down the spirited debate about the meaning and origins of Hip-Hop and the Hip-Hop generation, especially considering that the very next week we would read "Hip Hop's Mama," Imani Perry's spirited clarification of Hip-Hop's origin in African American musical and cultural tradition. But I chose not to silence the energetic group by claiming the authority of experience—of being a black girl who grew up in neighborhoods brimming with crack cocaine, gang violence, and chronic unemployment. At that time, I chose not to disclose how Hip-Hop enabled me to check the often overwhelming sense of isolation, paranoia, and despair that haunted my adolescent soul. Instead I wondered out loud, "What is at stake at preaching the meaning of Hip-Hop to a group of young people who have their own stories to tell about how Hip-Hop music and culture have shaped their lives?"

In this essay, I reflect on three years of teaching a 3000-level course in Visual and Popular Culture in the Department of Gender, Women, and Sexuality Studies at the University of Minnesota. I discuss how it is I have come to "know" and "be" Hip-Hop and how I have used this knowledge to educate a new generation of learners about the interconnected nature of race, gender, sexuality, and political economy. I present an overview of the problems and possibilities of an African American woman teaching and theorizing about Hip-Hop and feminism in predominantly white classrooms. I also discuss the pedagogical dilemmas of having to celebrate and critique a cultural form that is close to my heart. I argue that critically and systematically reflecting on one's positionality vis-à-vis Hip-Hop culture is a central task for both teachers and learners in a Hip-Hop feminist classroom. In this paper I take up the pedagogical virtues of promiscuity—of moving within and through a variety of texts, epistemic positions, voices, and geographic and cultural landscapes toward the aim of exploring Hip-Hop through a multiracial, critical feminist lens.

At the end of our two-and-a-half-hour evening class the frustrated young man came up and attempted an apology. "I hope you don't take what I said the wrong way." He made a point of letting me know in no uncertain terms that his best friend is the son of the only prominent black politician in Minnesota. "I didn't mean to be disrespectful because I am, as a white person, telling you, as a black instructor, that there is something wrong in not clearly grounding Hip-Hop in black experience." Indeed.

Thinking about my end of the semester evaluations, I smile, and tell him not to worry about his comment, "After all, everyone in the class begins where they are. We are all here to learn." I began packing up my laptop, unused books, and other course material to head to my car. My indifference vexed him. Not satisfied with my lack of anger and predictable black bitch defensiveness, this lovely young man follows me into the hallway and insists, "I know that there are problems with this, but I want to apologize to you. I know what I said was not right." He then goes on to explain how he knows about all about white privilege and, incidentally, Hip-Hop because of his black male best friend. "I understand if you're upset." I stop walking and turn to him and ask, "Would it make you feel more comfortable if I called you a racist?" He turns red, laughs nervously, and forces out a quiet no. "Good," I said, because I don't want all of our discussions this semester to focus on white privilege, white racism, and white guilt instead of the creative potential of Hip-Hop and Hip-Hop culture in its many guises."

Over-standing Hip-Hop

Hip-Hop is more that an art form or an amalgam of rap texts, it is a ubiquitous cultural practice that is distinctive in its ability to productively and pleasurably revel in the contradictions of late modernity (Sharpely-Whiting, 2007). Hip-Hop is radical because, at any point in time, it can take the things that we publicly repulse but privately love and present an innovative new aesthetic built with and in opposition to the most dangerous and elusive elements of expressive youth culture. Whether through turntablism, graffiti, spoken word, crunking, or explosive fusions of funk-jazz-soul-rap, Hip-Hop has undeniably, in some way, shape, and form, influenced the becomings of all of us born after 1965 (Cobb, 2009; Chang, 2006; Kitwana, 2002).

In Hip-Hop classrooms, students and instructors alike are forced to question our predispositions about Hip-Hop culture and politics. Important, we must learn to honestly acknowledge the ways *both* mainstream and oppositional Hip-Hop (not that these are always mutually exclusive) have shaped the political subjectivities and aesthetic sensibilities of two distinctive generations of teachers and learners: Gen X *and* Gen Y. My semester-long intergenerational exchange required that we all learn how to accede the proper homage to best and worst, the nastiness and the funk, and the most incisive and inane of Hip-Hop as a diverse, multigenerational cultural practice. Throughout the semester the built environment of the classroom is transformed into highly combustible cipher—a "counter-hegemonic space," in which we all examine our vices and vulnerabilities, our failures and disappointments, and our pasts, our presents, and our futures (hooks, 1990). As an instructor, I encourage students to develop the perspective of an enlightened witness, a subject who possesses the literacy to discern the function and operation of ideology in the representations, worldviews, and commodities that are placed before us for consumption. My goal was to transform these eager young people who were willing to pay nearly $2,000 to learn about sex, politics and Hip-Hop for fourteen weeks into what Tricia Rose calls "politically thoughtful consumers" (2008, p. 217) of the culture. I had my work cut out for me because most seem convinced that they already were.

From a masculinist standpoint, many students are surprisingly familiar with the culture—they are able to drop the names of the intellectual dons and divas and easily recount the latest transgressions of the hottest artists. With this said, only a very few had seriously considered the development of their social identities in relation to Hip-Hop. As a result, my pedagogical goal has not been to recount a history. Rather my intent is to guide students toward a more systematic examination of the attitudes and ideologies informing their understanding of Hip-Hop culture, as well as to push them to examine diverse forms of Hip-Hop cultural praxis. My goal is to disrupt a unidimensional engagement with the culture—either as art or entertainment—and to provide students with tools to infuse their own various life emancipatory aspects of Hip-Hop. In this, we share ways that Hip-Hop can inform writing practices, pedagogy, civic engagement, as well as one's career path. My political work in the Hip-Hop classroom is to enable students to envision ways that Hip-Hop culture can provide voice, confidence (swag), and creativity toward the aim of pursing a life path that is connected to social justice. As Marc Lamont Hill argues, Hip-Hop is treated as the intellectual and cultural terrain through which we all begin to confront the complexity, inevitable anxieties, dead-ends, and, sometimes, new frontiers of identity and identity politicking. In the feminist studies classroom, Hip-Hop is the site in which multiple configurations of race, ethnicity, age, ability, class, diaspora, sex, sexuality, gender, family, religion, and nationality are examined. We consider how structures of power and privilege shape how Hip-Hop gets consumed, practiced, absorbed, sold, distributed, and politically deployed.

Hip-Hop Standing in a Black Feminist Cipher

From a black feminist standpoint, it is impossible to overstate the importance of subjective engagement with Hip-Hop culture. Hip-Hop feminisms, specifically, require each of us to delve into the affective dimensions of Hip-Hop by writing our personal histories into the culture and placing our bodies inside of the cipher. The classroom becomes a transgressive space in which students and instructors together closely examine our complicity in the marginalization, silencing, victimization, and negation of each other (hooks, 1990). By emphasizing the oppositional political possibilities that Hip-Hop makes visible to us, the classroom becomes a place in which the raced, gendered, class- and nation-based power differentials are exposed, challenged, and reconsidered. Through Hip-Hop we explore and analyze the role of state in stigmatizing the personhood of black and brown single mothers, the role of popular Hip-Hop videos of objectifying and commodifying black sexuality, as well consider emancipatory possibilities of Hip-

Hop porn (Brown, 2009) The point here is to engage: to observe how power and ideology operate within the texts that Hip-Hop produces and mainstream media delivers and to identify new ways to interrogate, subvert, and transform socially mediated practices and ways of seeing that contain, dehumanize, and exploit Hip-Hop culture, politics, and bodies—especially black bodies.

As Carole Boyce-Davis writes, "Feminist politics is a resistance to the objectification of women in society, in literature, art and culture. It is also an articulation of a critical and an intellectual practice which challenges all patriarchal assumptions and norms. It is also a politics of possible transformation" (1994, p. 20). Hip-Hop feminist praxis is shaped from the "kitchen table feminists" of my grandmothers and great-aunts, as well as my homegirls who found a way to survive and thrive within, through, and in spite of Long Beach crip culture. With regard to Hip-Hop, my scholarship and teaching seeks to expose inner workings and interconnectedness of racism, heteropatriarchy, sexism, misogyny, racialized poverty, and unchecked capitalist exploitation and expansion. An extended engagement with Hip-Hop culture and politics helps us make linkages between abstract hegemonic organizing structures and the "every day."

After reading Patricia Hill Collins's *Black Sexual Politics* (2005), I find that students have an easy time and even delight in analyzing performances of hegemonic gender ideology in popular culture. However, students have a difficult time dealing with the deluge of emotions that come over them when they are faced with repercussions of hegemonic gender practices in urban communities. So, as a teacher of Hip-Hop, I must find ways to force them not to look away from the real-life repercussions of hegemonic gender ideology in people of color communities. For many in the Hip-Hop generation, who come of age in neoliberal ghettos, the "every day" is tragic when viewed through an intersectional, Hip-Hop feminist lens. Students are made to consider the gendered dimensions of racialized poverty. Hip-Hop feminism requires that we make direct, undeniable, and often painful connections between destructive representations of black masculinity and black femininity and lived experience. While students learn how to analyze the workings of hegemonic gender ideologies, they are also asked to tie them to real-life situations that demonstrate the necessity of gender progressive politics in urban communities. Consider the following stories: (1) a thirteen-year-old African American girl walking home from school is called bitch because she won't respond to a disrespectful attempt to initiate conversation by a stranger (2) a ten-year-old boy is called a sissy and is then held down and beaten with a leather belt by his stepfather because he lost a fight with a neighborhood rival (3) a fifteen-year-old girl is gang raped by five neighborhood boys she knew after passing out drunk at a party (4) a fifteen-year-old lesbian is stabbed to death in front of her friends in the streets of Newark after rejecting the advances of a twenty-eight-year-old black man. For white students, it is exciting and even pleasurable to analyze how destructive racial-gender ideologies shape representations of Hip-Hop generationers; however, the fixation on critique shields them from widespread patterns of contemporary social violence that are produced by racist-sexist hierarchies in which they are implicated. For this reason, when I teach Hip-Hop culture it is always necessarily intertwined with movements for social justice within the Hip-Hop generation. Hip-Hop serves as a way to educate and inform, as well as empower and transform. While these terms are contested, the Hip-Hop feminist classroom is a homeplace for thinking about and doing resistance.

As a Hip-Hop feminist educator, the university classroom necessarily becomes both a space of creativity as well as an intellectual and political space to challenge norms, expectations, and the basic rhythm of the university. In "The Future of Our Worlds," Grace Hong (2008) argues, "This is the terrain on which we struggle to re-imagine the university as a site where different kinds of methodological, epistemological, and intellectual projects, as represented in black feminism, might emerge" (p. 98). I use the intellectual terrain of Hip-Hop to explore these issues while speaking from the "I" outward (Durham, 2007). Hip-Hop is the intellectual context in which to interrogate how interpersonal encounters curtail our ability to connect with each other on meaningful levels, limits our ability to see past corporatized representations of racialized, gendered, and classed bodies, and, most important, to begin to understand just how these representations inhibit our ability to think past the "I" and toward the "we." The contradictions of late modernity dampen the possibilities of radicalized collective social and political action, not so much because we don't understand the pernicious nature of social inequality and domination but because our praxis takes place within those very institutions that isolate us and render our politics ineffective.

Body Knowledge and Performance Pedagogy in the Classroom

In *Teaching to Transgress: Education as the Practice of Freedom* (1994), bell hooks argues that engaged pedagogy requires teachers to be actively committed to a process of self-actualization that promotes their own well-being. The texts I assign, the exercises we do, and the ideas and stories that students and I share should not just promote critical awareness of the social world but also have the potential to heal. Healing requires honesty about pain, loss, misunderstanding, and even the ways in which the most pernicious stereotypes shade the ways we all see the world. It took more than ten years for me to learn this lesson. Students didn't want to hear about the readings from me, they wanted to hear from *me*. They wanted, needed even, to hear my ideas, my opinions, and my honest assessments of their ideas and opinions. In short, they needed me to be as vulnerable as I asked them to be, and as a result, they needed to critique me as many of the readings critiqued their power and privilege in society.

Most African descendant students generally felt comfortable with, although quietly skeptical about, the rejection of the "banking model," and self-consciously anti-racist-oriented white students were comfortable with this. White students who claimed a colorblind perspective, or who only managed to apologetically confess their whiteness, were angered and insulted by this process. They felt like they were being cheated—because I didn't give them "the Truth." Rather, I toyed with the endless possibilities of knowingness in relation to Hip-Hop—exploring the temporal and spatial iterations of hip culture—the patterned ways in which certain elements of the culture become normalized and eventually dated. My refusal to staunchly stake out a particular Hip-Hop aesthetic sensibility was often infuriating and confusing. Put simply, the students' inability to read me made it difficult to know how to intellectually perform for me. My hope was to enable the student themselves to find an anchor to the culture based upon critical examination of Hip-Hop culture and politics in their own lives instead of their interpretation of mine.

On the first day of class we do the "interruption game," an exercise that I hijacked from an art-based, spoken-word collective called Voices Merging, to introduce ourselves. During the interruption game, one person stands up to introduce themselves and as soon as another student hears that have they something in common with the speaker they interrupt the speaker and begin to introduce themselves. And on we go. The game begins with false bravado and awkwardness as students are unable to resist the urge to be polite and allow classmates to finish speaking. As the game continues, students gain confidence and take control of their frightened bodies and voices. As we share, a palpable rhythm merges. The short stories that are told range "I also grew up in . . ." to "my name is _____ and I also come from a home with domestic violence" to "I'm _____ and Immortal is *my* favorite artist!" After about eight or nine minutes (that's about how long it takes for everyone to build up courage to participate or get tired of hearing the same folks talk) we have collectively formulated a narrative based on vulnerability, incoherence, triumphed fear, and necessity. Within this cipher, we have invoked space and place, as well as publicly enunciated a self-narrated story. We have begun to demystify our outer manifestation of knowingness as students physically struggle to steady their voices, tell a story they know will be cut short, and keep the beat. It is this exercise that creates the context through which Hip-Hop pedagogically emerges as a creative site of cultural engagement.

In Sex, Politics, and Hip Hop the classroom is transformed into a space of improvisation, creative exchange, and disruption. This is as true for me as it is for my students. No matter how much students may get pissed off from the process, students never seem satisfied unless they feel like they *know* me, Professor Isoke, who they always end up affectionately or exasperatedly calling "Zen-zee-lay." As we debate the origins of the art form, and the dilemmas and possibilities of Hip-Hop and feminism, we all reveal our stakes in the culture. Rather than self-righteously rejecting hypersexual popular imagery, and the caricatures of black and brown youth industry capitalizes on, we explore political agency within performances that push the boundaries of the aesthetics of the upwardly mobile students. In this complex and ambiguous milieu, it becomes obvious that it is not enough to learn how to just analyze the culture—media literacy is the first step not the end goal. Rather it becomes more important to learn how to be with Hip-Hop, and be in solidarity with its practitioners. In the end, students want to know how they can *do* the knowledge.

Before getting to this point, it soon becomes clear that we have to demystify what is meant by *knowledge*. Knowledge for most sophomores consists of being able to reliably and intelligently regurgitate complex ideas, identify falsities, and convey a degree of certainty about "the facts." In the context of Hip-Hop, knowledge about the culture does not follow such a neat and predictable model. In actuality, people "know" Hip-Hop in very different ways. Some are heavily exposed to Hip-Hop in popular media: paid advertisements, music videos, and sitcoms. Others know the culture by listening to and following the careers of specific artists from particular regions. Others are practitioners of one or more of the four standard elements, and they have developed an affinity for the culture by actively participating in it. Students, like Hip-Hop scholars, "know" the culture differently. To make this point within the first weeks of class, the students and I co-construct a knowledge spectrum about Hip-Hop that emphasizes the intellectual and affective proximity of "knowing" Hip-Hop.

Important, students' curiosity of Hip-Hop and culture does not end with text. They want to know how I analyze it—not intellectually but personally, intuitively, affectively. After all, I teach them how to identify, explore, and speak life to their desires. They want to decipher my pensive scowls and poorly concealed grins as they struggle hopelessly to politically correctly convey a political incorrect point. As they got used to my heavy sighs and dramatic nods, they eventually took a risk and tried simply to be honest. As they figure out that I respect honesty more than I do political correctness, or even theoretical savoir-faire, they come to expect the same from me. And they don't buy the academic foot shuffling of "hmm . . . that was a very interesting point," or "let's bracket this point until..." Rather, they expect me to engage, they expect me to exert the kind of political agency that the texts I assign illuminate. This form of intellectual intimacy requires that I be ready, almost at the drop of dime, to deliver a short lesson on why calling African American and Latino/as "colored" is a way of expressing solidarity with 1950s racial apartheid. Why dismissing gangsta rap as ignorant, vile, and relentlessly sexist is synonymous with dismissing blues as a culturally irrelevant, backward discourse. Spontaneity requires that I move into freestyle, step on toes, and get appropriately checked for my lack of critical regard for Nicki

Minaj and my inability to tune in weekly to analyze the cultural impact of the *The Boondocks*. Knowledge moves both ways. But what is most important is an honest account of how it is we have actually come to think we *know* Hip-Hop. Which, of course, begs the question of what it means to *know* something at all?

As instructor or facilitator of this process, I resist occupying the role of the authoritative Other—the one whose sole role is to point out and critique distortions about Hip-Hop or the one who claims to know Hip-Hop better than younger bodies who sit before me. Rather, I assume that they understand how Hip-Hop shapes their world more than I do, and I seek to elicit careful, conscious, and politically aware articulations of *how* it shapes their worldview. In other words, I aim to facilitate the process of examination of how and where students exist in relation to the culture—so that I and other students can better understand the ways in which Hip-Hop can be used toward transformative social ends. The process of learning then is more of a process of self-discovery rather than taking in, processing, and regurgitating information. The classroom setting then, to say the least, is unpredictable and, when truly successful, an explosive forum in which we all leave wounded warriors in our efforts to understand each other.

The Hip-Hop feminist classroom is a space where we do everything political correctness tells us not to do and our political astuteness tells us to do anyway. In other words, we strive to making teaching and learning a co-intentional process—a process that is driven by the interests, passions, predispositions, and expertise of all present. The dialectic process creates the knowledge that is produced within the boundaries of the classroom. Within this framework, over the course of the semester, what students come to "know" about Hip-Hop culture and politics is less important than what they come to understand about themselves, each other, and the society in which they live.

Personal Disclosure

My worldview on Hip-Hop is rooted in being raised in a tree-lined drug hood in Los Angeles County, as well as coming into my womanhood with dark brown skin, brown eyes, and "naturally curly" black hair. As much as it pains me to say, while I could listen to some of the unapologetically raunchiest of gangsta rap (yes, I used to bump dubbed versions of DJ Quik and Second 2 None), I couldn't stomach *Video Soul* on BET. I could take the incessant bitch and ho name-calling antics because, in my twelve-year-old mind, I understood that they couldn't possibly be talking about me since I was still (supposedly) a virgin. What was unbearable to me was the fact that the handsome young man singing my favorite love song, "You Can Have a Piece of my Love," was destined to fall in love with the ethnically ambiguous, light-skinned golden girl wearing a black spandex dress in the music video that got played twice an hour for weeks on end. Gangsta rap, in some sense, became a way to avoid my persistent disappointment with R&B, and NWA's "I don't give a fuck, cuzz I'll keep 'bellin,'" was a way to shake off the insults and sexual innuendos thrown my way by roughnecks of every persuasion by virtue of me walking down to the street to visit a friend.

Through dialogue, debate, personal storytelling, *and* careful and critical consideration of the assigned readings, we all work through the diverse world that Hip-Hop and late modernity has shaped. Our own sense of being in a world that can distill the most precious and dear to our hearts and transform it into a commodity—for me that was Ice Cube. While I could pass as a fly girl (on a *very* good day), I could never freely enter the male-dominated space of the house dancer because I didn't have the long ponytail to sling around as I dipped and spun like those Puerto Rican and biracial girls who would always manage to wow the crowd. Okay, I didn't have any skills either, but that's beside the point. The point is that I used my women of color, Hip-Hop generation, and subjectivity strategically to reveal the ways in which racialized and gendered dimensions of power shape the way we see ourselves and relate to each other. It was through Hip-Hop, and Hip-Hop activism more specifically, that I was able to understand, value, celebrate, and theorize aspects of myself in relation to larger systems of power in this world. As a teacher and learner, in the classroom I use Hip-Hop to get others to do the same thing.

The Virtues of Promiscuity

I share this story to lay out the complexities of Hip-Hop feminist pedagogy, specifically, the inevitable difficulties that young, black, dark-skinned feminists may have in engaging Hip-Hop in the university classroom. Most of us who have been so fortunate as to be able to put food on our table by teaching college kids about Hip-Hop have not been so deeply immersed in the culture that anyone would ever mistake us as "Hip-Hop head." While I can say that Hip-Hop was my first love, it was never my one and only, nor was it the most important one in my personal development. What I can say is that Hip-Hop culture and activism has changed my life and, in one case, probably even saved it. What I can say is that while politics is my passion, Hip-Hop is what keeps the flames blazing. Hip-Hop is a space where I can pop shit unapologetically, and drop black feminist knowledge that can make people think less about consumption and more about community. For me it, it is a way to get young people—and myself—to think more carefully about the ways in which misogyny and racism are so deeply intertwined in contemporary American culture, and how deeply we all have internalized both. My classroom is one in which we are asked to question what we love, and how we love, and therefore question what we do and how we do.

Final Thoughts: Identity and the Hip-Hop Feminist Classroom

Repositioning feminist and queer perspectives in Hip-Hop from the periphery to the center requires a strident rejection of logocentric and phallocentric tendencies of Hip-Hop studies, and Hip-Hop culture more generally. It requires creating an oppositional space that effectively exposes and destabilizes interlocking systems of domination and the cultural practices that keep these systems intact. In *Chicana Without Apology: The New Chicana Cultural Studies* (2003), Eden Torres lays out the dilemmas of women of color using the ideas of Paulo Freire uncritically in a majority white classroom. She writes, "While Freire speaks extensively on the problems associated with internalized oppression, he only gives us a vague clue on how to deal with internalized dominance—the peculiar intellectual infection that tells students that only college professors who are white, male, heterosexual and U.S. born deserve to be taken seriously" (p. 78). With regard to Hip-Hop, there also exists a similar tendency for students to valorize the experiences of men who write, study, and teach about Hip-Hop culture while minimizing the perspectives of feminists of color who embrace a sometimes contradictory, tenuous, and seemingly idiosyncratic perspective on Hip-Hop and Hip-Hop culture. The women's studies classroom becomes an exciting institutional space in which phallocentric perspectives on Hip-Hop and culture are challenged and that power relationships between students and instructors can be retheorized. In my classroom the power exchange within and between students is multidirectional, dynamic, and spiraling. What this means is that my authority derives from the students' explicit agreement to meet the requirements of the course and be graded accordingly, but my *power* in the course is exercised not over students but emerges only through my ability to enable students to find themselves in Hip-Hop discourse, to locate their own vulnerability with respect to the culture, and to use the culture to create critical knowledge about the social world.

When young feminists engage Hip-Hop, we are doing more than analyzing lyrics, historicizing the genre, or even illuminating and politicizing a distinctive worldview. We are also engaging the often visualized but less often articulated gendered politics of love, sex, and family relationships. The issues are often painful and often force us to confront our own complicity in the reproduction of destructive stereotypes. Hip-Hop becomes a site where we can flex our critical muscles and make relationships between macrolevel structures of intersecting oppressions and our own personal struggles with abandonment, victimization, and hardship with respect to love. In Sex, Politics, and Hip Hop, not only do we think carefully about how state-level policies have resulted in the widespread incarceration of people of color, but we also think about the ways in which majority black and brown communities have had to create alternative relationship models that made up for the lack created by aggressive incarceration practices.

After spending a good week on policy, we spent another week with Asha Bandele's *The Prisoner's Wife* (1999), toward the aim of laying out the impossible dilemmas of loving a prisoner, the painful futility of clinging to Eurocentric notions of romantic love for racialized minorities, and, most important, directly engaging notions of personal transformation. Hip-Hop is used to impart the importance of triangulating among theory, policy, and personal (inter)subjectivity if we are ever to effectively change an oppressive status quo.

REFERENCES

Bandele, A. (1999). *The prisoner's wife.* New York: Simon & Schuster.

Boyce-Davies, C. (1994). *Black women, writing and identity: Migrations of the subject.* New York: Routledge.

Brown, R. N. (2009). *Black girlhood celebration: Toward a Hip-Hop feminist pedagogy.* New York: Peter Lang.

Chang, J. (Ed.). (2006). Total chaos: The art and aesthetics of Hip Hop. New York: Basic Civitas.

Cobb, W. J. (2009). *To the break of dawn: A freestyle on the Hip Hop aesthetic.* New York: New York University Press.

Collins, P. H. (2005). *Black sexual politics: African Americans, gender, and the new racism.* New York & London: Routledge.

Durham, A. (2007). Using [living Hip Hop feminism]: Redefining an answer (to) rap. In G. D. Pough, R. Raimist, A. Durham, & E. Richardson (Eds.), *Home girls make some noise! Hip Hop feminism anthology.* (pp. 304-312). Mira Loma, CA: Parker.

Hill, M. L., & Billings, G. L. (2009). *Beyond beats and rhymes: Hip Hop pedagogy and the politics of identity.* New York: Teachers College Press.

Hong, G. K. (2008). The future of our worlds: Black feminism and the politics of knowledge in the university under globalization. *Meridians: Feminism, Race, Transnationalism, 127*(8), 95–115.

hooks, b. (1994). *Teaching to transgress: Education as the practice of freedom.* Boston: South End.

hooks, b. (1990). *Yearning: Race, gender and cultural politics.* Boston: South End.

Kitwana, B. (2002). *The Hip Hop generation: Young blacks and the crisis in African American culture.* New York: Basic Civitas.

Miller, J. (2008). *Getting played: African American girls, urban inequality and gendered violence.* New York: New York University Press.

Neal, M. A. (2005). *New black man.* New York & London: Routledge.

Rose, T. (2008). *Hip Hop wars: What we talk about when we talk about Hip Hop and why it matters.* New York: Basic Civitas.

Sharpley-Whiting, D. (2007). *Pimps up, hos down: Hip Hop's hold on young black women.* New York: New York University Press.

Torres, E. (2003). *Chicana without apology: The new Chicana cultural studies.* New York & London: Routledge.

CHAPTER FIVE

For Oya: I Love Myself Dancing … and Then Again When I Am Boxed in and Overwhelmed[1]

Ruth Nicole Brown

(1)
Third child
socialized by night shifts and talk of the low down front office.
Regimented by sound
bells, calls, body tolls.
A factory worker's daughter,
canned courage, the motivator of routine and discipline.
I write at night.
In his absence she never explicitly announced her expectation
even as she raised me for it.
Sold milk for a quarter,
selfless sacrificial giver and avid reader,
never just a lunch lady but a people's librarian.
Besides swim lessons, reading well was a necessity.
She resisted capitalism.
Taught me everything sold is not worth being brought.
Our capital
look at me.
She dislikes the spotlight.
Still learning.

---

1 This title is an intentional riff on Alice Walker's reader, *I Love Myself When I Am Laughing... and Then Again When I Am Looking Mean and Impressive: A Zora Neale Hurston Reader* (The Feminist Press at CUNY; First Edition. 1993).

(2)

I was talking about something completely scientific and being all scientific about it. I was interrupted, "this is not a performance ethnography Ruth Nicole."

The ceiling fan circles above my head. My eye twitches. I feel the wind starting to pick up.

(3)

SOLHOT is a space for black girls and women to celebrate black girlhood. This semester commitments have taken me away from this space I suggested—my presence is not regular. When I return I am a visitor. Amid other homegirls Treva encourages all to act. From her I learn that SOLHOT is dedicated to keeping the Hip-Hop feminist and feminine traditions alive. "Check-in" is the way we start.

Today I am in SOLHOT and Chelsea brings light with the force of lightning to the cipher by calling herself "C-killa," sharing stimulating stories of Sir Matthew, both her nemesis and boyfriend no more, to skipping thoughts and cajoling her audience/fan club/mentors/and friends with a poem consisting of title only; "Bipolar Niggas."

Her candy-coated clear cacophony of black girlhood chaos creates charismatic choruses of "CLEARLY"; Chelsea checks those constantly cheapening and cheating on coffee-colored cuties, like herself.

It's war. I clearly want Chelsea on my team.

(4)

We meet over meals and I was fed.

Candy at my side,

Chamara at my head.

Questioning and finding out the answer to their questions about qualitative methodology, interpretive methods, arts-based inquiry, and performance studies.

We started with Zora Neale Hurston and ended with them.

(5)

Dear Black woman, there is no security in interdisciplinarity. Love, me.

(6)

Mothering

a daughter, Maya Sanaa, who tolerates my need to write, to be alone, and to fry chicken. My students invite her to class. She learned how to do the batty dance in SOLHOT. Incensed wisdom at age two—she watches us call on those we want known and remembered. She came to theater rehearsal to watch Taylor especially because she loves her. She teaches me every time she falls out, loose back, lungs obviously working, that in this life there are things worth fighting for. If it is time to eat, it is time to eat. If it is time to sleep, then give me a bath, put my pajamas on, and say goodnight. My daughter reminds me that I should do only the things I will fight for.

Approach the stage with mothering warrior courage.

(7)

Nikky Finney. She speaks truth and beauty, compassionately. *Postscript to the poet*: thank you for teaching me how to be ready.

(8)

My Aunt Dottie: one of the greatest performance ethnographers, ethnodramatists I know. Aunt Dottie and Uncle Jack lived in Detroit so I was able to visit them a lot while in graduate school. Through impromptu rituals and iterations of repetitious family gatherings, block parties, church functions, doctor's visits, and everything else, the politics, pedagogy, and liberation embedded through song, her life really the verse:

"What a fellowship, what a joy divine, leaning on the everlasting arms; what a blessedness, what a peace is mine, leaning on the everlasting arms . . ."

(9)

Fast forward.

In their own time, in their own protest to group think, at the park Dom, Chamara, and Grenita choreographed a dance to Erykah Badu's "Window Seat." They are dancers with various amounts of formal training but mostly they love to dance. Grenita came with her son, Dom came with the radio and music, and Chamara came with her presence.

They want SOLHOT to perform at the award ceremony and Grenita can't make it.

I think I volunteered to take her place. I met them at the park and they taught me. My body is disciplined to sit and type. Now I must dance and move. I learned. I meditated. It is funny how you get to know a song differently once you have intentionally danced to it with loved ones.

I get to know Chamara, Dominique, and Grenita through our bodies. Mostly what theirs can do and mine does not. I was the novice. They taught me the meaning of a song I loved and thought I already knew.

Photo by Claudine Taaffe

It is time to perform. In this photo, we are dancing.

I want to redance this same dance to the same music now and again and again.

I am thankful for muscle memory and students who teach me, what it feels like to be free.

But I am nervous. Right before the performance, Dom told me, "This is how it feels Dr. Brown . . ." when I push them to do the impossible and the new.

It felt like I was falling off the edge of the world and growing wings at the same time.

Part 2

Justice

My life has taught
me to defy other
folks' expectations.

Introduction

Yearnings for justice are at the core of our pedagogy. In part 2, the issues declared important to writers and scholars of the Hip-Hop generation are named and analyzed. Black girls' and women's bodies, the food we consume and grow, our sexuality, and beloved affiliations are matters of life and death.

"The Black Girl Body as a Site of Sexual Terrorism," by Adilia James, addresses a topic too often looked over and understated: the trauma black girls face as a result of physical and sexual violence. By connecting discourses of terror, black girlhood, and violence, James persuasively documents and identifies the harsh realities many girls face as a result of sexual terror.

In "The Politics of Representation for Black Women and the Impossibility of Queering the New Jersey 4/7," Christina Carney analyzes the case of the Newark 4/7, a media spectacle that wrongly criminalized queer black women who were victims of street harassment and violence. To honor the women whose lives were severely and permanently changed, Carney explains the impossibility of legal redress for queer, black, young women subject to state surveillance and racism.

Keeping it crunk, in "Camp Carrot Seed: Reflections on a Critical Pedagogic Project," Sheri Davis-Faulkner shares lessons learned about food justice. A personal and political documentation of her experience with youth making food, Davis-Faulkner opens up a necessary discussion about how we may critically engage youth in organizing efforts centered on being well.

"Dr. Theresa Bayarea: Dancing to Make Freedom," by Chamara J. Kwakye, relies on oral history to represent the life of a black woman dance professor. The politics of black women in the academy is historically perilous. For black women professors who grew up with Hip-Hop, their stories are eerily all too similar to those who situate jazz, blues, and spirituals as their generational soundtrack. Yet, the ability to literally move, jump, and spin one's own story and, therefore, life makes this dancer's narrative aesthetically Hip-Hop, inherently feminist.

"Freedom Schools and Ella Baker," by Shaunita Levison, discusses the enduring legacy of Ella Baker. Levinson demonstrates how the adoption of culturally relevant pedagogy benefits all students and recalls Baker's legendary achievements in community education.

CHAPTER SIX

The Black Girl Body as a Site of Sexual Terrorism

Adilia James

There are feminist activists who advocate that we rename the act of verbal-physical sexual harassment. Their suggestion for substitution: *sexual terrorism* (Davis, 1997; Sheffield, 1997). They contend that by drawing this comparison to such political acts of terrorism as assassinations, we finally acknowledge the seriousness of this sexual oppression that women in our society have grown accustomed to enduring in silence. Indeed, the ever-present threat of sexual invasion and domination that women face presents viable parallels to political terrorism. In addition, particular physical sexual attacks, such as rape, are violent tactics that terrorists across the world actually use to intimidate their enemies. Yet, some would question whether other assaults like catcalls, vulgar gestures, and groping are severe enough to be labeled *terrorist*. I take young black girls as my subjects here and illustrate how the sexual violence they encounter, as well as the threat of such physical violence, inflict psychological and embodied harm. I consider their trauma within the historical context of black female sexual politics in this country.

Terrorism Hits Home: Domestic Terrorism and the 9/11 Terrorist Attacks

ter·ror·ist /**tér·rist**/ *n.* [also *attrib.*] person who uses violent methods of coercing a government or community. **ter·ror·ism** *n.* **ter·ror·is·tic** *adj.*
 • subversive, radical, insurgent, revolutionary, anarchist, nihilist, bomber, arsonist; hijacker; thug. (Jewell, 2002, p. 866)

There is no one definition of terrorism that academics unanimously accept. There is much debate about what acts count as terrorism (Coady, 2004; Waldron, 2004) and what factors cause terrorism (Crenshaw, 2000; Ehrlich & Liu, 2002). For this reason, I will develop and use a cultural—or intuitive—definition of political terrorism based on our American experience. For decades, U.S. residents regarded terrorism as a threat that they were largely unlikely to encounter on their soil—some barbaric scare tactic regulated to truly war-torn foreign locations like the borders of Israeli and Palestinian territories. Two major events have recently reshaped our cultural conception of terrorism. First, Americans were blindsided by the 1995 bombing of the Alfred P. Murrah Federal Building in Oklahoma City. Not only did a 4,800-pound bomb kill 168 individuals and injure almost 900 more (many of the victims were children), but the terrorists were none other than two white males who were born and bred in "proper" American homes (Thomas, 1997a, 1997b). Timothy J. McVeigh, a decorated Persian Gulf War army veteran and the chief architect of the terrorist plot, apparently sympathized with right-wing antigovernment groups that feared the rise of an oppressive police state. These underground coalitions cited several highly publicized incidents in support of their assertion, including: (1) the Federal Bureau of Investigation's 1992 raid on a white supremacist's cabin in Ruby Ridge, Idaho; (2) the Bureau of Alcohol, Tobacco, and Firearm's 1993 raid on a Branch Davidian compound in Waco, Texas, that left more than eighty members of the Protestant sect dead; and (3) Congress's 1993 passage of the Brady bill, which requires a five-day waiting period for the purchase of a firearm (Thomas, 1997a). Both McVeigh and his accomplice, Terry L. Nichols, were apprehended shortly after the bombing. A federal jury sentenced McVeigh to death on charges of murder and conspiracy. Many of the survivors and the victims' family members could not find closure to their grief until they witnessed his execution in 2001 (Belluck, 2001). During McVeigh's trial, the prosecution emphasized that McVeigh was not being criminally charged for his radical antigovernment ideas—not in this land of free thought and speech—but for the violent method he employed to propagate his beliefs (Thomas, 1997a).

The Oklahoma City bombing was the most destructive terrorist attack in U.S. history until September 11, 2001. On this date, a group of Middle Eastern Muslim fundamentalists hijacked commercial airliners and flew them into the World Trade Center (WTC) in New York City and the Pentagon in Washington, D.C. Their mission was to cripple the economic, political, and defense structures of a nation they believed to be corrupt, arrogant, and too intrusive in foreign politics. New York City bore the brunt of the damage. Nearly 2,800 people died in and around the WTC towers (commonly referred to as Ground Zero), and hundreds of thousands of people were injured by the debris, exposed to environmental contaminants, and witnessed traumatic events (Farel et al., 2008). Given the extent of the damage, the U.S. government set up the WTC Health Registry to track the health of those individuals directly affected by the attacks, such as witnesses to the crashes, the injured, rescue workers, and neighborhood residents. When Mark Farel and colleagues (2008) evaluated the 71,437 interviews conducted by the registry two to three years after the 9/11 attacks, they found that 67% of adult participants reported new or worsening respiratory symptoms, including shortness of breath, wheezing, and sinus irritation. This evidence confirms the obvious link between a violent attack and immediate physical injuries endured by those within close proximity. However, there is also research that suggests that the mere threat of a violent terrorist attack can cause normally healthy individuals to report poor physical health (Shirom, Toker, Shapira, Berliner, & Melamed, 2008). The stress induced by terrorism takes a physical toll on the body.

Equally as important to note, terrorist attacks also inflict psychological harm upon their victims. About 16% of the adults interviewed in the Farel and colleagues' study on 9/11 victims reported that they were diagnosed with posttraumatic stress disorder (PTSD) and 8% had been screened for serious psychological distress (SPD). These symptoms persisted from two to three years after the event. In addition, those interviewed who sustained physical injuries were more inclined to develop PTSD than those who did not (35% vs. 13%). Other studies show that the looming threat of an attack can also affect a community's mental health. Richman, Cloninger, and Rospenda (2008) conducted a mail survey of Midwestern residents before 9/11 and again in 2003 and 2005, and these researchers discovered that that the attacks on the East Coast led their centrally located respondents to exhibit increased psychological distress and alcohol use post–9/11. Terrorism creates an atmosphere of fear that attacks the psyche.

In summary, as a nation we have come to understand political terrorism as an act in which an individual uses physical violence to express his or her ideological opposition against a government's policies or a community's behavior. Although since the 9/11 attacks, media outlets and conservative interest groups have portrayed the "typical" terrorist as a foreign radical, a terrorist can also be the neighbor who grew up next door to us. A terrorist attack usually occurs without notice—it can happen anytime and anywhere. A violent attack, or the threat of an attack, can lead to the physical harm of bystanders. In addition, an attack, or the threat of an attack, can inflict fear and psychological strain. A terrorist event is so powerful that the survivors' resulting medical trauma can last for years.

Ground Zero: The Black Girl Body

Feminist scholar Carole Sheffield (1997) writes passionately about the ever-present threat of in the lives of women. She defines sexual terrorism as "a system by which males frighten and, by frightening, control and dominate females" (p. 110). Sexual terrorism techniques include physical sexual violence, as well as the threat of violence. Women can experience it at anytime and anywhere. Sheffield understands sexual terrorism to be a gendered power structure because her research exhibits that men largely do not fear rape or sexual mutilation in their everyday lives, while women do. On the one hand, this finding seems difficult to refute; but it is also important to note that the violent deaths of gay youth like those of Larry King (Setoodeh, 2008) and Matthew Shepard (Matthew Shepard Foundation, 2010) demonstrate that males who do not adhere to the norm of dominant heterosexual masculinity also live in fear of sexual(ity)-related violence. In any respect, Sheffield contends that sexual terrorism's pervasiveness as a heteropatriarchal tool is supported by the criminal and judicial systems' unwillingness to seriously consider reports of sexual harassment and the tendency of these institutions to blame the victims. Here, I expound on Sheffield's theory of sexual terrorism by exploring the dangers encountered by individuals who live at the intersection of underrepresented identities in feminist sexuality literature: youth and black females. Or, perhaps it would be better to say that I am studying black girls beyond the context of teen pregnancy and provocative sexual expression (e.g., Edin & Kefalas, 2005; Sharpley-Whiting, 2007). I bring forth evidence from such areas as psychology and phenomenological theory that suggests that both sexual violence and the threat of sexual violence are likely to lead to embodied and psychological harm. My discussion of sexual terrorism in black girls' lives is limited to two forms: school hallway harassment and dating violence.

What makes the sexual terrorism experienced by young black girls different from the sexual terrorism experienced by other identity groups? First, black feminist scholar Deidre E. Davis (1997) insists that such forms of sexual terrorism as street harassment remind black women that the ideologies of slavery are still very much alive. During the era of U.S. slavery, white male slave owners concocted rigid biological and social distinctions between their own wives and African women in order to justify their inhumane exploitation of the latter group. White, middle- and upper-class women were propagated to be pious, pure, and submissive creatures in need of white male protection. African slave women were understood to be sexually aggressive beasts in need of white male domination. Rape, beatings, and verbal threats all became permissible tools for white men to use during the process of breaking in their African female slaves (Collins, 2000;

Gaspar & Hine, 1996). Today, the white men who target black women with their acts of sexual terrorism are perpetuating these racist and sexist stereotypes. Black men now also participate in this system of domination, although their impact is fundamentally different because of their relatively subordinated position to white men in the racial-gender power structure. Davis does not mean to assert that black women are the primary targets of sexual terrorism in our culture. Rather, she purports that black women's understandings of sexual terrorism are distinct from those of other women because of our particular political history of subordination and our unique struggle for freedom.

Additionally, the acts of sexual terrorism that black girls face serve as yet another reminder that their childhoods are far from innocent. In (2008), Dr. Ruth Nicole Brown joined historian Wilma King (1995) and sociologist Joyce A. Ladner (1995) in alerting us to the fact that black females have never really experienced a carefree girlhood, unless "one was intentionally created for them" (Brown, p. 39). Most black girls confront a number of so-called adult issues on a daily basis, including racism (Masko, 2005), (racialized) sexism (Fordham, 1993; Grant, 1994), and classism (Evans-Winters, 2005).

Thus, I conclude that sexual terrorism is similar to political terrorism in that male perpetrators use physical violence (e.g., molestation, rape) or the threat of force (e.g., catcalls, groping) to subordinate and denigrate women. Although a political definition of terrorism emphasizes the stated (or implied) intent of the terrorist, I place greater emphasis on women's reactions to sexual terrorist attacks. Thus, a man who whistles at a woman walking down the street may believe he is only flirting or showing his appreciation for her beauty; but for many women whistling is also an indicator that their bodies are always being evaluated and monitored for possible sexual invasion. Sexual terrorists can include strangers on the street, peers from school and work, and dating partners. Thus, a woman can encounter a sexual terrorist attack just about anywhere and at any time. And, of course, sexual terrorist attacks can leave behind physical and emotional scars. What is also important to note is that women may possess different interpretations of their attacks depending on the particular intersection of their identity markers.

Terror in the Halls

Sexual harassment in schools is similar to political terrorism in that the threat of invasion is ever-present for young girls. Students are more likely to face harassment from their peers rather than from teachers or administrators. The specific nature of the tactics ranges from lewd jokes to rape. The most common in-school locations for sexual harassment are hallways, classrooms, and cafeterias (AAUW, 2001). The American Association of University Women (AAUW) has conducted some of the most comprehensive empirical reviews of sexual harassment in our nation's schools (1993, 2001). Their latest study, (2001), which consists of survey data from a representative sample of public school students in eighth to eleventh grades, revealed that 81% of their respondents experienced sexual harassment in their school lives often, occasionally, or rarely. Girls were slightly more likely than boys to have ever experienced sexual harassment (83% vs. 79%, respectively). There were significant gender and race/ethnicity differences in students' reports of nonphysical harassment. Girls were more likely than boys to say that they had faced sexual comments, jokes, gestures, or looks (73% vs. 59%). More males than females reported being called gay in a derogatory manner (49% vs. 42%). Additionally, black girls were less likely than white girls to have someone call them lesbian (20% vs. 32%). There were also significant social differences in students' responses to questions about physical harassment. A higher proportion of females than males shared that they had been touched, grabbed, or pinched in a sexual way (57% vs. 42%). Fewer girls than boys reported that someone had pulled down their clothes (12% vs. 19%). However, black girls were more likely than both white and Latina girls to have experienced unwanted touching (67% for blacks vs. 51% for Latinas and 56% for whites), to have had someone tug at their clothes in a sexual manner (50% for blacks vs. 30% for Latinas and 32% for whites), or to have been forced to kiss someone (28% for blacks vs. 18% for Latinas and 15% for whites). AAUW's estimated rate of sexual harassment in secondary schools is simply startling.

Admittedly, there are other studies with much more moderate results regarding sexual harassment in schools. The report (Dinkes, Kemp, & Baum, 2009) is an annual joint report of the U.S. Departments of Education and Justice that synthesizes national school violence data. This government publication shows that during the school year that AAUW collected its data for the report, 36.3% of U.S. public schools reported incidents of sexual harassment, 2.5% sexual battery other than rape, and 0.7% rape or attempted rape. About 3.0% of public school principals stated that they had to discipline students for sexual harassment of other students at least once a week over the course of the 2007–2008 school year. And in 2007, 1.0% of male students, as well as 1.0% of female students, reported that they were targets of hate-related words regarding to their sexual orientation. Actually, AAUW researchers can pretty easily explain the low rates of sexual harassment in schools presented by this government report: Only 40% of students who participated in the study said they would be likely to complain to a school adult if they were sexually harassed by another student. In addition, in her legal review (1999), scholar Nan Stein contends that even when students report sexual harassment to their teachers or principals, these adults often trivialize the incidents or try to neutralize tensions with quick and simple punishments—thus, fewer claims reach the status of formal complaints. These discrepancies reveal that in-depth studies of U.S. school culture, rather than a cursory collection of census data, will provide us with the information needed to properly evaluate the extent of sexual harassment as a social problem in schools.

In much the same way that a political terrorist attack inflicts psychological harm on its victims by cultivating an environment of violence and fear, sexual harassment in schools leaves students with serious emotional scars. About half (47%) of students included in the report who had experienced sexual harassment in their school lives stated that they felt very or somewhat upset right after the episode. Girls were more than twice as likely as the boys to have such feelings (66% vs. 28%). In addition, significantly more female students than male students said that they felt self-conscious (44% vs. 19%), embarrassed (53% vs. 32%), afraid (33% vs. 12%), or less self-assured (32% vs. 16%) by their encounters with either nonphysical or physical harassment. Sexual harassment also places limitations on girls' freedom. As a result of these gender differences in emotional response to sexual harassment, a higher percentage of girls than boys shared that they changed their behavior as a result of sexual harassment. The most common changes for girls included avoiding the person who harassed them, changing their seat in class to get farther away from a harasser, and not talking as much in class.

These survey results reflect the real experiences of LaShonda Davis, the young black girl from Forsyth, Georgia, who brought her case of peer sexual harassment all the way to the U.S. Supreme Court (Biskupic, 1999; Copeland, 1999; Kopels & Dupper, 1999). During her fifth-grade year, a male classmate teased, groped, and stalked LaShonda. When her teachers and principal ignored her complaints, LaShonda wrote a suicide note. That's when her mother, Aurelia Davis, took her case to the courts. In 1999, the Supreme Court declared that under Title IX, school officials must provide financial compensation to victims of peer sexual harassment if they are "deliberately indifferent to sexual harassment, of which they have actual knowledge" and the harassment is "so severe, pervasive, and objectively offensive that it can be said to deprive the victims of access to the educational opportunities or benefits provided by the school" ("The Supreme Court: Excerpts from Decision on Sexual Harassment," 1999, p. 25). There is ongoing debate about whether this ruling is too vague to implement any effective measures in actual schools (Rich-Chappell, 1999; Weiss, 2007).

Using a phenomenological perspective, I also assert that the physical female body reacts to the threat of sexual harassment. Specifically, Iris Marion Young's essay "Throwing like a Girl: A Phenomenology of Feminine Body Comportment, Motility, and Spatiality" (2005) is a good point of departure for this venture. In this essay, Young relays formal and informal observations of females in late twentieth-century industrial Western societies, commenting on the restraints girls and women place on their own physical movement. Young introduces three modalities of feminine motility in this essay that are based on fellow phenomenologists Simone de Beauvoir and Maurice Merleau-Ponty's theoretical musings: (1) ambiguous transcendence, (2) inhibited intentionality, and (3) discontinuous unity with the surrounding environment. First, ambiguous transcendence refers to females' constant feeling that their bodies are not their own. Since males often treat women's and girls' bodies as objects to be looked over and handled, females often try to hide their bodies by clasping their arms close to their chests or walking hurriedly through the streets. Second, inhibited intentionality is females' reluctance to approach and complete a given task. Young offers as example girls who shyly climb the pitching mound and half-heartedly toss a ball as if they do not have faith in themselves as full human subjects who have control over their own bodies. Third, Young describes discontinuous unity as the phenomenon in which females use only one or two parts of their body when approaching a task. While young boys usually step into their pitches, using the full force of their legs, arms, and torso, girls merely lift up their arm and throw the ball a short distance. To Young, it appears as though girls are protecting their "fragile" body by keeping it mostly motionless.

Young's primary objective in this essay is to describe the manner in which society's gender ideologies objectify the female body. However, she also recognizes that these ideologies leave females feeling worried about threats on their personal space. Young writes:

> She also lives the threat of invasion of her body space. The most extreme form of such spatial and bodily invasion is the threat of rape. But we daily are subject to the possibility of bodily invasion in many far more subtle ways as well.... I would suggest that the enclosed space that has been described as a modality of feminine spatiality is in part a defense against such invasion.... The woman lives her space as confined and closed around her, at least in part as projecting some small area in which she can exist as a free subject. (2005, p. 45)

Therefore, Young concludes that women embody sexist ideology and the threat of gendered sexual violence as is best exemplified by their visible hesitance in the movement of their bodies in public spaces. Much as the survivors of a bomb or shooting rampage, a girl who survives a sexual terrorist attack—particularly a physical one—is likely to experience a period of emotional shock that makes her especially cognizant of the possible dangers around her. And this self-consciousness can be easily read on girls' bodies.

The stories of schoolgirls like LaShonda Davis serve as evidence that few children today experience "innocent" childhoods. Persistent and violent sexual harassment is becoming an increasing problem in grades kindergarten through 12. What is different about LaShonda's story is the possibility that her case exhibited undercurrents of racism. Perhaps LaShonda's harasser targeted her specifically because he had been socialized by his favorite rap artists or peers that black girls are "easy" and "say, 'No!' when they really mean, 'Yes!'" Additionally, LaShonda's principal admitted that he had received a complaint from her at least once, but for some unspecified reason he failed to take any action to remedy the situation (Copeland, 1999). How did she interpret this total disregard for her suffering? Was she concerned that her principal was ignoring her complaints because he possibly believed that black girls are especially flirtatious and "fast" (i.e., they sexually mature faster than others)? LaShonda's harasser may have pursued her simply because he was attracted to her, and her principal may have ignored complaints from girls of all races, but LaShonda's interpretation of events certainly shaped the course of her trauma.

On November 6, 2009, the Caribbean female recording artist Rihanna (age twenty) sat down for a much anticipated television interview with journalist Diane Sawyer (Martz, Rhee, & Zak, 2009). It was nearly nine months to the date since her boyfriend Chris Brown (age twenty), a black male R&B star, had violently attacked her during a car ride home from a Grammy Awards party. Within hours of the assault, someone leaked a photo of her swollen and bruised face to the press. For weeks, new reporters, talk show hosts, and bloggers circulated the haunting image and debated the ramifications of the incident. Both Rihanna and Brown escaped into seclusion while numerous speculations about that night were bounced around the media outlets. In her interview with Sawyer, Rihanna explained that it all began with her confronting Brown about a text message on his cell phone from an old girlfriend. She begged him to admit that he had been lying about the nature of their relationship. As Rihanna put it, she just "wouldn't drop it." Rihanna went on to further explain, "So…. it escalated into him being violent towards me and… it was ugly." Brown punched, bit, and shoved Rihanna, in addition to putting her into a headlock that was so severe that she had difficulty breathing.

This incident clearly reflects the broad definition of political terrorism: Brown used physical violence to demonstrate his opposition against Rihanna's dating policy and behavior. Specifically, he used force to express his anger with Rihanna's insistence that their dating relationship be exclusive as well as her dissatisfaction with his violation of the rule. Dating or intimate relationship violence is a prevalent form of sexual terrorism in this country. A critical finding of the National Violence Against Women Survey (Tjaden & Thoennes, 2000), cosponsored by the National Institute of Justice and the Centers for Disease Control and Prevention (CDC) was that 25% of the women surveyed (n = 8,000) said they had been raped or physically assaulted by a spouse, cohabiting partner, or date at some time in their lifetime. Analysts project that this translates to mean about 1.5 million U.S. women experience violence in intimate relationships. And since many women are victimized more than once, the estimated number of attacks against women is 4.8 million annually. Women of color are significantly more likely than white women to face an attack; but among women of color, American Indian/Alaska Native women are at the greatest risk. Interestingly, the Youth Risk

Behavior Survey of 2007 (CDC, 2008), which monitors the lives of our nation's high school students, found that a slightly higher percentage of young men than young women reported being hit, slapped, or physically hurt on purpose by their boyfriend or girlfriend during the twelve months before the survey (11.0% vs. 8.8%). Yet, an overwhelming larger proportion of girls than boys said that they had been forced to have sexual intercourse (11.3% vs. 4.5%). These findings have led several government organizations to declare violence against women a serious criminal justice and public health concern (Tjaden & Thoennes, 2000).

Like an act of political terrorism, Rihanna's attack occurred without notice. Rihanna expressed confusion about how a verbal argument escalated into battery. In describing the moments directly after the blows, Rihanna told Sawyer:

> I was battered. I was bleeding. I was swollen in my face. So there was no way of me getting home except for my next option was for me to get out the car and walk. Start walking in a gown and bloody face. So I really didn't know what was my plan. I didn't have a plan. That whole night was not part of my plan.

Indeed, victims of political terrorism rarely learn about a terrorist's plan in time to escape danger.

The physical harm that Rihanna endured was indisputable to anyone who viewed the photo of her battered face. What Rihanna revealed in her interview was the emotional torment she had been struggling with over the course of several months. When Rihanna was shown a video of the apology that Brown had posted on YouTube.com, she eloquently responded:

> I know that he felt really bad about doing it. I just didn't know if he understood the extent of what he did. The thing that men don't really realize when they hit a woman is the face, the broken arm, the black eye—it's gonna heal. That's not the problem. It's the scar inside. You flash back and you remember it all the time. It comes back to you whether you like it or not. And it's painful.

During the days that the incident dominated the news, Rihanna preferred to remain alone and felt too embarrassed to speak to friends or family members. She felt incredibly lonely as a result and spent much of her time crying. Rihanna was on an emotional rollercoaster. Three weeks after that infamous night, she actually flew to Miami to vacation with Brown. She still loved him, and she was afraid to lose "this empire" that she had built with Brown by her side. Not only did her resentment toward him begin to challenge her love for him, but she also was afraid that by returning to Brown she was sending a wrong message to girls that could actually cost them their lives. According to a CDC national report on violent deaths (2009), intimate-partner violence was a precipitating factor in 52.2% of the total female homicides reported in 2006 (16 states, or 26% of the U.S. population, were included in their final analysis). The consequence of staying in a violent relationship can be grave.

However, there were many young girls, largely from Brown's fan base, who were quick to suggest that Rihanna must have known that her persistent nagging over the text message would cause him to get violently angry. When a reporter (Hoffman, 2009) asked two ninth-grade girls from the Bronx, New York, why they defended Brown even after seeing the photo of Rihanna's face, one student responded, "She probably made him mad for him to react like that. You know, like, bring it on." The other girl believed that Brown shouldn't have been criminally prosecuted since Rihanna had recently joined him in Miami and they appeared to have reconciled: "She probably feels bad that it was her fault, so she took him back." These reactions so plainly illustrate Deidre E. Davis's assertion that sexual terrorism serves as a reminder to black women that the ideologies of slavery still structure their lives. These girls, along with numerous other individuals speaking out on blogs and YouTube videos, perpetuated the racially sexist stereotype that black women are sexually aggressive monsters in need of taming and subordination at the hands of a strong man. Many contend that that Grammy night would have ended on a beautiful note if Rihanna would have ignored the text message from Brown's ex-girlfriend (giving Brown the benefit of the doubt) or if she had stopped asking him about it the first time he asked her to drop the subject. But she just had to learn the hard way what happens to a woman who does not pay deference to her man. Studies suggest that this may be a relatively common view among black youth. When Sara B. Johnson and her colleagues (2005) completed focus groups with 120 urban, predominately black youth (ages fourteen to twenty-two) to gather their perspectives on violence and fighting, gender-based violence became a central part of the discussions. Participants in the female focus group often agreed that girls do things to make boys want to hit them. As one young woman offered: "It's understandable why men abuse women . . . women do not know how to be quiet" (p. 176). In accordance, both female and male focus groups proposed that men sometimes abuse their girlfriends as punishment for being disrespectful. Some female participants also speculated that girls identify abuse as acts of love, the logic being something like, "If he didn't love me and didn't want to be with me, he would just leave me instead of expressing what he expects out of this relationship." Many of the participants explained that they had learned this lesson from watching their parents' fights.

Feminists' use of the term to describe the sexual harassment faced by women everywhere and every day is not an unfair proposition, for in this essay I have illustrated that sexual harassment against females inflicts psychological and embodied harm in much the same ways as violent political terrorist attacks. But I will also add that those who live under the constant threat of terrorism do not always crumble under the weight of fear. In fact, a range of research projects using a multiplicity of methodologies demonstrate that a population's self-esteem is more positive when mortality salience is high rather than when it is low. "Ironically," Gurari and colleagues (2009) wrote, "it seems that implicitly, people may feel better about themselves in the face of terrorist attacks designed to demoralize them" (p. 494). We saw extravagant displays of patriotism and optimism directly after the 9/11 attacks in the form of American flags on every suburban lawn and urban storefronts, and the White House administration's urge for citizens to get back to their everyday routines. Similarly, in spite of the threat of sexual violence, many girls still confidently arrive at school with provocative clothing and look for new love after breaking up with an abusive boyfriend. Black women have traditionally sought transcendence from the racialized sexual stereotypes that threaten to control their lives by singing the blues and writing novels (Collins, 2000). Today's black girls are defining their own images of themselves by building online forums (e.g., blogs, social networking sites) (Stokes, 2007) and participating in unique advocacy spaces like SOLHOT (Brown, 2008). More research needs to be conducted with young females to understand the nature of their resilience so that parents, teachers, school counselors, and other adults who work with students can aid those girls who are grappling with the negative effects of sexual terrorism.

REFERENCES

American Association of University Women Educational Foundation. (1993). *Hostile hallways: The AAUW survey on sexual harassment in America's schools.* Washington, DC: American Association of University Women Educational Foundation.

American Association of University Women Educational Foundation. (2001). *Hostile hallways: Bullying, teasing, and sexual harassment in school.* Washington, DC: American Association of University Women Educational Foundation.

Belluck, P. (2001, June 12). The McVeigh execution: The scene; calm at execution site and silence by McVeigh prove unsettling for some. *New York Times.* Retrieved January 19, 2010, from http://www.nytimes.com/2001/06/12/us/mcveigh-execution-scene-calm-execution-site-silence-mcveigh-prove-unsettling-for.html?scp=2&sq=The%20McVeigh%20Execution&st=cse

Biskupic, J. (1999, January 11). High court reviews student sexual harassment, *Washington Post*, p. A6.

Brown, R. N. (2008). *Black girlhood celebration: Toward a Hip-Hop feminist pedagogy.* New York: Peter Lang.

Centers for Disease Control and Prevention. (2008, June 6). *Youth risk behavior surveillance—United States, 2007.* Morbidity and Mortality Weekly Report, 57(SS–4). Retrieved March 13, 2010, from http://www.cdc.gov/mmwr/PDF/ss/ss5704.pdf

Coady, C. A. J. (2004). Terrorism and innocence. *Journal of Ethics,* (1), 37–58.

Collins, P. H. (2000). *Black feminist thought: Knowledge, consciousness, and the politics of empowerment* (2nd ed.). New York: Routledge.

Copeland, L. (1999, January 11). Court tackles harassment in schools, *USA Today,* p. 1A.

Crenshaw, M. (2002). The psychology of terrorism: An agenda for the 21st century. *Political Psychology, 21* (2), 405–420.

Davis, D. E. (1997). The harm that has no name: Street harassment, embodiment, and African American women. In A. K. Wing (Ed.), *Critical race feminism: A reader* (pp. 192–202). New York: New York University Press.

Dinkes, R., Kemp, J., & Baum, K. (2009). *Indicators of school crime and safety: 2009* (NCES 2010–012/NCJ228478). Washington, DC: National Center for Education Statistics, Institute of Education Sciences, U.S. Department of Education, and Bureau of Justice Statistics, Office of Justice Programs, U.S. Department of Justice.

Edin, K., & Kefalas, M. (2005). *Promises I can keep: Why poor women put motherhood before marriage.* Berkeley & Los Angeles: University of California Press.

Ehrlich, P. R., & Liu, J. (2002). Some roots of terrorism. *Population and Environment, 24* (2), 183–192.

Evans-Winters, V. E. (2005). *Teaching black girls: Resiliency in urban classrooms.* New York: Peter Lang.

Farel, M., DiGrande, L., Brackbill, R., Prann, A., et al. (2008). An overview of 9/11 experiences and respiratory and mental health conditions among World Trade Center health registry enrollees. *Journal of Urban Health, 85* (6), 880–909.

Fogg-Davis, H. G. (2006). Theorizing black lesbians within black feminism: A critique of same-race street harassment. *Politics & Gender, 2,* 57–76.

Fordham, S. (1993). "Those loud black girls": (Black) women, silence, and gender "passing" in the academy. Anthropology & Education Quarterly, 24 (1), 3–32.

Gaspar, D. B., & Hine, D. C. (Eds.) (1996). *More than chattel: Black women and slavery in the Americas.* Bloomington: Indiana University Press.

Grant, L. (1994). Helpers, enforcers, and go-betweens: Black females in elementary school classrooms. In M. B. Zinn, & B. T. Dill (Eds.), *Women of color in U.S. society* (pp. 43–63). Philadelphia: Temple University Press.

Gurari, I., Strube, M. J., & Hetts, J. J. (2009). Death? Be proud! The ironic effects of terror salience on implicit self-esteem. *Journal of Applied Social Psychology, 39* (2), 494–507.

Hoffman, J. (2009, March 19). Teenage girls stand by their man. *New York Times.* Retrieved March 19, 2009, from http://www.nytimes.com/2009/03/19/fashion/19brown.html?_r=1&scp=1&sq=teenage%20girls%20stand%20by%20their%20man&st=cse

Jewell, E. J. (Ed.). (2002). *Oxford pocket dictionary and thesaurus* (2nd American ed., p. 866). New York: Oxford University Press.

Johnson, S. B., Frattaroli, S., Campbell, J., et al. (2005). "I know what love means": Gender-based violence in the lives of urban adolescents. *Journal of Women's Health, 14* (2), 172–179.

King, W. (1995). *Stolen childhood: Slave youth in nineteenth-century America.* Bloomington: Indiana University Press.

Kopels, S., & Dupper, D. R. (1999). School-based peer sexual harassment. *Child Welfare, 78* (4), 435–460.

Ladner, J. A. (1995). *Tomorrow's tomorrow: The black woman.* Lincoln & London: University of Nebraska Press.

Martz, G., Rhee, K., & Zak, L. (Producers). (2009, November 6). *20/20* [Television broadcast]. New York: American Broadcasting Co.

Masko, A. L. (2005). "I think about it all the time": A 12-year-old girl's internal crisis with racism and the effects on her mental health. *Urban Review, 37* (4), 329–350.

Matthew Shepard Foundation. (2010). Matthew's life. Retrieved January 25, 2010, from http://www.matthewshepard.org/site/PageServer?pagename=mat_Matthews_Life

Rich-Chappell, M. (1999). Child's play or sex discrimination?: School liability for peer sexual harassment under Title IX. *Journal of Gender, Race, and Justice, 3* (1), 311–342.

Richman, J. A., Cloninger, L., & Rospenda, K. M. (2008). Macrolevel stressors, terrorism, and mental health outcomes: Broadening the stress paradigm. *American Journal of Public Health, 98,* 323–329.

Setoodeh, R. (2008, July 19). Young, gay and murdered. *Newsweek.* Retrieved January 25, 2010, from http://www.newsweek.com/id/147790

Sharpley-Whiting, T. D. (2007). *Pimps up, ho's down: Hip hop's hold on young black women.* New York: New York University Press.

Sheffield, C. (1997). Sexual terrorism. In L. L. O'Toole & J. R. Schiffman (Eds.), *ender violence: Interdisciplinary perspectives* (pp. 110–128). New York: New York University Press.

Shirom, A., Toker, S., Shapira, I., Berliner, S., & Melamed, S. (2008). Exposure to and fear of terror as predictors of self-rated health among apparently healthy employees. *British Journal of Health Psychology, 12,* 257–271.

Stein, N. (1999). *Facing sexual harassment in K–12 schools.* New York: Teachers College Press.

Stokes, C. E. (2007). Representin' in cyberspaces: Sexual scripts, self-definition, and Hip Hop culture in black American adolescent girls' home pages. *Culture, Health & Sexuality, 9* (2), 169–184.

The Supreme Court; Excerpts from decision on sexual harassment. (1999, May 25). *New York Times,* p. 25.

Thomas, J. (1997a, June 3). The Oklahoma City bombing: The overview; McVeigh guilty on all counts in the Oklahoma City bombing; jury to weigh death penalty. . Retrieved January 19, 2010, from http://www.nytimes.com/1997/06/03/us/mcveigh-guilty-all-counts-oklahoma-city-bombing-jury-weigh-death-penalty.html?scp=1&sq=The%20Oklahoma%20City%20Bombing:%20The%20Overview&st=cse

Thomas, J. (1997b, June 14). The Oklahoma City bombing: The verdict; McVeigh jury decides on sentence of death in Oklahoma bombing. *New York Times.* Retrieved January 19, 2010, from http://www.nytimes.com/1997/06/14/us/mcveigh-jury-decides-on-sentence-of-death-in-oklahoma-bombing.html?scp=1&sq=McVeigh%20jury%20decides%20on%20sentence%20of%20death%20&st=cse

Tjaden, P., & Thoennes, N. (2000, July). *Extent, nature, and consequences of intimate partner violence: Findings from the national violence against women survey.* Washington, DC: Centers for Disease Control and Prevention and National Institute of Justice.

Waldron, J. (2004). Terrorism and the uses of terror. *Journal of Ethics, 8* (1), 5–35.

Weiss, B. I. (2007). Title IX versus Canadian human rights legislation: How the United States should learn from Canada's human rights act in the context of sexual harassment in schools. *UC Davis Journal of Juvenile Law & Policy, 11* (1), 55–100.

Young, I. M. (2005). Throwing like a girl: A phenomenology of feminine body comportment, motility, and spatiality. In I. M. Young(Ed.), *On female body experience: "Throwing like a girl" and other essays* (pp. 27–45). Oxford: Oxford University Press.

CHAPTER SEVEN

The Politics of Representation for Black Women and the Impossibility of Queering the New Jersey 4/7

Christina Carney

On the night of August 18, 2006, at approximately 1:55 a.m., in front of the Independent Film Center Theater in the historic neighborhood of Greenwich Village in New York City, Terrain Dandridge, Renata Hill, Venice Brown, Patreese Johnson, Chenese Loyal, Lania Daniels, and Khamysha Coates were stopped by independent filmmaker Dwayne Buckle while walking toward the Metro to return to Newark, New Jersey. Though the defendants' and their accusers' stories differ, according to the women, Buckle was sitting in front of the IFC and made the following remark toward Patreese Johnson: "Let me get some of that" (Hartocollis, 2007). Afterward, the women claimed that Buckle called them homophobic slurs and threatened sexual assault (Hartocollis). From there a physical confrontation ensued between the women, Buckle, and several men (who remained unidentified) that resulted in the bruising of several of the women and the stabbing of Buckle. The defendants were originally charged with assault (which carried gang citations) and attempted murder by New York City prosecutors. While three of the women accepted plea bargains, four decided to go to trial. All four were convicted in April 2007. Dandridge (twenty years old at the time) was sentenced to 3.5 years, Brown (age nineteen) to 5 years, Hill (twenty-five years of age) 8 years, and Johnson (age nineteen) to 11 years. Buckle claimed that he was the victim of a "hate crime against a straight man" (Hartocollis). The incident raises these questions:

- How and why were the NJ4/7 not able to seek the redress that they desired?
- How is the discourse of the NJ4/7 as inherently pathological constituted and maintained ideologically and discursively?
- Are there any other sites, besides the U.S. courtroom, that offer alternative political possibilities?

The NJ4/7 incident serves as a lens of how blackness as a discourse and legality demonstrates that the theory of universality is an impossibility for black queer women. Representations of the black community, which are gendered, are reinforced through representations of black women as mammies, welfare queens, and black lesbians as inherently criminal has further validated violence (Collins, 1999; Lubiano, 1997). Seeking alternatives to rights-based perspectives promotes other possibilities that limit violence based on identities structured around the normalization of gender, class, sexuality, and race.

The NJ4/7 incident is not exceptional but serves as an example of the general predicament not only queer black women face on a daily basis but also black men and other peoples of color. The impossibility of the black female body to embody virtue and a respectable womanhood is discursively structured relationally to white femininity (Hartman, 1997). Street harassment and the violence it produces (especially upon refusal of a sexual advance) serve as a reflection of greater investments in heteronormativity. This case also serves as proof that rights for black lesbian/gay/bisexual/transgender/ queer (LGBTQ) identities do not guarantee that redress will be allocated properly because of the discourse of blackness as a distraction to juridical universality (Silva, 2001).

Unfortunately, a prime example in the investment of blackness as abject is reflected in contemporary queer politics. Though spaces such as the Village in New York City or Hillcrest in San Diego may serve as an example of contesting heteronormativity, they also produce another problematic discourse—homonormativity (Duggan, 2003). Nationally these new economically revamped spaces have become hubs for entertainment, nightlife, and other forms of consumerism for all people. These urban spaces have served as the primary center for generations of young men and women (queer and straight) who have grown up primarily in suburban spaces and, unlike their parents, have returned back to the city to reclaim space and economic investments. Black and brown bodies serves as the entertainment and but are not welcomed as desirable neighbors. Again, blackness as abject is reinforced even in queer spaces and politics.

It is my hope that this case and similar situations like the NJ4/7, but whose stories remain invisible because of discourses that reinforce them as worthy of the violence against their bodies, invoke urgency toward the continued trajectory of racialized violence. While the stories of Matthew Sheppard, a Casper City, Wyoming, teen murdered because of his sexuality, generated a significant amount of national attention and the introduction of hate crime legislation, many women and men of color are not allocated the same attention, space, and ethical crisis. The women of the NJ4/7 articulate a vulnerability because their sexuality was an impossiblity. It was impossible because a discourse of blackness, in the particular context, negated a claim of lesbian/gay identity. Instead lesbian/gay identity as space is constructed as white and preferably male (patriarchal). Instead, women as victims are automatically labeled as perpetrators. The black body and space (e.g., adjacent neighborhoods to the Village) yet again become symbols of violence and excess—regardless of gender.

The Headlines

During my search for print media I noticed that many alternative black press sites, in general, failed to address the incident. Likewise, mainstream LGBTQ newspapers were generally nonresponsive to the incident. However, more mainstream newspapers, such as the and , profiled the incident from its beginning until the New Jersey 4/7's sentence. The *New York Times* (NYT) was the newspaper that initially wrote about the NJ4/7 incident.

The headline for the article, August 19, 2006, reads: "Man Is Stabbed in Attack after Admiring a Stranger." According to the article,

> It all began harmlessly, the victim, a 28-year-old man from Queens said, with a comment he made to a woman who walked past him early yesterday on a Manhattan sidewalk. But things quickly escalated into an ugly and ultimately violent confrontation that led to the man, Dwayne Buckle, being stabbed in his abdomen with a steak knife, and the arrest of seven women, ranging in age from 18 to 31 who are accused in the attack, police say. (Buckley, 2006)

It was not until April 14, 2007, five days before the NJ4/7's conviction, that the *NYT* decided to offer the perspective of the women.

On the day following the publication of the initial article, on August 20, 2006, the headlines read "'Hatred' by Lez Gang; Straight-Bash Claims" (Akram, 2006). Two months later, a new article was released titled "Lesbian Gang-Stab Shocker" (Italiano, 2006). In the August 20 publication, Buckle claimed that a large number of gay women attacked him. He even argued that he was the victim of the confrontation. The spectacle of racialized violence, especially between parties of the same race, was thus normalized and individualized. The concentration is on the spectacle of women's refusal to be objectified, not Buckle's sexual advances, which are actually normalized in this case.

The hysterical fear of girls and women of color is not unique to the NJ4/7 case, but follows a trajectory of sensationalized new coverage of women of color as criminal (Eliason & Chesney-Lind, 2006). Mainstream U.S.–based feminism, centered on an investment in a politics of recognition is articulated by law enforcement and criminologists as a risk that assumes that the constructed inherent violence of men (especially men of color) will now be appropriated by women. Women of color are contesting this assumption of an access to power by reason of its supposed deviant embodiment. During the 1990s several newspapers reported the link between women's empowerment and the current generation's epidemic female criminality (Eliason & Chesney-Lind).

The *Post* and the *Times* did not differ significantly in their responses to the NJ4/7 incident. Both privileged the position of Dwayne Buckle as the victim. The *Post* sensationalized the incident throughout. In addition to their failure to add an alternative perspective to the incident, because of the reality of daily street harassment, the *Post* and *Times* also contributed to a discourse that positions queer communities as safe only for white upper-middle-class inhabitants (gay or straight). Additionally, the link between women of color and criminality was heightened during the 1990s along with sensationalized representations of the fictionalized increase in violence perpetrated by women of color. Eliason and Chesney-Lind (2006) have noted that the discourse of female masculinity was heightened with the inclusion of its supposed performance by black and brown youth. The increased incarceration of black and brown youth in the post–civil rights period affected both male and female youth. However, the discourses that rationalized their constructed criminality differed. For black men, it was business as usual. For example, black and brown men as sexual aggressors served as trademarks for decidedly inherent qualities. However, for black women, their fall from virtue was the refusal of heterosexual desire.

In reviewing the media's analysis of the incident, it is also important to discuss attempts to construct a counternarrative by the women involved in the incident. I have decided to use the trailer, accessed from YouTube.com, for analysis. This four-minute, six-second clip focuses on the reality of the Village in NYC as not always a safe space for LGBTQ youth of color.

Renata speaks on what attracted her and her peers to the Village of NYC: "I like to go to the village because there is nothing but gay people . . . people I never thought would be gay . . . like wow, I didn't even know they had gayness out in like 1920. You got people like 80 years old that's gay" (Doroshwalther, 2011). Renata continues on the Village, "You're around your own kind, you don't have to worry about getting judged by people" (Doroshwalther). However, this space turned out to not be so safe for these women. Their articulations of verbal and physical abuse were made invisible. Though the Village offered a sense of comfort regarding their sexual identity, it did not offer the same comfort in regard to race and police response to the crisis. Terrain Dandridge comments on street harassment of women "as far as a man trying to get female's attention, which is being outrageous with the way they do it, I don't think that will ever change either" (Doroshwalther). Venice Brown, one of the New Jersey 4/7, adds, "No means no, just take no" (Doroshwalther). Renata's mom concludes, "This goes on every day in our neighborhood. It's called 'gay bashing,' but they won't call it that . . . they will call it everything but that" (Doroshwalther). Patreese Johnson's mother, Dell, comments on the tension between the black community and police: "Patreese has seen how her brother and cousin has been harassed by the police. So I guess it took away a lot of trust. After the fight she thought it was over and it was no need to call the police" (Doroshwalther). Hill adds, "If we would have been able to call 911, instead of defending ourselves, one of us would have been dead" (Doroshwalther). The trailer ends with the question: "Who does justice work for?" (Doroshwalther). Justice, in the form of police and legal authorities, does not work for women of color. For the NJ4/7, gay bashing not only happened in the place where one would think it would be rare, the neoliberal queer space, but also in their neighborhoods along the outskirts of New York City's most desirable neighborhoods. For the NJ4/7 and other queers of color, justice remains unequal and mostly invisible. The lack of outrage on the part of the greater LGBTQ movement reflects the statements of scholar-activist Cathy Cohen who remarked how Stonewall's central critique of police brutality and violence still remains invisible (Cohen, 1999; Manalansan, 2005; Hanhardt, 2008).

This analysis of the media serves as explicit examples of how the discourse of the black lesbians as the true culprits of crime is circulated and validated. The and were analyzed to not only show how they converge and diverge in discourse but also to explore the spatial politics of NYC and the Village that mark brown and black bodies as abject—even in a proclaimed queer space. This discourse of the criminality of girls is also code for deviant sexual behavior: lesbian desire. The counternarrative of conceptualizes the NJ4/7's realization that the Village was not necessarily an open and welcoming place for them. It was common sense for popular culture to demonstrate how black queer youth brought violence to a queer community. The discourse of the NJ4/7 as violent masks the everyday reality of violence against LGBTQ youth. Crimes against their bodies are irrelevant and their abject sexuality is centered as the main focus. Though mainstream press has always constructed the black male as always initially guilty (i.e., lynching, New York jogger rape case), this incident was different because of the involvement of black lesbians. Black lesbians have been constructed as criminal because of their performance of gender that is deemed as a threat to heteronormativity. By positioning adolescents of color as problems, it validates the state's and police's authority to carefully monitor women of color and then erase the violence on the account of a failed performance of femininity. This supposed redemption from abnormal gender identification is seen as the proper strategy that communities of color must adhere to if they want to insure their future generation's respectability. However, we know this is impossible. The work of Patricia Collins (1997) demonstrates that regardless of the actions of black women, they will continually be faulted for pathological behavior. This latter is justified explicitly through the scientific construct of black people as unable to live freely within the U.S. moral landscape. This ignores white and institutional culpability and places the responsibility on racialized communities. As such, self-actualization for women of color is fundamentally different. This discourse masks the continuing legacy of positioning black women as the culprits of poverty and obstructions to black people's success in the United States. The inclusion of racialized bodies remaps this cultural movement toward the criminal because the black body is already criminalized. The inclusion of people of color in the LGBTQ movement risks tainting the true goal of recognition toward a sovereign subjectivity. In addition to the positioning of mainstream criminology theory, queer spatial theory has articulated how queer spaces are complacent in antiblack racism.

REFERENCES

Akram, D. R. (2006, August 20). "Hated" by lez gang; Straight-bash claim. , Sports+Late City Final, pg. 21.

Buckley, H. (2006, August 19). Man is stabbed in attack after admiring a stranger. , Section B; Column 1; Metropolitan Desk, pg. 3.

Cohen, C. (1997). Punks, bulldaggers, and welfare queens: The radical potential of queer politics? , 437–465.

Collins, P. H. (1999). New York: Routledge.

Doroshwalther, B. The fire this time. Retrieved May 1, 2011, at http://www.youtube.com/user/TheFireThisTime#p/u/1/3D

Duggan, L. (2003). Boston: Beacon.

Eliason, M., & Chesney-Lind, M. (2006). From invisible to incorrigible: The demonization of marginalized women and girls. (1), 29–47.

Gregorian, (2008, June 20). 'She-Wolf' beat charge tossed. , All Editions; pg. 17.

Hanhardt, C. B. (2008, Winter). Butterflies, whistles, and fists: gay safe streets patrol and the new gay ghetto, 1976–1981. (100), Hartman, S. (1997). . New York: Oxford University Press.

Hartocollis, A. (2007, August 14). Woman in gang assault trial says man started the fight,Section B; Column 2; Metropolitan Desk; pg. 4.

Italiano, L. (2007, April 14). 'Crotching' tiger knifer says victim got a beatdown because he pointed at her privates., Sports+Late City Final; pg. 15.

Italiano, L. (2007, April 13). Gal's growl: Hear me roar 'puncher' raged: 'I'm not a woman.', Sports+Late City Final; pg. 19.

Italiano, L. (2007, April 12). Man 'felt like I was going to die.', All Editions; pg. 11.

Italiano, L. (2006, October 4). Lesbian gang-stab shocker., Sports+Late City Final; pg. 19.

Lubiano, W. H. (1997). New York: Pantheon.

Manalansan, M. (2005). Race, violence, and neoliberal spatial politics in the global city, 84–85.

Silva, D. F. (2001). Towards a critique of the socio-logos of justice: The analytics of raciality and the production of universality. (3), 421–454.

CHAPTER EIGHT

Camp Carrot Seed: Reflections on a Critical Pedagogic Project

Sheri Davis-Faulkner

Eric: We got this pizza right here, 'cause you know we got the pizza
Jonathon: Something something something, it's cheese . . .
Kwesi: Pizza pizza pizza
Bernard (videographer)

On the first day of Camp Carrot Seed four male participants started a cipher during their cooking class. Eric began the rhyme, Jonathon picked it up, Kwesi closed it out while also showcasing a pizza crust, and Bernard recorded the moment.

For their first cooking class, this coed group of seven teenagers made "healthy" pizzas nearly from scratch. Tameka worked on the sauce using canned crushed tomatoes, fresh garlic and onion, and salt and pepper. Keisha cooked the chicken sausage and Kwesi rubbed the crust with olive oil. The crew layered the crust with chunky marinara sauce, sausage, steamed broccoli, and topped it off with mozzarella cheese. In the background, Treston, one of the volunteer cooking instructors, guided Carl through making a frozen fruit smoothie with strawberries, blueberries, banana yogurt, and apple juice. While the pizzas cooked, the group shared the responsibility of cleaning the kitchen. There was NO pizza or smoothie left at the end of lunch.

I spent two days each week with my Camp Carrot Seed (CCS) crew and we packed those days with daily gardening and cooking, environmental service projects, neighborhood mapping, grocery shopping, sweet potato cake baking, corn and squash harvesting, a recording session, dance routines, mural painting, and a culminating teaching luncheon for friends, family members, and sponsors to share the results of our project. This participatory action research project was inspired by my doctoral research, which investigated how childhood obesity and youth food decision making gets presented in mainstream media in the United States. My time with this youth group demonstrated that youth are not poor food decision makers. In fact, I would argue that poor and working-class youth of color are good decision makers with poor options.

A few years ago my son was given a used copy of ,a children's book published in the 1940s. In this book, the youngest member of the family decides to grow a carrot. He puts a seed in the ground, he pulls up the weeds, and he waters it. His older sibling and parents intermittently express to him that the carrot will not grow; he carries on. In the end he harvests a carrot nearly the size of his body that he wheels away in a wheelbarrow. At no point does he ask for or receive help from adults, nor does he respond to his family's discouragement. This little boy wanted a carrot, he got the tools, he did the work, and he harvested his carrot. This book inspired me to have faith in the power of youth determination. It also directed me to develop an engaged research project whereby I shared my resources with a group of black youth in exchange for some of their experiential knowledge.

I spent eight weeks with this small group of youth between the ages of thirteen and nineteen years old. I observed their interactions with food, their available food systems, and worked with them to either make their favorite meals differently or to try new foods. I spent this time with them to gain experiential knowledge in order to further develop culturally relevant and age-appropriate resistance pedagogies. This essay is a critical race and gender conscious reflection on the many lessons I learned from my CCS crew and research experience.

Lesson #1: All that is free is not free.

I selected my research site for Camp Carrot Seed based upon five important factors. The location had a classroom, a kitchen, a garden, and a group of youth all on site. The most important reason I selected this site was when I asked to conduct the camp there the youth minister said, "Yes." Yes is a powerful word in participatory action research, especially when a black female researcher hears it from a predominantly white male–operated faith-based organization that services predominantly black families.

I learned early on that I could not teach seven to ten teenagers in a building with offices because the levels of noise and, consequently, surveillance were too high. Youth cannot comfortably interact with one another if they are constantly being told to regulate their speech, habits, clothes, and movements.

I also determined that white male adults have a tendency to ask more of black youth than they would reasonably ask of themselves. By this I mean, if on a daily basis youth make their own breakfast and clean up; maintain a garden and put the tools back in the warehouse; and make their own lunch and clean up, they should not be derided for not mopping the floor. To be clear the host organization provided much needed services such as shelter, childcare, health care, food, and job training for the surrounding community for free. They also provided me with free access to their spaces and the opportunity to work with the youth in their programs, but all that is free is not free. I raised funds to cover all of the costs for the camp and, collectively, my volunteers, the CCS crew, and I provided most of the labor to maintain our space.

Lesson #2: Youth bodies can be sites of struggle *and* security.

Most of the youth participating in the camp were displaced in that they were living in a shelter for women and children. Typically their mothers left the site during the day to look for employment, and my crew was left under the care of the faith-based organization (FBO) staff. The staff was primarily white and male. The stakes were high because the teenagers' behavior could impact whether or not their family could stay at the shelter for the duration of the program. The remaining participants lived in the surrounding area with their families or their friends' families. This group had been participating in the free youth programming provided by the FBO for more than a year. During the program they served as our "experts" on the FBO, and we all benefited from their experiential knowledge.

Over the course of the camp, two of the original participants stopped coming because their mother left the program and they moved away. Two new participants joined when their mother was placed in the shelter. Living at a shelter means they had no private home base, which potentially provides a comfort zone where they could be themselves. Constantly on display, I believe they looked for soothing activities that would not draw too much attention from adults.

Media matters when youth are displaced or feel out of place. Flipping through pictures on a camera, playing games on a phone, or even snacking continuously just after completing lunch are all forms of keeping busy. I believe this results from constant management of youth bodies down to their fingertips. Being able to select and watch YouTube videos and listen to Pandora stations when they do not have regular access to a television or computer is not wasting time; it's an opportunity to connect with a world beyond their physical environment. Keeping in touch with their network via Facebook and text messaging provides a secure form of contact that does not require them to reveal their living situation. Snacking on their favorite affordable food and beverage from the local convenience store is a simple pleasure and one thing they can control.

On a few occasions the FBO staff sent my kids to do another activity offsite at the last minute without discussing the decision with any of us. There were days when my kids came in the door angry or distant. There were days when they argued and even fought with each other. Every day we all managed our anger, disappointment, hurt, and insecurities within our crew. We also coped with microaggressions, for example, inappropriate comments or unfair uses of individual power by FBO staff and authority figures. But every day that my crew had the choice to come to camp they showed up and contributed.

Lesson #3: Black bodies considered small are not necessarily "healthy."

Every morning I provided a simple breakfast that adhered to a few rules. The cereal and jam had less than 9 grams of sugar per serving, the bread was whole wheat, the milk was organic, and the juice was 100%. I explained upfront the food decisions I made, why I chose certain foods, and that I was able to afford it because of individual sponsors. I did not regulate what they could eat, how they ate, or how much they ate. They could bring their own snack to camp and add as much sugar as they wanted to their food. What I did do was have them calculate the amount of sugar they consumed, and I made predictions about their morning attitude. I asked them how they felt throughout the day, discussed with them the impact I thought the sugar had on their emotions, and hoped that they would see a connection.

Together we learned that many of them consumed between 140 and 200 grams of sugar before 10 a.m. We also observed that many of them were irritable and tired by 11 a.m. Their recognition of this pattern did not necessarily change their food choices, but they did begin to challenge each other about their sugar consumption. In popular media there is this belief that we can "know" about bodies by looking at them. All but one of my participants would fall within the "normal" weight range based upon visual logics. However, I would argue they were all malnourished simply based upon their daily sugar and sodium consumption via snacks and beverages. Between 9 a.m. and 3 p.m., I provided them with breakfast, lunch, and snacks—mostly fruit. They would supplement with honey buns, soda, chips, sports drinks, lollipops, pork skins, candy, chocolate bars, and so forth, which they would eat sporadically throughout the day.

Toward the middle of the program I surveyed each participant about how they would spend $3 at the convenience store across the street, then I gave them each $3 for a shopping trip. They managed to stretch and pool their $3 to create a grocery list of items. Many of the items they selected had multiple servings in the package but my crew did not typically read the serving information or ingredients. They did not realize that one bottle of their favorite soda had 44 grams of sugar per 8 ounce serving and that each 20 ounce bottle had two and a half servings. Therefore one of my kids who often drank two bottles of their favorite soda actually consumed 220 grams of sugar in her beverage alone.

We learned about whole foods, as in nonprocessed, by growing them. But black kids gardening in the middle of July in the South raises a range of issues, particularly regarding skin color. I have not yet found a discussion about colorism in literature about garden projects that target urban youth. I'm a light-skinned, thirty-six-year-old black woman, who dresses rather young—jeans and tee-shirt uniform. Within the first few weeks at least half of my crew complained about being in the sun because it was going to make them "black." One stood under a tree for shade until given a specific task and then she returned to the tree; one explained that if they were my skin color it wouldn't be an issue; and another told me if they were my color they would be beautiful.

Doing this work meant rejecting a simple focus on food growth and the life cycle and engaging these recurring comments. The wrong way is to simply tell them, "You should love being black because I do." Unfortunately, we live in a world of hierarchies where privilege and discrimination is usually color coded. A much more powerful response is: (1) to open these moments for them to interrogate their interpretations; (2) to focus on their evidence from peers, family members, teachers, service providers, and so on, which tells them that having dark skin and brown skin means being deficient; (3) to challenge their evidence with them. Not talking about colorism does not make it go away, but not acknowledging how light-skin privilege works in that space is criminal.

Also, hot weather meant the girls and boys were more likely to lean against one another for support. This led to regular conversations that shifted back and forth from the accusatory "You gay"—that is, you're walking gay, you're talking gay, you're dressed gay, you're looking at me gay, you touched me gay—to the pre-action disclaimer "No homo." I did not make a habit of regulating their speech around me, even though we all performed a guarded form of public speech in the presence of FBO staff. However, "you gay" was considered a curse word in my presence. I explained that I believed the phrase placed unfair restrictions on the boys' movements and interactions. They still said it but they immediately paused and said, "Sorry, Ms. Sheri."

Hot weather also meant tank tops, short shorts, short skirts, and sandals were uniforms for some of the girls. I am happy to report, besides the negative comments about skin color, there were very few self-deprecating comments about body size or shape by the female participants. I intentionally did not regulate their clothing choices, and that summer in Atlanta it was 90 degrees easy by 11 a.m. every day. There was one rule about clothes: Wear comfortable clothes that you do not mind getting dirty in the garden. While others within and outside of the camp challenged the girls' choice of outfits, I let the work dictate their actions. They determined on their own that it was difficult to handle hoses and carry bins wearing sandals. They also found it more difficult to bend down and pull weeds in short skirts. The entire crew figured out through experience that it was nearly impossible to handle dirt and red clay in new clothes and sneakers without getting them dirty.

Eventually the gardening regulated all of the girls' and boys' clothing choices.

Lesson #4: *Gardening* is a benign term; growing food is mental and physical work!

Gardening is hard if you're not wearing the proper attire, but it is extremely difficult for youth that are not used to manual labor. First thing after breakfast we had to check the water barrel in the garden, which was usually empty or nearly empty. There was no water source near the garden so we connected about five hoses to the nearest water source, which required a wrench to turn on. It took almost half an hour to connect to the water source, another half an hour to fill the barrel because of low water pressure, and then we had to put all our tools and hoses back in the warehouse. It was all hands on deck; there were no explicit gender divisions of labor. Some people volunteered to get tools (so they could sneak snacks from the warehouse), some weeded the ten beds, some connected the hoses, some watered the beds, and they passed around an iPod Nano to record our work and the progress of the plants' growth.

Food takes a long time to grow. Our garden manager left one week into the program. We, complete amateurs, managed on our own for nearly a month. Some seeds never sprouted. Three amazing garden volunteers showed up midway through the camp and the garden started to thrive. But the experience of growing food has made me cynical about the way gardens are romanticized in the green movement as the answer to food insecurity. What I hear is, "There are not enough places in your neighborhood to access fresh produce so go grow it!" All seeds planted do not become food.

Before this camp I must admit that I thought of gardening as a peaceful, leisure activity that older white women do with cute gloves and cute hats. Now I think of gardening as labor. Pulling up kudzu, stretching out and wrapping up hoses, and even carrying watering cans back and forth from the water barrel is work, especially in 90 degree weather. There are many reasons why black people migrated from rural Georgia towns, where the predominant work was farm labor, to work in urban Atlanta. I am guessing one reason might have been the ability to work inside air-conditioned buildings.

Lesson #5: Black youth have local resources and skills that are largely untapped!

When developing projects, programs, activities, and field trips for youth look for and use local resources. There are numerous black working-class and poor communities that are rich in historical and natural resources such as hike and bike paths, creeks and waterfalls, forests, parks, fields, universities, libraries, archives, stores, small businesses, and community banks. By constantly taking black youth out of their community for field trips, you suggest that the best resources are largely available beyond their reach. By staying in or near their community my crew was able to teach and debate their social knowledge of their communities by mapping their homes, apartment complexes, and local stores. On our field trips they shared stories about their friends and families who lived in places on our route. They even talked about loved ones buried in local cemeteries we passed.

We exchanged our perspectives about the neighborhoods we traversed. They gave me a cultural tour of the stores and restaurants they frequented in their neighborhood. I showed them resources like the huge nature preserve, community garden, (free for youth) artist community center, and a major tributary in and around their neighborhoods, most of which are accessible via walking and public transportation. On our final field trip, we drove to a waterfall not far from the site and spent the afternoon talking about the camp, the upcoming school year, relocating to new neighborhoods, dating, and childcare.

I cannot report that they significantly changed their eating habits in eight weeks, but that was not necessarily the point. I wanted to know basic information such as would they willingly garden and go hiking if it was on the schedule? Would they eat fruit and drink water every day if it was available? Would they begin to function like a team over the course of the camp? Most of the answers were yes.

At the close of camp one participant presented about the mural we created; two led the garden tour; two prepared (with the support of their cooking instructor) a stir-fry and salad for a forty-person luncheon; everyone set up the event room; one presented on the Google map he created with each place we visited; one presented the results of our "make our favorite meal healthy" shopping trip; and I described the ingredients and sugar content on the snack wrappers and beverage containers collage we made from the $3 convenience store challenge.

Beat:	**Chorus:**
stomp, clap	What's good, what's good,
stomp, snap	whatcha thinkin in your head?
stomp stomp, clap	whatcha thinkin in your mind?
stomp, snap	Put it in a rhyme.

stomp, clap
stomp, snap
stomp stomp, clap   —Camp Carrot Seed Crew
stomp, snap   WonderRoot Arts Community Center

In conclusion, we conducted a limited multisited study of food growth, food products, cooking, and food landscapes. By working withyouth, I learned that they would never buy fruit like the strawberries, blueberries, blackberries, and grapes I provided for them from a convenience store because they do not trust that the fruit is handled correctly. Also they complained that fruit was too expensive at convenience stores so purchasing it would eat up most of their small budgets. Snacks and beverages, on the other hand, were considered safe because they were in sealed packages and were more affordable—35, 55, and 99 cents. There were more than four convenience stores and take-outs within a five-minute walk from the site. However, the nearest grocery store was a forty-minute bus ride plus the cost of bus fare. Youth are good decision makers with poor options. Camp Carrot Seed is a resistance pedagogy that insists upon adults recognizing the inherent wisdom in youth decision making before engaging them in programs that try to change their habits. We need critical race organizing projects (CROP) where youth are valued as powerful agents who can significantly change the options available for them in their communities.

CHAPTER NINE

Dr. Theresa Bayarea: Dancing to Make Freedom

Chamara Jewel Kwakye

I danced out of my mother's womb
And I ain't stop moving my feet since
Boom boom bit, boom bit

Since as long as I can remember
Dancing to everything from
Djembe's to the Elements September
Boom bit

Child of the Great Migration, Second Wave
I long for lazy summer Oakland days
When Panthers fed us breakfast,
Holding up Black power fists
Boom boom bit, boom bit

You see when the drum calls
My hips, they always respond
Boom bit
But back in the day I got in trouble
For that sh!t
Boom boom bit, boom bit

Mama said, "Dancing is only for social spaces."
Daddy said, "Can't do nothing with that. You won't go places."
Boom bit

But I saw the rhythm of Dance in everything
From celebrating Katherine Dunham
Or mourning the death of fallen soldiers from Malcolm to King
Boom boom bit, boom bit

I heard eight counts in my heartbeat
And saw dance moves performed by
The way Brothas walked down the street
Boom bit

You see I dance to make freedom
Whether it's my "I'm the only Black person in my department" pirouette
Or my single mother Grand jeté
I move my body
Boom boom bit, boom bit

I pliéd over tenure
And landed in polyrhythmic pelvic thrusts
With son by side and daughter on hip
When they said it couldn't be done
Boom bit

Should you enter my classroom
Ivory tower or in the 'hood
The tears from the middle passage,
Will be the danced sweat on your brow
Boom boom bit, boom bit

Your hips will swing like nooses from trees
Your feet will point to Mecca in the East
And your arms will hold
Elaborate Griot stories Centuries old
Boom bit

I dance for
Tired black domestic women
In rememories of the South
To round the way girls on
Brooklyn street corners with loud mouths
Boom boom bit, boom bit

For Negras determinata in Brazil
To ladies in brown, red, orange, yellow, green, purple and blue
I dance for you
And us when the rainbow ain't enuf
Boom bit

I dance for hopes of balance/disruption
Between artistry and the academy
Performance and academic jargon
And child support bargains
Boom boom bit, boom bit

And you'll know that I was
Here
For I danced for freedom without
Fear
Boom bit.

My time with Theresa Bayarea was active. Throughout our time together I was actively listening, actively writing field notes, and from her persuasion and insistence I was dancing or, as she says, "actively storytelling with my body." When I first approached her about participating in the project she daringly said, "If you want me to tell you my life history you have to tell me yours through dance." Of course I thought she was joking. She was serious. I had done ballet, modern, and African dance as a young child, but I had not danced seriously at all as an adolescent or as an adult. She challenged me, "What kind of researcher are you if you only take from your subjects and give nothing back? Giving back can't start when you start writing. Reciprocity has to be there from the very beginning." So I danced. When able, I participated in her dance classes at a university and a community center in Northern California and afterward she/we (the informal term she gave to our interview process), "You are conjuring your life through dance and sweat when you set foot in the class and I help you deliver that and I'm conjuring my life through words and stories and you help provoke my thoughts and help me deliver my life from the moment you push record." Unlike my time with Vivi, where we engaged as "kitchen poets" or shared information while simultaneously working together on different domestic tasks, Theresa and I took very clear delineated turns engaging each other. We did not re-create the binary of researcher and subject; neither of us functioned as expert; I was not the expert researcher and even with all her years of dance experience, she was not the "expert dance teacher." She dismissed the title at the beginning of each semester, the first day of class by stating, "If I'm the expert on dance then that means two things, one, that you have nothing to teach me and two, that you have nothing to teach your peers. We work, learn and teach together. I'm here to push us to learn and help deliver a final product that shows off everyone's growth, even mine." She said the same in an e-mail before we began the project,

> Chamara,
>
> I hope you realize that my challenge to you to dance before confirming my participation in your project was not a hoop jumping process to see if you were a serious researcher that understands reflexivity, reciprocity or ethics or to see if you're really serious about academia. It was more a challenge for you to give me the same trust with your life in dance that you are asking from me with my life in words. If I understand your project correctly you are asking me to share not just the things that I have experienced in the academy, but the things I have experienced in my life, including my personal life? I have had the luxury for so many years to communicate many of the things I have experienced through the art of dance, abstract theory and abstract text. Translating those things to words that will equal Theresa Bayarea's life story is intimidating and seems like the ultimate act self disclosure, something I know you already know is a double-edged sword in the academy. I will trust the process if you trust the process. Come dressed and ready to do some active storytelling with your body (when you come back out here) and I will come ready to TALK about my life. The process for both of us will be difficult but we will work, learn and teach together and hopefully end up with something that shows off our growth.
>
> Peace,
> Theresa

In this chapter, Theresa's life history is presented in her words via interview transcripts. While the interviews were not conducted in sequential order, they are presented in chronological order so as to show a progression of her life and expand our understanding of her life in context. The chapter begins with a discussion of her early childhood in California, highlighting social mobility and class tension within the black community. It then proceeds to a discussion of her decision to pursue dance move, with a discussion of black women's bodies and trauma. The chapter goes on to discuss her experiences as an undergraduate dance major and as a dancer in well-known dance company, including a conversation of mental health and body dysmorphia in the black community. Last, the chapter explores her experiences as a faculty member with a focus on the binaries of personal and private. Finally, the chapter concludes with Theresa's reflection on her participation in this project.

I was born in the spring of 1969 in Northern California. I was my parent's first child. My father was an accountant and my mother a nurse. My father was born in Texas and my mother was born in Louisiana, but they both moved to Northern California with their families when they were very young. My paternal and maternal grandparents both left the South for better job opportunities in the late 1940s. My parents have known each other since they were six years old and they went to the same grade school, junior high school, and high school but didn't start dating until after they graduated from high school. My mother says that Daddy asked her out every year since they were in grade school but she didn't take them him seriously because he was the class clown and a flirt. She said she finally took him serious one Sunday after church when he came over to her house and asked my grandfather if he could escort her to the church picnic the following Saturday. They've been together ever since.

Both my maternal grandparents and paternal grandparents graduated from high school and all of them had taken some college classes so my parents said they always knew that they'd go to college, without question. They both ended up going to the same college, a small private Catholic college in Louisiana. After they graduated they moved back to Northern California and immediately got married. My father interned at an accounting firm and not long after interning he started working there full time. My mother worked as a nurse with a prominent local black OB/GYN in a private practice. They were married for four years before they had me. My parents were both excited to find that my mother was pregnant and so were my grandparents; I was the first grandchild on either side. My parents used to go dancing every Friday after work; it was their ritual. My mother said that while she was pregnant they kept up the ritual and whenever they started dancing I started "dancing." She said I would still be "dancing" after they got home and that I'd keep her up half the night from all my movement. The doctor my mother worked with delivered me and he said that it was the shortest labor he'd seen. My parents both say it's because they had danced together in delivery room to help my mother get through her early contractions and by the time doctor came into the room I was ready and I danced right on out. They said I danced out of the womb.

I shudder to use the word but I suppose from the outside looking in we may have been, we were. I've always thought of us as working class because I knew that my parents worked very hard to take care of more than just the four of us, but even with helping both sets of grandparents and my mother's and father's siblings from time to time, we still owned our own home and managed to have money for lessons or activities that my brother and I wanted to do or were sometimes forced to do, plus Daddy was an accountant, he always kept our money affairs in order.

Growing up my parents kept us active. I went to a private Catholic school from primary through high school and I was active in clubs and activities at school at a young age. My parents encouraged it. They always told me and Paul [Theresa's brother] that "idle hands led to failure" so they made sure to keep us busy. I mean from the time I could speak I was in the children's choir at our church and once my brother could talk—he's four years younger than me—he was also in the children's choir. I never remember having a moment when I would even think to say that I was bored.

Even though Paul and I were in all of these activities we spent a lot of time with my grandparents. My mother's parents and my father's parents lived a few houses down from each other and we lived no more than ten blocks away from all of them. Many times during the week my parents worked late so my brother and I were either at Grams and Pops (my mother's parents) or with Nanny and Granpa (my father's parents). I credit them for giving me the education of real life. Granpa (my dad's father) always told me that he would teach me "all the things that the fancy private school wouldn't get around to, like common sense." He and my father argued constantly about what they thought was best for us. Granpa thought that Daddy was ruining me and Paul by making us go to private school with white children. One evening as Daddy was picking me and Paul up from Granpa and Nanny's they got into it. After we got home from school Granpa asked us how was school. I told him that a friend and I got in trouble for singing the black national anthem. One of the sisters said it wasn't appropriate for us to sing at school. My grandfather was livid. As soon as my father came into the house to pick us up he could barely speak before Granpa started telling him about the incident. I remember my Granpa saying, "Nothing they learn is going to stick out more than that they should hate being a Negro." There were other kids at the school, black kids, Latino kids, Asian kids, but still the school was 50% white and 50% kids of color. My grandfather knew that the school and the parish in general at that time really catered to the white students and white parishioners. "Ain't no Negro Sisters or priests at that school. Nothing like y'all had when you were going to St. Ann's; no one to protect them from racism. I hate that you think it's okay to send them there because of all the fancy buildings and activities. You'd sell their souls for a chance to get into a good college. They need to be around folks that are going to encourage them in their studies and help them be proud of who they are. You new Negroes think that money can buy you out of racism. It can't!" He and my father got into it all the time about the price of our education. Daddy said going to those schools would help us when it came time to apply to college. He said it was helping us and Granpa always said it was helping us but at a great cost.

My mother's family was less combative about their opinions of our education but Grams and Pops were also concerned that the only time Paul and I saw black kids were at our local church unaffiliated with our school or in the evenings when we got home from school. My mother's friends had helped to start a branch of Jack and Jill so my mother's compromise was to enroll me and Paul in Jack and Jill. By us being in Jack and Jill we did things with other black children, but for my grandparents [paternal grandparents] they still didn't think it was enough. Granpa decided to take matters in his own hands. At the time I didn't know if he took us to the Panther's free breakfast program to spite my mother and father or because he overwhelmingly believed in their mission. Regardless he took us to the free breakfast program. When I got older he told me he took me and Paul to the free breakfast program not because we didn't have enough money to eat or to spite my parents but because of the Panther's determination for us to be free. He said he would check out the brothers in Oakland and the work they were doing, staying within 50 feet and watching the police as they stopped brothers walking down the street and the things the Panthers outlined in the 10 point plan. He said he was scared of them at first but drawn to the fact that they were unafraid to stand up for us. By taking us to the breakfast program he knew that we would get more in that hour or so at the church with other black children and the brothers and sisters that were there than we would get all day from the white nuns and priests at our school. We would get a sense of pride in ourselves as black children that we would never get from them. He said that Paul I missed that sense of pride and togetherness that he had growing up in the South. He loved us and he just wanted us to be proud of being black. That was Granpa.

He and Daddy never saw eye to eye on their political views, especially when it came to black folks. My father was too passive and conservative for Granpa, and Granpa was too outspoken and liberal for my father, but they loved each other and respected each other as men. Watching their relationship and how they'd interact was the first poli sci class my brother and I had. That's how Paul and I knew what was going on. On Sundays after church and after we'd eaten lunch Daddy and Granpa would immediately settle themselves out on the front porch to talk about everything from apartheid to busing in Boston, to slavery to socialism in Cuba to race politics in Brazil to the Iran Contra scandal to the permeation of drugs into our community—nothing was off limits. Since Paul and I played in the front yard where they could see us we'd take a break from playing and sit on the porch and listen to them talk. We'd listen as long as we could before becoming bored but most of the time I was fascinated on how long they could go. They'd talk for hours on end only taking a break to do whatever favors Granma or Mama asked and then they'd pick up where they left off and go right back to it. They were always civil but every now and then you could tell if one of them got upset. When Granpa was perturbed his right eye brow would raise. It would be up so far that it looked like it was about to meet the start of his hairline. And if Daddy was mad his nostrils would flare; sometimes on that porch I thought I could see up to Daddy's brain, his nostrils were so flared. Even then, nostrils flared and eyebrows raised, they were always respectful. No yelling, no screaming, just tense. They were the type that had to agree to disagree. Granpa always joked and said he didn't know how Daddy was related to him since he didn't have a rebellious part to his sprit. Granma would always follow and say, "He is rebellious; he's the exact opposite of you and me, besides your kind of rebellion skipped a generation and landed on Paul and danced into Theresa."

I'm not sure where it came from, my passion to dance that is, but I've been dancing since as long as I can remember. My mother said not long after I could walk I was dancing. She signed me up for my first ballet class when I was three years old. My parents and grandparents all said anytime I would hear any kind of music I danced. As a matter of fact that's how I got my childhood nickname, Boogie, or Boogs as my father still calls me. They said if the radio was on and any type of song was playing whether it was a jingle, a Stevie Wonder song, anything with a beat, I was dancing. People have asked me repeatedly if anyone else in my family was a "classically" trained dancer or took lessons. No one that we've ever been able to find on either side of my family has ever been "classically" trained but I mean my parents danced as their thing to do with each other on the weekends and my grandparents told me how they used to dance, you know, socially, but no one ever seemed to be passionate enough about it to study it. I don't think anyone that really loved to dance and move and would ever study it like this; you spend so little time dancing that it only becomes a word, a noun not a verb. It was the first thing outside of my family members that I ever loved. It was fun, it was challenging, it was tiring, it was fascinating. I loved it and still do. I think my fascination with dance was because it became a way for me to express myself. I know that sounds cliché but my parents were very rigid; the parochial schools I went to were rigid, even the activities I participated in, Jack and Jill, Girl Scouts, they were all run by rigid people or governed by unyielding rules. I felt as if I was being controlled within every arena except when I stepped into the dance studio and my grandparent's homes. That's not to say that dance teachers I had were lax nor were my grandparents, but I was inspired and encouraged always to create my own identity in each of those places. No one told me who I was in those places. I was allowed to tell them, I danced who I was.

Even though I've been dancing ever since I can remember my love story with dance began very mundane. Initially, I started dancing because my parents hated the daycare I went to. When I was three years old I was in preschool for half days, from 8 a.m. to 12 noon. From there I would go next door to daycare, from about 1 p.m. to 5:30 p.m. Grams and Granma worked as domestics so whoever got off earlier would pick me up if it happened to be before 5 p.m. The daycare options were limited and my parents, out of lack of time, money, and any other familial options were forced to place me in a mediocre daycare. I was in daycare for about four months when Dr. Bell, the doctor my mother worked for, told Mama that his sister-in-law that had studied at Julliard was returning to the Bay to be a ballerina in a local company. He told her that she was starting a private dance class with other young black girls and that she should think about enrolling me in her class. My mother talked to my father about it and he thought it was a great alternative to daycare. So every day, as soon as A.M. session was over I ate lunch, went to chapel, and then Sister Francis walked me and two other girls one block down the street to a storefront that Ms. Janice turned into a dance studio. Ms. Janice had us from 2:30 p.m. to 5:30 p.m. When I think about it now, that's a long time for a three year old to be in class. That's three hours, but I don't ever remember complaining or hearing from my parents that I complained. They always told me that when they came to get me at 5:30 p.m. I was always up front standing right next to Ms. Janice mimicking her every move. I do remember sometimes when they came to get me I would cry, I didn't want to leave. I wanted to stay, I wanted to dance.

My parents supported my love of dance. They were at every recital, every contest, every rehearsal that they could make. If one of them had to work late, then the other one would make sure to show up early, and the times that they both had to work late, then they would make sure that both sets of grandparents were there. It wasn't until my freshman year of high school that they started to push me to "think about something other than dance." I ignored them and I mean I didn't get it, for me there was nothing other than dance. For me to think of something other than dance was like asking me to see myself as something other than human. It was the thing I woke up early for and the thing that I would be up until 11, 12 o'clock practicing. I knew that I wanted to be a dancer.

It was during the second semester of my junior year when I started to see that we really saw dance differently; my parents saw dance as my hobby and I saw dance as life, I saw it as life. One day after a dance rehearsal my mother and I were driving home from the dance studio and while waiting at a stoplight she asked me if I'd thought about what college I was going to attend. I told her I wanted to audition for Julliard, Alvin Alley, or apply to Temple. I remember the look on her face to this very day, it was deadpan and she was quiet. The light turned green and cars started to honk behind her. She finally started driving and calmly said, "Had I known you would go and screw your life up over dancing, your father and I would have never signed you up when you were three years old." I was horrified. It wasn't until that moment that I realized that my parents thought of this as a hobby, not something that I could do as a legitimate career. We got home, walked through the front, and my father greeted us and when we were both silent he knew something was wrong. He asked what happened and my mother walked out of the room without answering. I asked my father, "So you and Mommy don't want me to go to school and become a dancer?" My father pleaded with me, "Theresa you're an excellent student, you've always made the honor roll, you're bright, why do you want to do something that has no real future, especially a real future for a black woman?" Forget the fact that the woman that had been my first dance teacher had been a black woman and a ballerina and later a prima ballerina in a large dance company. Forget the fact that I had been teaching dance at a community center and getting paid for it since I was fourteen. Forget the fact that I had won scholarships for dance that helped pay my high school tuition. Forget the fact that they had encouraged me to dance in the first place. Forget all of that. "Your mother and I just don't understand how you're going to support yourself dancing. We didn't invest all this money in your education so you could be in and out of work. Plus the average dancer only dances until they're thirty, that's if they're not injured. What are you going to do? Retire at thirty? Is that the kind of life you want for yourself?" It was. I was young. I couldn't care less that the average dancer only danced professionally until they were thirty. Hell, I figured I had been dancing since I was three so dancing until I was thirty meant I would have twenty-seven years of experience, something my father or my mother couldn't say that they had in their own careers at that time. They tried to get folks to talk to me, Father Benjamin, Sister Francis, Ms. Janice, Granpa, Granma, Grams, Pops, my teachers, my school counselor. I refused to be swayed and Ms. Janice, Granpa, Granma, Grams, Pops all started their talk with, "Your parents want me to talk to you" and they ended it the same, "Theresa you should follow your own heart and live your own life." They supported me but even with all their support it still hurt that my parents were so upset about my passion to dance.

I spent the entire summer before my senior year of high school working two jobs, working the front desk at a doctor's office, Dr. Davis, and teaching dance at a day camp. My plan was to save money for college applications and money for college in general. My parents made it more than clear that they would not help me pay for college if I chose to do anything related with dance. I also started dating David, a drummer from my African dance class. I was seventeen, he was nineteen. My parents didn't like the fact that he was nineteen, but he was in college and was a history major so they allowed me to date him, thinking that our spending time together would influence me to follow suit and "major in something more traditional and stable." No such luck; instead, our spending time together led to me getting pregnant. The first month I missed my period I thought it was because I had been working so hard and pushing myself so hard physically. Since I had to send out audition tapes that fall I wanted to make sure I was in great shape and I was using that summer to prepare my body. I just thought missing my period was due to those changes, but when I missed a second period I knew I was pregnant. I asked one of the nurses at the doctor's office if she could give me a pregnancy test without Dr. Davis knowing. He knew my family. She agreed and so one day I came into work early and took the test. The results came back the next day confirming that I was pregnant. I was horrified, not because I was pregnant but because my relationship with my parents was already strained because of my choice to pursue dance, but this would kill them. I told David and he was silent. He said he would support me in whatever decision I made, but he also told me that he wasn't ready to be a father either. I was crushed, not because I had some grand idea that he and I would run off and get married and raise a family, but because even though we had had sex, I was the one that had the decisions to make.

I found out that I was pregnant at the beginning of August. By the end of August I decided that I was going to keep the baby. I didn't tell David. He was going back to college back East and we hadn't really talked since I told him that I was pregnant. I figured it would be easier for me and the baby if I didn't guilt him into being a parent. I thought about abortion. Having an abortion meant that I could continue on my path to dancing without any interruptions, but there was something about having an abortion that didn't sit right with me. I don't really think it was the whole being raised Catholic thing, you know, the Catholic girl guilt. I just felt that being a mother was something that I wanted to do. I felt blessed to be given the opportunity to have life grow inside of me; to be a vessel for something other than dance, for something other than myself, for someone else. I was looking forward to being a mother. I figured I could go to school and major in something that would provide me with stability and still dance on the side or dance later. I just knew I didn't want to have an abortion. Plus, I had a few friends that had had abortions and I knew I didn't want to live with the sadness I saw in their eyes, I didn't want to experience loss in that way or to turn my back on being a mother. Truthfully I was excited to be pregnant but I still hadn't told my parents. I wasn't sure how to tell them. I told Paul, he was excited that he was going to be an uncle, but he said that "this is going to kill them."

It was Labor Day weekend and I had just finished cleaning my room, I was preparing for school to start that Tuesday when my mother came in and told me that she had made a doctor's appointment for me on Tuesday after school for my annual physical. I didn't think anything of it since I had to have one each year for dance, so no big deal. So after school that Tuesday my mother picked me up and took me to the doctor. I wasn't paying attention as she was driving so I hadn't noticed until I felt her put the car in park and looked up that we were at different office than usual. She turned the car off and I remember she was still gripping the steering wheel and looking straight ahead when she asked, "Theresa, are you pregnant?" I was shocked. How did she know? What was I going to say? I wanted to lie but all I could muster was a soft, "Yes." She started crying and told me that she was ashamed of me, and angry that I could do such a thing. I wanted to tell her that I hadn't planned it, that I was sorry, and that I wanted to keep the baby. She stopped crying long enough to tell me, "Well the people in here are to help you take care of your nasty, not to mention girlish, foolishness." I didn't even have a chance to ask her what she meant before she got of the car and told me to do the same. At this point I was scared to death. I had no idea what was about to happen or what was going on. Somewhere deep inside I knew I was about to have an abortion but I just didn't believe and never expected that my mother would do something like that. I felt like I was in a movie everything was moving so slowly but so quickly at the same time. We walked into the building that we had parked outside of but I remember we walked into what I felt was like a side entrance or an employee entrance. I remember staring at the door we walked through as my mother and I were sitting in a hallway. I only remember seeing people with name tags and scrubs or white coats walk through the door. I remember people asking me questions, but I don't really remember answering them. I don't know if you've ever felt like this? But I felt like my voice was trapped in my throat. I just kept swallowing. My mother answered most of the questions for me and she filled out any paperwork that they needed. We waited for a while and finally a woman that I didn't recognize, but I could tell my mother knew, led me and my mother into a room and she handed me a gown and told me to change clothes. I changed clothes. I put on the gown. I lay down on the table and stared at the ceiling. I don't remember much after that. I know I heard the doctor say the word , but I don't think he was speaking to me. I don't know how many people were in the room. I don't remember really seeing anyone either. I could only see fragments of people, an elbow, a mouth, a wrist, a nose, eyes; never a complete face or a whole body. I don't remember much after they administered the anesthesia. I felt like all my senses just shut off except for the music in my head and the sound of this loud vacuum noise. My body didn't belong to me. That day I felt like it belonged to my mother, to David, to my father, to the doctors, the nurses, it belonged to everyone except me, it didn't belong to me.

I was heavily drugged so when I fully came to I was home in my bed. When I looked around I saw Peter sitting at my desk doing his homework, like he usually did. He said I was trying to get up from the bed and he asked me, "Tee, what do you need? I can get it for you." He says I told him, "I need my body back. I need to dance." I don't remember saying that but I do remember feeling like the only way I was going to become whole after that experience was to dance and never again allow anyone to control my body. It's like the day they took my little girl from my womb, she was a girl, they took the little girl in me.

I'm not sure what my parents told my grandparents or our other family members but no one really spoke about the abortion. I still couldn't believe it happened. I told no one. I didn't tell my friends, I didn't tell David. The abortion itself and not being able to tell anyone out of fear made me feel silenced. I felt silenced because having an abortion was a choice that was made for me. When I tell people to this day, folks ask why didn't you scream, or run, or tell your mother no, or call the police? They ask the questions that will haunt me forever. I don't know why I didn't do those things. I felt I couldn't. I felt powerless, like I had no choice, but I know because of that feeling of powerlessness I was adamant about my choice to dance. The trauma of abortion and the trauma of my mother choosing abortion for me changed me forever. At that moment it felt like I controlled so little. I was seventeen years old. My parents were attempting to control my career choices; my mother was controlling my fertility. So when it came time for me to assert myself and reclaim all the power I lost on that day, in those months, I chose to dance. Choosing to dance didn't just mean going to class after school, it meant that I applied to the schools that I wanted to go to for college; it meant that I worked to make sure I had enough money to pay for application fees; choosing to dance meant that I made the decision to become independent and not in the cliché way where you think you're grown, but I was womanish in a way that was real.

I don't remember much between the abortion and starting college that fall. I felt like a zombie, a robot. I was on autopilot. I know I went to school and finished high school, I know I danced but I don't remember much else. I do remember that about two weeks after the abortion I did move in with my [paternal] grandparents. I'm not sure if they knew and didn't want to say anything or if they believed what I told them when I said I needed to live with them because things had gotten too hectic with Momma and Daddy. Regardless of what they knew or didn't know, they welcomed me with open arms and I appreciated every moment with them. They loved on me, not doting on me or spoiling me, but they were supportive in a way that my parents weren't. I don't think my parents knew how to be supportive in that way, the way that my grandparents were. My grandparents had a way of being that was completely different from my parents. Their only expectation of me was to be happy with the person that I was to become and give back to this world in the same way that God gave to me. They'd say, "So, baby, if God gave you the gift to dance, then you dance for the world the way that you would dance before God. You don't short change nobody." Theirs was very much a way of "do what makes you happy and shine" versus my parents way of "do what will make money and provide security." Being around Granpa and Granma at that time was very healing, but I was still hurting. Deep inside, I was still hurting. Even though the physical scars healed, inside my spirit and my mind I carried the pain.

When I started school in the fall I was still carrying that hurt with me but I kept the love that my grandparents had given me near and dear to my heart along with the love and support of my brother. When I left for school I could tell that my parents were still upset that I had chosen to dance and that I had moved so far away, to them the East Coast may as well have been another planet, but they begrudgingly gave me their blessing. They didn't say much, other than "take care of yourself and we're always here if you need us." I told them thank you, but I was upset that all they could muster up was take care and we're here. I wanted them to apologize. I wanted my mother especially to say I'm sorry for taking away your right to give life. It would be years before my relationship with my parents would be anything more than civil.

When I left for school I had no idea what to expect. I enrolled as a ballet major and took elective courses in other forms of dance and also took a full academic course load. At that time very few dancers took anything other than dance classes, but I wanted to challenge myself physically and mentally so I had three academic classes and four dance classes. One was an introduction to dance discipline so we weren't doing anything physical but the other three were physical. When I left high school I was in the best shape of my life. Ms. Janice and I had developed a sort of dancer's boot camp that she helped me with beginning the summer before my senior year and we continued it right up until the day before I left for school. During that time she mentored me on dance, physicality, nutrition, and technique and she talked to me about what to expect from my instructors and colleagues, but I don't think anything can fully prepare a young black woman to become a ballerina.

I was always confident so when classes started I wasn't shy about being upfront or in the middle of the bar and mirror. I felt about assured about the training I'd had up until then especially since I had had numerous opportunities to dance with companies back home and even a few offers to join some of them right after high school graduation but being at this school was something different. First off, of course, it was all white; many of the students there had been in school together since they were young; their parents were donors or contributors to the school; they knew the instructors; and the majority of them were upper class, the class distinction was clear. They were quick to tell me and the four other people of color that we were the tokens and had only gotten in because the school needed some color. I mean they were blatant. I remember by the second week of class they started referring to us as the zoo pack. The zebra, the monkeys and the hippos. The zebra was a guy who was Japanese and Puerto Rican, the monkeys were the two brothas, and the hippos were me and this other sistah, you know because of our ass. We'd all started hanging out together because we had five classes together and because it was strength in numbers. None of us wanted to be caught by ourselves and be harassed. So when they saw us together they'd start making monkey noises or pretend like they were at the zoo and pretend to take pictures of us or throw food at us and pretend that they were feeding us.

I tried to ignore it at first. I ignored it mostly because I knew I didn't want to get put out of school for fighting. Plus I loved dancing more than anything and being sent home would have only made my parents all too happy. So I refused to let them throw me off. Eventually we did start to talk back, I mean we were scared.

We weren't punks. When they started up with the noises or little comments I would always ask them if they were afraid of a hippopotamus being a better dancer or make little remarks like that. I made it clear that if they wanted to get to me they'd have to do it on the floor and the stage. I dared them to be better than me. I thrived off that kind of competition. For a while it would stop them from talking shit. They'd see us in dance class and see that we were serious. We'd match them turn for turn, jump for jump, leap for leap. I think we were a little rough around the edges in terms of form, but our execution was just as good if not better than theirs. They knew we could dance and for the most part they left us alone. Their taunts however didn't make the other types of racism any better. Our instructors were the worst. They'd see us in class at the bar, and they'd ask if we had taken any other dance classes like jazz, or tap, or "tribal dance" as they called it, instead of African dance, they just assumed we only knew those forms of dance, the forms that they associated most closely with black people. Once we told them that we had been formally trained in jazz, tap, African Dance in addition to ballet they'd say things like, "Well no wonder you all are so big, you're never going to be able to delicately execute these moves. Ballet is about being delicate, soft." Or when we did execute the moves properly they'd still say things like, "There's too much power and force in your movements!" or "You're bodies are difficult for ballet" or "Your body doesn't agree with ballet" or "You're body has too many curves, too much muscle." It was hard. I had loved ballet up until then. My teachers back home never talked about our bodies in a negative way and they prided themselves on mixing in techniques from other forms of dance with our ballet training. What I had been trained to see as a positive thing, being well versed in several different types of dance, being well rounded and well versed as dancer, was frowned on when I got to college. It was like being able to speak multiple languages and then being told to only speak one and never speak any of the rest. So I literally began to code switch between all the forms of dance that I knew; in particular I'd code switch between ballet and all the other forms of dance that I knew.

It's funny because I can honestly remember thinking before ballet class, "Okay discount each part of your body. Stiffen up. Be rigid so you can be soft"; and then before tap, or jazz or African dance I would think, "Okay, relax. Be fluid. Move together. Remember all of your body." When we did shows it was the worst. I remember during the fall semester of junior year we were doing. Our dance teacher would say aloud during rehearsal, "I don't know what I am going to do with these large buttocks and dark skin. How am I going to make them resemble anything close to a swan?" This is what we'd have to hear after going through six hours of grueling rehearsal on top of attending all of our other classes. On the day of the performance our director had me and another sista go in early for makeup before the show so she could have the makeup artist's make us as pale as possible. She told them, "I want these black ducks to be transformed into beautiful pale swans." Just like that. So plain. Like it was nothing. I was angry not just at that incident but I was angry in general. I was being thrown so many things at one time. Being away from home, being away from my support system, and on top of that I never really dealt with all the pain from the abortion and then the difficulty of transitioning from high school to college but on top of it the racism that was coupled with it at times was unbearable. I remember thinking that if I couldn't make it through all of this then I'd failed and for that reason I really felt like I had no choice but to put up with the things going on at school. I wanted to dance so badly and I wanted to be accepted there so badly. I just felt like if I cracked under the pressure then they would've thought, "Oh well, she's was just one more black girl that couldn't cut it as a ballerina, as a dancer." I think in my mind if I failed there then it meant that I couldn't make it as a dancer anywhere. It would've meant so many things to me at the time. It would've meant that I had chosen the wrong career path, it would have meant that I was being silly to think that I could take the thing I was passionate about and turn it into something more than a hobby, and it would've meant that my parents were right. (Laughing) I think that's the part that bothered me the most.

To cope I started binging and purging... yes I was a walking stereotype and a contradiction. The stereotype was I was a dancer that had an eating disorder. No surprise there. The contradiction was that I was a black girl with an eating disorder. People act like black women are somehow immune from things like that. For me, binging and purging was a way for me to feel in control of something. I know that sounds crazy but the routine of overeating and then vomiting felt like it was the one thing at that moment that no one else was doing to me. I controlled it. I did it to myself. When I was upset, sad, angry, worried, anxious, almost any emotion outside of happiness I binged and purged. It was rare when I was happy. I used to feel all my emotions through dance but once I felt like I wasn't good at that anymore I channeled all my emotions through B[inging] and P[urging]. I was five feet ten inches tall and at my sickest I weighed ninety-seven pounds, but that seemed to be when I was the most successful in ballet class. I even scored a solo in the spring of junior year. One of my teachers said, "Your body is finally beginning to resemble that of a ballerina's and less of a brick house." I was horribly sick but I was being rewarded by what I thought was acceptance because I got a two minute solo. I nearly killed myself for two minutes. No one said anything either. I wanted so badly for someone to notice how sick I was but even though I know people knew I was binging and purging no one said anything. I think it was the culture of that particular school and of professional dancers, period. You don't ask and you don't tell about eating disorders. My parents and family never came to visit. My parents claimed they had to work and my grandparents were getting older and didn't want to fly. I rarely went home. I always told them I was in rehearsals, working, or had exams coming up. My whole four years I only went home three times to visit. When I did go home to visit, I always made sure to wear layers of clothes and no one ever really suspected anything. They commented that I must have been working hard because I was thinning out but no one said anything beyond that.

I finally did get in trouble for binging and purging. I passed out during rehearsals during the beginning of my senior year. We were in seminar doing leaps and I remember it was my run and I remember jumping but I don't remember landing. When I woke up I was in the hospital hooked up to a machine. The nurses told me I had collapsed in class and that I was being treated for dehydration and malnutrition. One of the deans came to the hospital and asked who I wanted to notify. I just remember not wanting them to call my parents so I had them call Ms. Janice. She had moved to New York that summer to start teaching for Dance Theatre of Harlem that fall and so she came to the hospital to get me. She saved my life. She didn't berate me, she just took care of me. I stopped out of school that year and lived with her. She made me call my parents about a week or so after I got out of the hospital and they came to see me. I could tell they were mad at me, but they were more worried about the way I looked so they acted civil. Ms. Janice told them she didn't think I should go home with them and convinced them to let me stay with her and for some unknown reason they did. I think they trusted her. She was an extremely spiritual woman, a child of Yemaya, no one could say no to her. She and her Iya nursed me back to health. I knew what I was doing to myself was wrong and that I wanted to get well so I didn't fight them helping me. Ms. Janice made sure that I ate and she made sure that I went to therapy. I didn't want to go. I was like most black folks, I thought therapy was either for white people or for "real" crazy folks but she went with me. I needed her there and I was thankful that she was there. That was the first time, in therapy, that I was able to really talk about the abortion. I was able to recognize and acknowledge the anger, the fear, the loss, everything. (Laughing) I ain't knocked therapy since.

As I was feeling better physically I went with Ms. Janice to the classes she taught at DTH. I loved them. It felt like home, not just because I was around mostly black people but because I got to see dancers create. They had to talk about their pieces. Why they chose the music they chose, what emotion they were tapping into to create. What was going on in their life that inspired their movement choices? That was what was missing from my time at school. The first two years we learned the fundamentals but when we did have the opportunity to create our own pieces they were so constrained by all these other things, donor's thoughts, traditional ballet. I had no freedom to explore who I was as a dancer. I stayed with Ms. Janice during the entire year of what would have been my senior year of college and it was during that time that I got better and figured out how I was going to approach dance from then on out.

The next year I went back to school and finished my senior year. I pretty much kept to myself and did what I needed to do to graduate. I wasn't cured of the eating disorder, you never really are, so of course I relapsed to binging and purging, especially around the time I started going on auditions for dance companies. I had done dance company auditions before right out of high school so I knew what was expected in terms of the actual audition itself, but I didn't anticipate casting directors and instructors being upset about my age. Some wouldn't even see me because at twenty-one they thought I was "too old" or "untrainable." Getting a college degree had fucked me over in the world of dance. All those old feelings of anxiety came back, and I started to binge and purge again. It killed me. It wasn't about my body or my skin, supposedly. It was about the fact that I decided to get a degree and I was old. I was absolutely crushed.

Once again Ms. Janice showed up. We'd remained in close contact after I returned to school but she was amazing because I didn't have to say anything. She just knew that I was in trouble. She called me one week and I hadn't returned her call that whole week and she just showed up at my apartment one day after she was done teaching. I opened the door and she just looked at me. I put my head down and started crying and she came in and told me it was no time to cry, it was time to figure out what I was going to do to get my dancing feet back.

She asked me what I wanted for myself. I told her I wanted to dance and I wanted to be well. She asked me what I loved about dance and I told her it was beyond movement but all the things that dance could do. I reminded her of the things we'd (me and some of her other students from the dance studio back home) choreographed back in Oakland. We'd done dance to protest dress codes at school, police brutality in our neighborhoods, city wide curfews, etc. She told me well it sounds like you don't just want to dance; you want to intellectualize your movement, politicize your body. I said yes. She said well then, you have to study dance from all angles, not just movement.

I had no intentions of going to graduate school. I thought that discussing dance and not dancing was a waste of time. So Ms. Janice had me go and see some folks at some different schools and talk to them. I checked out a few graduate programs on the East Coast, a few in the Midwest, and some back on the West Coast and really liked how a few programs had infused both physical aspects of dance with theoretical and anthropological articulations of dance, so I applied to five schools and got accepted to four. I was thrilled. I felt like I was finally finding my space as a dancer.

To be frank I started graduate school thinking I knew everything—I didn't know shit. The summer after I graduated from undergrad I went on tour with this dance company and spent three months in Europe. I got paid a ridiculous amount of money and they paid for all of my lodging and the majority of my food. You couldn't tell me I wasn't hot. In addition I received two fellowships so I didn't have to pay for school at all. I decided to start my PhD in anthropology and worked on an MFA in dance at the same time. It was pretty cool because I was allowed to count some of my classes from the MFA for my doctoral course work so I thought I was hot shit to say the least. I was extremely arrogant. I knew most of the folks that came into the anthropology program were older than me and I assumed they hadn't had as much experience dancing as I had, and I knew that the folks in the MFA program weren't working on their PhD so I thought I was fly. I got slapped back into reality real quick. I was always a good student and most things related to academics came so naturally, so of course when I saw how many books I had to read that first semester I didn't think it was a big deal at all. I thought I had it all figured out. What I didn't account for was how demanding the MFA program would be coupled with my doc classes. I expected my MFA dance classes to be similar to what I had done in undergrad. They weren't. I had to put together a show from scratch. Cast people, choreograph, light it, set design, wardrobe, a lot of things other people had done in the past I was now responsible for doing and learning how to do it well. On top of that I had to stay on top of my actual reading and assignments for my other class. I realized this wasn't going to be as easy as I thought. I got over myself real quick and managed to do well enough in my classes that they didn't kick me out. (Laughs) My advisor, a friend of Ms. Janice, told me he didn't think I was going to make it but was glad I had dropped the attitude and started to really work hard.

He was my saving grace. He had taken the same route as me in many ways. He was a dancer and then went and gotten his MFA in dance and PhD in anthropology. He and Janice had danced in the same company for a while and when I went to visit schools he agreed to be my advisor if I chose to come to school there. That was the first time that I ever worked closely with a white person, a white man specifically. I mean of course I had white professors before but he was the first white professor that I ever worked directly with. (Laughs) I didn't trust him at all initially. Again a part of my arrogance. Part of being a student is humbling yourself enough to learn and it was clear in hindsight that Ms. Janice would not have introduced me to Tim if she didn't think I could learn something from him. I just had to be ready. He was extremely patient with me. He let me make mistakes, which was infuriating at times especially since there were times I felt like he could have saved me from heartache. You know don't take a class with this person or take a class with this person or apply for this not that. Focus your energies here. Not that I would have done or believed what he said early on anyway but it was a learning process. We had to learn to trust each other. I had only been in places where white people demanded that I change who I was in order to be successful. Tim had no intentions on changing who I was. Maybe the arrogance but he didn't want me to deny who I was as an artist to become a scholar or vice versa. He wanted to show me that what I brought to our department was something unique. That's what he wanted to show all of his students. I'm still thankful for him for that reason. You can't underestimate the power of good mentors and advisors, regardless of what they look like.

Don't get me wrong, grad school wasn't a cake walk because Tim was my advisor. At the time I started he was still junior faculty, he was starting his fourth year when I started my first, so he didn't have any tremendous amount of pull, but he was an awesome teacher and his colleagues knew that. He was also committed to doing excellent research and molding scholars that wanted to do the same. He couldn't shield me from racism or sexism. He was always very honest about it, though. He was honest about it existing, something I don't think I expected this white man to ever be honest about.

I remember after a seminar with this one professor that was notorious for being an ass, especially on anything critiquing race, I was in tears about what he said about my research project. My project looked at dance, race, and sexuality in Brazil and, as we're going around talking about projects, he laughed as I was talking about my research and said flat out, "Take note, this research will not make any significant contribution to the field. There is no place for dancers that call themselves researchers." I was too naïve to understand that this was not just a dig at me but at Tim too. When I walked in his office after class I was in tears. I told him what happened and I will never forget what he said, "So you think he took something from you by saying that? Look, you are and always will be a black woman. Off the bat these bastards are going to give you shit for it. Nothing I say or do and nothing you can do will protect you from other folks' ignorance. The beauty of it is that you already know that this ignorance exists, you just arm yourself with knowing your stuff and don't apologize for it." I don't think in the moment his words made me feel better but his words that day are still something I use to survive the academy to this day.

I left graduate school with two degrees, a job, and pregnant. I got pregnant on my last trip to Brazil. The trip was right before I defended. I went back because I helped plan a festival in a favela in São Paulo and so I went back to celebrate. I will spare you the details but Bailey's father was a drummer and I could never resist the call of the drum. When I came back to defend I was about two months pregnant. I didn't know I was pregnant and just assumed the morning sickness was nervousness about defending, and my periods had gotten more and more irregular as an adult so I wasn't alarmed. I didn't know I was pregnant until I went to the doctor for a change in my asthma medication. As always they ask you a million times if there is a possibility if you're pregnant. I didn't think so but they ran test anyway when they took a blood sample and I was pregnant. I was happy and sad. I was happy because I knew that I was keeping this baby, but I was horrified because I didn't know what having a baby would do to my career. Plus Bailey's father still lived in Brazil and we had no intention on being together. Needless to say it was hard. My new job was back on the West Coast but it wasn't close to my family so they couldn't help me with him on a day-to-day basis. It was hard.

The academy is not a place that is kind to people in general that give a damn about their families and it's especially harsh to single parents, particularly women. And of course no one is ever outright nasty, I mean sometimes they are, but I know how to deal with folks like that. It's the nice nasty that becomes a problem. I had Bailey during my first semester on the job. So I taught the first few weeks of the semester and then went out on maternity leave. The following semester I was right back to work. I'd found childcare for him but I had been pressured to teach one of my seminar's in the evening to accommodate more students so I didn't have childcare after 5 p.m., so Bailey was right there in the dance studio or in the conference room. I was breastfeeding so I would pump during office hours if I could. I would get occasional stares. Apparently some of my students complained about him being there but I was in a city, I didn't know many people, and childcare in the evening would have meant that more than likely I would have to leave him with someone. It was rough. I loved my job but I loved my child and I wasn't just going to leave him with anyone.

Eventually I got it together and found good extended childcare for him, but not before my commitment as a scholar was questioned and my commitment as a teacher and my commitment to service were questioned. My first annual review was horrible and the third-year review was a bit harsh too but I survived. I was deeply angry about that. I know how much guilt I had about not doing all the things I wanted to do with Bailey and for Bailey because my job at times came first so for my commitment to be questioned was like a slap in the face.

I definitely think my life outside the academy and prior to the academy prepared me for life in the academy. It wasn't until this process of talking about my life that I was able to see how much I was prepared to be in this space. The abortion was something I will never forget. Your body never forgets trauma like that. But I can say that experiencing something like someone taking something from you was unbearable. There is nothing that the academy could ever take away from me that could hurt like that. Nothing. On the flip side I have learned to fiercely protect anything I have given birth to. So to translate that into the academy, I fiercely defend any idea that I give birth to. I don't let anyone tell me no about show ideas that my students and I come up with or conferences or anything else. Even if it means that I have to find resources on my own. Which I usually do, but once it's done it always turns it out to be fabulous. I always say during faculty meetings if you don't like it now you'll fund it later and they always do. I just refuse anyone to ever take away something that I give birth to away from me ever again, even if they don't agree with it. I refuse to be silenced like that ever again.

I can definitely say that havin an eating disorder helped me find my voice again. I had learned somewhere along the way that pleasing people is what mattered more than anything and silenced myself because of it. I wanted to fit into a dance culture so much that I was willing to kill myself in all senses of the word in order to do so. I think Ms. Janice and Tim were instrumental in helping me find that voice again. They forced me to speak my own truth and not be ashamed. I've learned that I can't be silent here, especially since a place like this was never meant for people like you and me. They expect us to be silent. My life has taught me to defy other folks' expectations.

CHAPTER TEN

Freedom Schools and Ella Baker

Shaunita Levison

In the summer of 2009, I became aware of a program that focuses on high expectations for all children, strengthens their sense of self-worth, and affirms that they are loved. This program is known as the CDF Freedom Schools. This extraordinary program uses a curriculum designed to connect the children to African American history and enlarge their world and develop potential. As a servant leader, I was charged to encourage the children in reading various children's books throughout the entire summer. The books we used focused on heroes, heroines, as well as settings that reflected the children's very own cultural history and images.

Unbeknown to me, the driving force behind this magnificent program was Ella Baker. As a servant leader, I was taught about Baker; and while I learned in great detail exactly how she contributed to the civil rights movement, I remember her most as a model servant. Baker was a woman who had devoted her entire life to service in fighting against injustices. The structure of the relationship of a servant leader to their students was very similar to the ways in which Ella Baker interacted with her social action students because there is a strong emphasis on learning being relational among all participants (including the authoritatively constructed person). Baker suggested that if a person has it within their power to do so, then they should act on their authority and know that change can and should start with them.

Ella Josephine Baker was devoted to social change. She was an educator. She used her leadership skills in various social action organizations to teach people how to guide others. In 1946, she joined the staff of the New York Urban League. She aided in the founding of In Friendship in 1955, which was a support group for Southern school desegregation and the bus boycott of Montgomery, Alabama. The term was a strategic component of Baker's pedagogy as she communicated and related to the students with whom she worked; it was significant that their relationship was filled with camaraderie and closeness as friends might.

Ella Baker was an African American woman whose work with youth of color deemed her as an activist community educator. Her life's work involved not only advocating for social justice but also encouraging younger people to work at enacting fairness and inclusion for all people. Similarly, culturally relevant programs often facilitate the chance for people to question, wonder, and analyze critically, all while offering education that is for freedom. It was Baker's student-centered approach that not only highlighted her dedication to freedom but, more significantly, her solidarity to young people who also wanted to change the condition of African Americans.

In my decision to advance the education of African American students using an approach that is more centered on student learning, it first took my conscious effort to realize that the structure of learning may not be as effective as it could be for African American students. Based on my admission that the students were lacking opportunities that could influence their intellect and what it means to learn, I felt that this combined pedagogy approach would be a way to mend what was broken in classroom spaces.

Ella Baker advocated for curricula that was socially relevant and emphasized a fluid and interactive relationship between students and teachers (Ransby, 2003, p. 359). Consequently, Trent (1990) argues that since there are a growing number of white female students that will teach the growing number of diverse students in schools, then it is more imperative that race and ethnicity, too, are considered in designing curriculum for students to then be taught. Teachers should be a daring change agent in the classroom. To truly embrace an individual's purpose of educating their students, an educator has to be open and armed with the flexibility to engage all students present within their classrooms. Bridging the students' commonalities and differences will greatly influence the classroom atmosphere. Baker had the ability to teach her student activists as she served as a consultant for various organizations by encouraging them to be change agents.

Ella Baker's pedagogy was democratic and reciprocal. Barbara Ransby suggested that Baker "viewed education as a collective and creative enterprise requiring collaboration and exchange at every stage" (2003, p. 362). Baker's approach is often compared to Paulo Freire, a Brazilian educator and influential theorist. Both Freire and Baker demonstrated a deep reciprocity between teacher and student.

If educators think in terms of teacher-student and student-teacher—that is, a teacher who learns and a learner who teaches—as the basic roles of classroom participation, then the classroom space should create the possibility of progress for all participants.

Ella Baker was a facilitator. Baker preferred that everyone be equally accountable to one another. This approach influences critical thinking skills as well because if the instructor positions themselves as a facilitator versus the authoritative leader who holds all the answers, then students will began to look to one another to work collectively through the matter at hand. Students are very capable of discussing issues when given the opportunity. Enacting this type of approach within the classroom fosters collaboration.

I believe using both an adult and community education (ACE) pedagogy and class responsibility collaborator (CRC) model can enhance the learning experiences of African American students. Having these approaches in place gives students the opportunity to deconstruct negative stereotypes about themselves and uncover praiseworthy aspects of their history and culture (Sealey-Ruiz, 2007). Schools should reevaluate their curriculum and classroom practice in efforts to meet students where they are. By doing so, it benefits everyone. If an ultimate objective has to be spelled out, it would be my hope that students in structured spaces are reorganized to influence the inclusivity and growth of all students.

How can educators make a difference? We can certainly start by knowing our students and assigning readings that are relevant to their lives. We can all learn from Ella Baker!

REFERENCES

Ayers, W. (1989, November). 'We who believe in freedom cannot rest until it's done': Two dauntless women of the civil rights movement and the education of a people. *Harvard Educational Review, 59* (4), 520–528.

Ransby, B. (2003). *Ella Baker & the black freedom movement: A radical democratic vision.* Chapel Hill: University of North Carolina Press.

Sealey-Ruiz, Y. (2007, November). Wrapping the curriculum around their lives: Using a culturally relevant curriculum with African American adult women. *Adult Education Quarterly, 58,* 44–60.

Trent, W. (1990, Spring). Race and ethnicity in teacher education curriculum. *Teachers College Record, 91* (3), 61–369.

Part 3

Performance

My legacy
of imagination
is not lost.

Introduction

Performance is central to all things in Hip-Hop feminism. Whether the performance is improvised, freestyled, or choreographed, our imaginations are alive and well. Along with everything else, we create.

"The Almighty and Most Powerful," by Porsha Olayiwola, is a sensual cascade of melodic Hip-Hop feminism at its very best. To hear Olayiwola recite her poetry is to hear a young woman take ownership of herself, her body, and her beauty and invite others to do the same.

"I AM A WOMAN," written by Loy A. Webb, is a play to be produced and performed. Recalling the relevance of the civil rights movement, Webb addresses the full humanity of black women through a familiar and simple declaration, "I am a woman."

"Body Cypher Love," by Tanya Kozlowski, Irene Christine Zavarsky, and Christina Armstrong is a visual feminist statement that employs Hip-Hop feminist aesthetics. "Body Cypher Love" provides an example of how the introduction of technology need not inherently displace relationships—meaningful relationships—that benefit from coming face to face, hand to keyboard, in person, and on the screen.

Rap doctor Blair Ebony Smith brings the message in "Black Girl Night Talk." A poetic reflection of all things sincerely Hip-Hop, Smith writes in rhyme to remind us to listen. Prophetic, spiritual, and personal, this contribution acknowledges what it means to be a woman in a Hip-Hop world.

What is the purpose of Hip-Hop feminist pedagogy if it does not seek to promote healing and wholeness? Queering Hip-Hop makes us attentive to the ways sexuality, identity, race, and religion are constructed on the continuum of inclusion and exclusion to see who we are and who is with us in solidarity. "Acting Out: A Performative Exploration of Identity, Healing, and Wholeness," by Durell Callier, is an ethnodrama based on personal experiences and political possibilities.

The booty. The butt. The backside. Shake it left to right. Watch it slide. The way we move to the music we love necessarily implicates certain bodies more than others. In "Get It Girl Moments: A Reflection on Dance and Research," Grenita Hall, provides an ethnographic performance narrative that reminds us of the interconnectedness between song and dance, sound and movement.

CHAPTER ELEVEN

The Almighty and Most Powerful

Porsha Olayiwola

"I couldn't find anything to write about . . ."
But this morning, I took a long hot steamy shower
And as the water cascaded over my face
Down my back, and past my waist
I picked up the slippery bar of soap
With the hope that the lathery smooth suds would soothe me
And as I washed every hidden space and intimate space of my body
I sang softly
Gently washing my toes, legs thighs
My fingertips, arms and shoulders
Over my chest—between my breasts and down my stomach
The only thing left to clean was my hidden exquisite African violet
"So that's what I decided to write about"
My VAGINA
That punani—that clit—that nana
Them cookies—my goodies
My kitty—my candies—that good stuff
That sho' nuff gon make you scream
My peaches and cream
That goodness—my whispering eye
My vertical smile
The almighty and most powerful—pussy
See, now-a-days that's what they refer to my African violet is
And I don't wanna talk about how the days of chivalry have long passed

But rather how my vagina has become the #1 commodity
Exchanged and rearranged like it's somebody else's property
They say sex sells
Well, I guess Imma have to rebel
'Cause Today, my vagina ain't for sale
Nor is it a means of obtaining and sustaining a man
Man, she kill me when she say
"Pussy don't fail me now"
How you gon depend on your vagina to get a man
And they demand my African violet like
It was created solely for the pleasuring of man
They Command *"Girl, Give me that"*
They want to beat it up—tear it up
And do it rough
By my vagina is not a violent altercation
So refrain from the degradation of the creation of man
See, My African violet is the location of the creation of man
In fact, I gave birth to a nation of man
It's the almighty, and most powerful . . .
But because America is always on hard
They find it hard to see it as more than an object
Nothing but commodity of high quality
And since supply meets demand
Woman and Man have agreed on an equilibrium price
She gets the clothes, the car, and the cash
And he gets what's priceless
See, I lose respect because
They think it's okay to consider my African violet an object
So he misses the best part of me—My intellect
And if America stopped for 2 seconds
To listen to me
They would see me reflect on pieces of genius in me
But instead, they want . . .
That punani—that clit—that nana
Them cookies—my goodies
My kitty—my candies—that good stuff
That sho' nuff gon make you scream
My peaches and cream
That goodness—my whispering eye
My vertical smile
The almighty and most powerful—pussy.

CHAPTER TWELVE

I Am a Woman

Loy A. Webb

I wrote "I AM A WOMAN" in the summer of 2010 while in Memphis, Tennessee on vacation with my family. We had gone to the National Civil Rights Museum, and there, we watched a documentary on the Memphis Sanitation Strike. The men who participated in the strike explained that they wore signs around their neck, which simply read "I <u>AM</u> A MAN" to declare their humanity. As I began to analytically dissect this film, I said to myself, if the syllogism is "A man is human. I am a black man. Therefore, I am human," when will saying "I <u>AM</u> A WOMAN" be enough to declare one's humanity as well? In an essay written in 1966 titled "A Woman Playwright Speaks Her Mind," Alice Childress stated, "The Negro woman will attain her rightful place in American literature when those of us who care about truth, justice and a better life tell her story, with the full knowledge and appreciation of her constant, unrelenting struggle against racism and for human rights." I hope, even if only faintly, this short play resembles what Ms. Childress had in mind.

Be blessed,
Loy A. Webb

CAST OF CHARACTERS
Woman 1: Sapphire
Woman 2: Tragic Mulatto
Woman 3: Welfare Queen
Woman 4: Mammy

SCENE
A barren land filled with the unused fertility of black women.

TIME
Distant Present.

SCENE I
The lights rise on WOMAN 1, WOMAN 2, WOMAN 3, and WOMAN 4. The women stare into the audience silently. Demanding the audience to hear their silence until it becomes awkward. Suddenly WOMAN 1 screams, with an "I Exist" sort of scream. Then proceeds to shake the other women one by one to get their attention. The women show no response. The rest of the women do the same thing individually, contagiously following WOMAN 1's lead.

Woman 1: I am sick and tired of screaming and no one hearing me
All: But me.
Woman 4: I am sick and tired of existing and no one seeing me
All: But me.
Woman 3: My life feels like I have on Harry Potter's invisible cape.
Woman 2: Man it feel like God pushed record, but your girl didn't tape.
Woman 1: More like being tapped in a space where I can't escape.
Woman 4: No matter how loud I scream, in the background all you hear is
All: (Silence) them crickets.
Woman 2: I wish I could kill them fucking crickets!
Woman 3: I'm sick and tired of being sick and tired of them damn crickets!
All: I am a woman, birth from the womb of mother Africa. I was, ripped from my mother's breast and forced to live with my abductor.
Woman 2: My abductor is responsible for this shit! This
All: I'm lookin for a yellow bone long haired star/ Thick in the hips come and get in my car.
Woman 2: Type shit! I wouldn't wish this, held-down-my-foremothers-and-raped-them-then-discarded-them-like-used-condoms-shit! On nobody. And I'm suppose to go around bragging and shit. 'Cause my skin lighter than a paper bag... Sheeet. You must be out yo damn mind. I want to

expunge all this rapist blood from me, and be that kinda fine. I'll forgo a couple of men yelling

Woman 3: Aye! Aye! Aye girl!

Woman 4: Wassup lil mama?

Woman 1: It's like that? Bitch you ain't that cute anyway.

Woman 2: To go back in time and erase the pain that created this piece of shit…that I am. But then again, the majority of our race wouldn't exist.

Woman 1: See my dad told me that the world would be my oyster because I was

All: black and a woman.

Woman 1: So I worked hard to get to the top of the ladder of success, only to find that I couldn't go beyond the glass ceiling. Don't be fooled looks are deceiving. My credentials, experience, and ability to do my job has no clout when I walk in a room, automatically they assume My black-woman-ness, makes me less qualified. I'm like a dog on a leash, I can only go as far as the leash will let me. I'm qualified to work below, but not above. And don't let me begin to speak out about this injustice. My claim is then dismissed as another

All: Frivolous feminist, trying to state a cause of action that doesn't exist.

Woman 1: But just because I care about the state of my sistah's does not make me a feminist. I shouldn't have to be a feminist or womanist, to care about women. Shouldn't it be enough that I am a woman myself, and that I care about myself? I, am, just a woman who understands what it feels like to sit in a room full of people who don't look like her in either race or gender, and be ignored. And be told that I'm too loud. Or too aggressive. Or too opinionated. If God didn't want a black woman to function like an ordinary human being he wouldn't have given her a brain. But I got one, and as long as it's working properly, I'm going to use it. Not caring whether or not it makes you feel uncomfortable. (pause) That… that doesn't make me less of a woman. That doesn't mean that I'm trying to emasculate anybody. It means that I'm human. And I have the human right to change the world, just as you do, with the power of my mind.

Woman 1: Once upon a time…

Woman 4: Not too long ago…

Woman 2: A queen was born in the …

All: C-H-I-C-A-G-O.

Woman 3: My kingdom was called the projects. My court was my six kids I had by six different daddies. My riches came from the king of all kings, his name was Uncle Sam. Taxpayers hated me. They said

All: We are sick of paying money for her to sit on her—

Woman 3: *Ask* about me. They just jealous cause Uncle Sam gave me just enough to get me a Cadillac with a…

All: "Diamond in the back, sunroof top/ Diggin the scene/ With a gangsta lean/ woo-ooh-ooh.

Woman 3: Or at least that's what they think. They didn't see that in addition to the check full of pennies, I worked my behind off trying to provide for my family and still came up short. I was simply the face of welfare, not the body. The body of welfare is the companies that make millions of dollars in profit, yet still get governmental handouts. If you're a student and got loans from Uncle Sam, that's a form of welfare baby. If you're a company and you get governmental subsidies, that's a form of welfare. I'm-not-going-to-mention-any-particular-car-companies-or-bank-that-received-welfare-checks-a-trillion-times-more-than-mine-and-instead-of-buying-Cadillacs-they-take-private-jets-and -vacation-at-spa-resorts... But that's neither here or there. While I enjoyed being their queen, I had to resign my throne. No longer will I lend my face, to somebody else's body.

Woman 1, Woman 2, Woman 3: Apologize!

Woman 4: For being a woman.

Woman 1, Woman 2, Woman 3: Apologize!

Woman 4: For being black.

Woman 1, Woman 2, Woman 3: Apologize!

Woman 4: For being fat. I can say that and it rolls off my tongue like the Niagara rolls into the sea. See, if you looking for a sob story from me, you're not going to find one. I'm not like any of the depressed women in the commercials, cause my fat doesn't define me. My only negative feeling is toward the view of me as seen through the eyes of society. We live in a world that glorifies glitter rather than gold, and if you want to survive you got to exchange your soul, for less than it's worth. They make you feel like from your birth, you owe them an apology, and G, I'm not apologizing anymore for the (*Inset actresses height and weight if comfortable*) woman that I am. I have spent my entire life apologizing, cause folks refuse to accept me as I am. Just cause I don't look like you, doesn't mean I belong like some animal caged in a zoo.

Woman 1: Look at me I am human.

Woman 2: Look at me I am human.

Woman 4: Look at me I am human. This is for everybody who has had to apologize for being you. Stop it. Stop apologizing.

All: Stop fucking apologizing.

Woman 4: The only person we owe an apology to is our imperfectly perfect selves. For not accepting all of our perfectly imperfect selves.

All: We have spent our entire lives apologizing for our existence.

Woman 1: They try to make us feel like illegitimate children. Blaming us for something they laid down and created.

Woman 3: But there's a revolution going on.

(Woman 1 starts chanting "left, right" she starts marching and the other women follow one by one.)

Woman 2: Cause we ain't taking this shit no more!

(Marching continues.)

Woman 4: I exist because black women fought for me. Sun up to sun down they fought for me. Sun up to sun down my foremothers fought for me!

(March continues.)

Woman 4: My foremothers had them rough hands. Hands not meant for a "woman," but worn on the black woman. They were rich with the scars of toil, that built this nation from the ground up. So for my foremothers that labored for me, side by side with my forefathers, today we draw the line when the world tries to disgrace the lineage of your legacy.

All: I draw this line to declare I am simply a human being. Rather than a human in female form, I am sick of the female alternative forms!

Woman 2: No a diva is not a female version…

All: Of a hustla, of a of a hustla, of a of a hustla.

Woman 2: I am not a damn diva.

All: I repeat I am not a diva!

Woman 3: I don't want to be. I embody the definition of what it means to work hard to provide for my family. I, a woman…

All: Black.

Woman 3: Have earned the right to be…simply a hustla.

All: I'm drawing the line to re-define myself. No longer will I accept the world's definition of me.

Woman 4: This is a warning.

All: I repeat this is a warning!

Woman 2: Anybody cross this line your ass is grass. I ain't ya hood rat. I ain't ya gold digger. I'm not ya chick, chickenhead, pigeon or any other type of bird. I'm not your broad. I'm not your trick. I'm not your butterface. I'm not ya butch. I'm not your jump off. I'm not your yellow bone, red bone or any other type of bone. I'm not even your damn female. Do we go around saying—

Woman 3: These males is tripping.

Woman 2: I'm not your heifer. I'm not your hoochie or hussy. I'm not ya shawty. Oh yeah Young Burg, I'm not your fucking dark butt. I'm not ya baby. And Plies, I am Not! your damn bust it baby.

Woman 1: I'm not your b-word.

Woman 2: My girl means we ain't yo bitch. Barbie bitch to be exact.

Woman 3: Slut or hoe.

Woman 2: I ain't yo tragic mulatto.

Woman 1: I'm not your sapphire.

Woman 3: I'm not your welfare queen or jezebel.

Woman 4: And I'm definitely not your mammy.

Woman 1: I am a Woman.

Woman 2: I am a Woman.

Woman 3: I am a Woman.

Woman 4: Let the whole world hear that…

All: I am a Woman!

Woman 3: Maybe not the type you imagine.

Woman 2: Cause I ain't reached your mountain top.

Woman 1: But let me remix Frederick Douglass for a moment. Judge a man.

Woman 2, Woman 3, Woman 4: Strike man, put woman.

Woman 1: Not by the heights in which he has risen.

Woman 2, Woman 3, Woman 4: Strike he, put she.

Woman 1: But from the depths in which he has climbed.

Woman 2, Woman 3, Woman 4: Strike he, put she.

Woman 1: New sentence reads.

All: Judge a woman not by the heights in which she has risen, but from the depths in which she has climbed.

Woman 4: Me and my sistahs will continue to climb. See society marks us as the lowest on the totem pole, supposedly because we are weak.

All: But the real reason is the strength in our feet.

Woman 2: An army of sistahs has risen to fight on the front lines of this war. To my sistah that doesn't realize that her perfectly imperfect self is the reflection of God, we march for you!

Woman 3: To my sistah that's a single mother that's doing all she can to provide for her children, we march for you!

Woman 4: To my abused and forgotten sistah who is disillusioned by her circumstance and feels that the glass ceiling of failure is unbreakable, we march for you!.

All: Right, left. Right, left. Right, left. Right, left.

They aim ready to shoot.

All: To all those who cross this line beware.

(Lights fade to black.)

THE END.

CHAPTER THIRTEEN

Body Cypher Love: A Remix: A Hip-Hop Feminist Project

Tanya Kozlowski, Irene Christine Zavarsky, and Christina Armstrong

An Intro: Another Remix

i'm already tryin 2 4get i'm damaged
cuz the undertow of silence mouths
"y do we have 2 defer our dreams?"
my mere presence evokes conflict within u
ur lack of self luv & fear manifest into hateful rhetoric mirrored by
    neo-liberal appropriations delivered in condescending gestures
the imperialist delusions permeate like smog
i must not wait!
don't tell me it's not my turn!
i resist ur teachings
no i will not run in place!
my legacy of imagination is not lost
it is not in my disposition to lie
i rebel as I speak walkin steady towards 2mrw

Before you read the text, we recommend that you watch our video on YouTube, Body Cypher Love: A Remix: A Hip-Hop Feminist Project.

Putting Irene, Tanya, and my pictures, words, music, lives, and ideas together was a beautiful cipher. Tanya, Irene, and I are beautiful women with similar yet diverse backgrounds and experiences. We literally cross the globe. We freestyle witty and wonderful punch lines out of the air. We took our lives, knowledge, and experiences and created a beautiful creative empowering video. The stories and messages in the film are wonderfully layered and tied together. Tanya would mention how it was great when our three selves came together at one point of the piece. For an instance, it was my words, Tanya's music, and Irene's video. We created re-imaginations. (Christina)

* * *

Our film project consists of three concepts that we found ourselves compelled to remix, namely, the cipher, the Hip-Hop cultural text, and the bodies of womyn of color. In this text, as in the video, we will speak as individuals and as one. Remixed. We—Christina, Tanya, and Irene—met and hung out for a few hours in early October 2009 to try to get to know each other beyond our first names for the purpose of generating topics that could be used in a group project. After walking to dinner and chatting in the living room of Tanya's apartment, we were able to make some decisions and began creating ideas for our project. We wanted to engage a wider audience than our class because our individual experiences and subjectivities have been shaped significantly by spaces outside of the university. The five-minute multimedia film is centered on the bodies, cultural texts, and ciphers developed among womyn of color; however, men, children, white womyn, adolescents, and the elderly will all be able to critically engage with our project. (Tanya)

* * *

When I became part of this project, I was very excited and very scared. Both Tanya and Christina are awesome women and I am still proud to work with them, to be part of our team. I did not know much about Hip-Hop when we began. I listened to it, same as I listen to a whole bunch of other music rock, pop, alternative, classic, country. . . . Now, I know more about Hip-Hop. I listen to it. Same as I still listen to other music. What have I gained by being a part of Body Cypher Love? I met great scholars, beautiful people, engaged in fruitful discussions, and produced an awesome video that I do not want to stop watching. In this video, there are so many parts of ourselves (re)mixed together. Some sequences are influenced by all three of us; in others only one or two speak. Important, you cannot decipher whose idea or contribution is in each part of the video. The beautiful thing about our video is that it is us, in all our diversities and similarities. Even if you wanted to, you could not take it apart. When I look back at that project, I am still excited, I am still scared. I am, for sure, very proud. (Irene)

Come on, It's Hip Hop -
Let's Break Some Rules!

"Sometimes I feel like I don't belong anywhere... Sometimes I feel like I gotta no home."
—Alicia Keys, "Prelude to a Kiss," *As I Am* (2007). Negro spiritual, "Sometimes I Feel" (like a motherless child).

My first semester of graduate school was not what I thought it would be. I came with high hopes that I would make new friends quickly and be active and involved in organizations. Where I found myself was alone and lonely in my apartment. I was living alone for the first time in my life. Living alone was not really the best choice. The way society is structured it does not reward and value introverted people like me. I began to regress. I felt out of place and weird and different again like I did when I was younger.

In the past, I had some man present in my life to buffer the pain, insecurities, and difficulties during hard transitions. Now, there was no one but me. I missed my former boyfriend and questioned every day why I broke up with him. I yearned for intimacy and affection. Recently, I received my master's degree from Harvard. I yearned for the close friendships and life I left behind in Cambridge-Boston. If not for the support of family by way of phone calls, an old friend who was in the same city, and an occasional retreat home to see old friends, I fear I might have gone crazy. (Actually, I did a little bit.) But then I discovered some strength and resilience in me. Things got better.

In the midst of dealing with my new reality and rediscovering the strong parts of me, I was taking a course, Hip-Hop Feminism. I was beginning to get to know people. Tanya, Irene, and I went out to dinner to get to know each other before we started making the video. It was a night of female bonding that I needed that entire semester—just talking, learning about each other, and eating dinner. The process of making this video was intertwined with the spaces or bodies we were in—my place, Tanya's place, and a coffee shop. This cipher, this bonding, and the time in our class are the kinds of "food for the soul" that I needed. You can see pictures from our class in some of the photos in the video. (Christina)

The Concept(s) Moves Us

The concept of the cipher is central to our project. A cipher is a space of knowledge production. Ciphers generate knowledge. We created a cipher to analyze womyn of color representations in Hip-Hop films. We chose an interview of Tupac, an episode of the famous television series *Full House*, and an episode of *The Simpsons* to remix specific clips and insert our voices while simultaneously erasing the voices of the original characters. In contrast to the representations of womyn of color in mainstream media we address this concept with our own personal creations of self in text, music, and video.

Picture Me Rollin' by Black Artemis (2005) drove my participation, imagination, and motivation in creating our project. No matter how many times I watch our film, I smile, laugh, think about something new—and I cry. I cry every time because it hits me every time I watch it, that for six minutes of life, thanx to the technology of YouTube, I am celebrated and not silenced, or called a dykespicbitchcuntdissapointmenttomyfamilywasteofspacefemaleloser. I smile and laugh because I think of all the fun Irene, Christina, and I had in meeting together to make the film. All of us are so different that to think three of the most different womyn could come together to create a dynamic ass video, in less than three months, still leaves me in a state of utter awe and pride. Suddenly three strangers were a group with no idea what to do or what to say to each other. Rather than meet at the library or at a campus building, we remixed our group project strategy. I suggested to Irene and Christina that we just go out to dinner and chill together for a bit on a Sunday night and make a cipher of womyn, not focus on a group project formulated by the curriculum. Along the journey we found beauty in both the process and the product of creating our video; and that's hard to do in the academy. That's hard to do in life, period. The task of using multimedia to make a film with strangers was not only daunting because it was being graded, but daunting also because rarely are womyn asked to contribute, let alone create, something new within the academy. The music, the photos, the videos, the text, the order in which images were arranged, the disruptions and contradictions were our collective re-imaginations. Christina singing excerpts from artists Alicia Keys and Sweet Honey and the Rock prior to showing our class our project made time stand still and held hope in our hearts. You just had to be there to know what I'm talking about. (Tanya)

"Bilder bilden; so oder so. Die medialen, gesellschaftlichen, persönlichen Spiegelungen von body cyphor love provozieren Vervielfältigungen"/"Compositions compose and/or educate; either way. The media-based, social, personal reflections of body cipher love provoke multiplications. My conclusion is to love myselves."
    —Christine Rabl, Department of Education and Human Development, University of Vienna

Cypher—how are our surroundings shaped by ideas? We live and work at a university that defines which programs are worth funding and which are not. What buildings are worth mending and what buildings do not even exist. That defines what is to be considered academic and what is not. I studied political sciences at the University of Vienna, Austria. Since the very beginning I struggled with the problem of fitting into that university. My interests weren't outlined neatly along mainstream political science. I was interested in cultural studies: Why do people live how they live? Why do they listen to the music they listen to? Film analysis: How do films shape our values, our ideologies? Can I go to the movies and just be entertained? Or am I always taught something? Gender studies: Why is it that women are seen differently? And why does different always mean less important? And what does all that have to do with my life? With me—being a woman, a daughter, a friend, a lover (seldom), a buddy (way more often!) a political person, a scholar? Only few courses granted that type of discussion. The only professors (mostly women) who taught courses like that are still stuck somewhere in the middle of the academic career ladder, with a glass ceiling right above them. Whenever I tried to be inventive, I was questioned. My ability to write about these topics as a political scientist was and still is questioned. That makes me angry and sad. I have something to say, people just don't care to listen. Especially people who already have all the academic honors and just *know it all.*

Surrounded by symbols I did not pick and I do not want to contribute to, reciphering the spaces I live in is a revolutionary act. It happens when I come together with other people, women claim space, share thoughts and feelings, and define that space. Speak up against injustice, against the policy of knowing-everything-better, racism, against not listening, sexism, and homophobia. We ciphered a lot. Constantly. It was for sure one of the best classes I've ever taken. It taught me, it touched me, and it spoke to me. Recipher the space you live in! Make it your space. (Irene)

I had no idea how messed up the academy was prior to entering it formally in the fall of 2007. When I made the decision to try to get into a PhD program I was rejected three times, and each rejection seemed to manifest feelings of uncertainty, increase feelings of insecurity, and break my spirit. Back in 2005, I thought the hardest part would be just getting into a system that creates no expectations or seeks scholarly contributions from lesbian womyn of color. But I was so naïve because the hardest part of my PhD journey is being a lesbian womyn of color and learning every day new ways imperialism, colonization, and cultural logics, like heteropatriarchy, continue to manifest in the daily lives of everyone. The final important piece to the creation of our group project is knowing that the opportunity didn't have to happen at all. Do you know how long it's been since someone older than me cared about, truly cared about, my life, my struggles, my hopes, my dreams, and took a genuine interest in me? I don't remember and I can't forget that. I couldn't believe this brilliant, genuine, and talented womyn of color scholar actually thought I had something worth saying and sharing. This professor renewed my faith not only in myself by asking me to tell a story and share that story with others, but she also renewed my faith in womyn loving other womyn on the spectrum like Audre Lorde talks about. A lot of professors—a lot—say they are down completely with supporting PhD students; but in practice they ain't down with nothing but supporting themselves and their careers. As a professor of Hip-Hop feminism, she had faith in all of her students, not just me; and she challenged us all to believe in ourselves, in the possibilities of love, and the beauty in each other. That little bit of courage made all the difference in me; and I hope it shows in our film. (Tanya)

We are also leaning on and engaging with the arguments of womyn, especially womyn of color scholars such as bell hooks, Judith Butler, and Audre Lorde, in the creation of our film. We posit that it will be very powerful and productive to engage with these scholars. Engaging their work will push us to work together more collaboratively. It will keep love at the center of our inquiries; allow us to use our erotic power collectively as diverse womyn. It will encourage us to be critical in creating a project that will continue to add to the production of knowledge about issues of girlhood, gender, identity formation in the public sphere, and Hip-Hop feminism.

The video transformed my personal experiences and pictures into something new when music and text were added—the remix. We had a section themed "movement" with video from my trip to Ghana mixed in with the Graduate Employee Organization (GEO) rally (graduate students went on strike at the university in fall 2009) and driving to and from the city. This idea of movement felt to me like the ever-present stride toward the hope that we can change the world. It is the hope of better days that we move toward in spite of all that is sad and cruel in the world. The beginning of the film displayed how women are negatively portrayed and viewed. Then, we in response show the beauty and lives of great women. It shows the movement for change.

Also, there were photos from the inauguration. No matter what you might think of Obama's policies or how well he is doing in office now, on that lawn in Washington, D.C., in January 2009, there was intense joy and spirit. It was historical, spiritual, and communal. It felt like my "I Had a Dream" moment to talk about with my future children. Getting Obama in office was a movement. (Christina)

All my life, I was trying to fit into labels: being a good daughter, a good pupil, a good friend, a good scholar, and a good woman . . . However, some labels never quite fit. I was often too loud, too untamed, too curious and inquisitive, too much like a boy, became too dirty when I played outside—mud up to the elbows and tree gum in the hair (I was lucky I had so much hair, my mother just took scissors and cut it out). Only later, I understood better why things did not fit for me. Labels are produced by a patriarchal society and give the one who labels the power over the labeled body: boys can be wild and fierce; girls should be gentle and quiet. Labels are dangerous. They put me in a box I don't want to be in and don't let me out again. They tell me what to look like and how to dress. Instead of getting to know each other we work with prejudices. Instead of getting to know me, people label me quickly and then stop investigating: *She is very independent, she does not need help. She is a strong woman; nothing can hurt her, no need to be gentle.* By trying to measure up to the (assumed) expectations of my social surroundings, I forgot how to live.

I spent so much time in my life worrying about my looks: *I should not eat that chocolate bar; I am trying to lose weight!* I think I've tried to lose weight since I was twelve years old. For one year I counted calories and was so proud of myself when I managed to eat only one tomato in the whole day. I could not sleep that night because I was so hungry and threw up the next morning. I still was very proud of myself. Every weekend I sat at our family dinner table, grinding my teeth, sipping my mineral water, and trying not to be seduced by fresh bread, ham, butter, and cheese. I was not a very delightful person at that time. Grumpy during dinnertime, hungry all the rest of the time. After half a year I lost twenty pounds and for the first time in my life a boy was interested in being my *boy*friend (I always have had boy-*friends*, but he wanted to be my *boy*-friend. That was different!). However, I did not want to be his girlfriend, and I didn´t know how to get rid of him—I had no experience! Eventually I stopped dieting and gained weight again. A part of me still wants to get back to the very slim woman I once was. A part of me is still convinced that that is the way to get men interested. (Irene)

Around the time of the making of the video, I was hit by probably the hardest emotional blow that I have ever experienced. Tanya and Irene didn't know specifically what I was going through, which makes the film all the more special. I was heartbroken. I felt inadequate as a woman. I physically got sick. Plus, this had to be the time when all types of articles about too many black womyn being single and there being no black men just appeared again out of nowhere. It just made me feel even worse about the whole situation. I let go of and lost a good black man going for a PhD. He was loyal, intelligent, and caring.

As a single black female pursuing a PhD, loving myself is the only option. The film made me think about what was important to me. The pictures in the video were representative of things I loved and cared about. For instance, there was a picture of my time in an a cappella group. I love music. I love to sing. Being a part of this group helped me develop a stronger presence and confidence on stage. (Christina)

Her Love Moves Me

Film and TV, fiction and fantasies tell us how to love. What a good heteronormative husband looks like, how a good heteronormative wife behaves. How our heart knows our true love and how music will swell as soon as you lay eyes on him or her. In real life, there is no music that tells us when we've found the one. The first kiss is the most important moment in a young woman's life. It is told to be the most beautiful moment. As far as I am concerned, it was mostly awkward and wet. Telling streamlined stories about streamlined relationships that all head for a happy ending—since all endings have to be happy—is what covers up all the diversity in relationships that exist in the world. Love is nothing that happens once in one way. Love is as diverse as the people who love. (Irene)

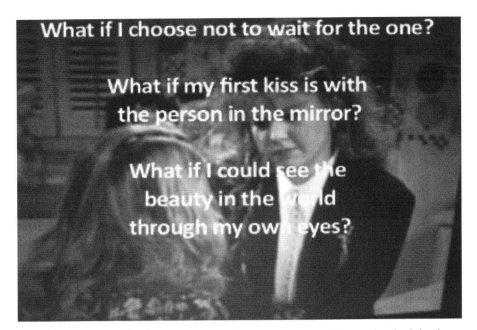

What if I choose not to wait for the one?

What if my first kiss is with the person in the mirror?

What if I could see the beauty in the world through my own eyes?

The constant rush of cars hurrying past my apartment hitting the slush built up in the potholes in the streets is ever present. The aging breaks being pushed down upon by the bus driver as the bus approaches the corner stop are so loud I catch myself jumping up to avoid the bus coming through my dilapidated windows. My Mexican flag, pride flag, and GEO Union sign sit patiently in the window ledge fading from the sun's visits. The light masks the emptiness in the room somewhat as I lay on my bed trying to remind myself here (on the university campus and in the PhD program) there is no time to sleep, there is no time to be afraid, and there is no time to cry. There are papers to grade, e-mails to answer, treadmills to run on, rent to pay, snow to shovel, buses to catch, meetings to attend, food to cook, laundry to do, and I'm already late giving my contribution to the artist statement for the video I helped make. The air seems colder now and everything seems loud and obnoxious when we are apart. The sheets are still holding on to her scent and I lay next to the pillow remembering the happiness, which held itself in my eyes as I looked over at her lying next to me when I woke up this morning. I have memorized the texture of her breath as she parts her lips in between dreams. The smell of her soft brown skin invigorates my pulse while distracting me from academic concentrations. I can taste the warmth of her body on my tongue and in my mouth, and I long for nothing else but to retreat back into her arms just once more. In times of struggle, I go back to that feeling of possibility I get every time she smiles at me and how I secretly ask my butterflies to stir slower when she slips her hand in mine. Still looking for my y'chi, I roll over and breathe out slow tears because she is gone, again. To tell you that I miss her would be a great lie because there is not a verb with enough depth and character in any language to describe how I ache for her when we are apart. (Tanya)

But where is the script for me?

Chorus:
All I wanted was a boyfriend
To get my first kiss and hold hands
Just like every teen girl on a sitcom I saw on TV
I wanted a prince charming magical fairy tale for me

I spotted him looking out the school bus window one day
Thought he was kind of cute but would never look my way
That was what I reasoned with every boy I saw
Because all I could see about me was all of my flaws
Not pretty like the other girls who seemed to have it all
Big boobs, nice hair, big butt, waist small
He got on the bus and actually said hi to me
Gave me a smile, thought it couldn't be for me
But he saw something about me that he seemed to like
Maybe it was my smile; maybe he saw something arousing on TV last night
Whatever it was it was some kind, some kind of chemistry
Some kind of meant to be, or some kind of love mimicry
Within days he asked if I would go with him

Made the decision was too soon, I wish I could go back to then
I was so desperate for the romantic images in my head
Didn't see the danger signs to be played out soon ahead

The first day was a little strange
Trying to figure out how my body was to be arranged
Laid my hairy legs on his lap for a little while
Not a girly girl, no special grooming, not even nail to the file
Relied on his expertise, I followed his lead
He asked me if he could kiss me and nervously I told him in time we'll see
What I'd been waiting for so long
Was coming as soon as I made the call
But I was hesitant because I hadn't known him long enough
Barely knew anything about his life or all the important stuff
But then I let it happen and it wasn't what I thought
Felt his teeth on my mouth and our two tongues fought
All I could think was how slimy his tongue felt in my mouth
My first kiss didn't feel like magic, it was gross by all accounts
I reasoned that magic feeling had to be make believe
Cinderella stories are only for those girls on the screen

He started suggesting some things I hadn't even thought about
Wanted to grab hold of my butt and breasts that hadn't even sprout
Is this what happened in everyone else's relationship?
I hadn't had one before, but I thought it was more innocent
I was self-conscious and too embarrassed to let it get that far
Plus on my breast I had an ugly discolored scar
Details hazy, I communicated no and I thought he would respect my wishes
But soon enough I found out he still would keep persisting

Never said yes, but before I knew it his hand was in my shirt on my bra
The most X-rated movie I had ever saw
Thank goodness it was really padded or he would have had it
I told him no again and he still made a quick grab at tit
He reached inside the cup holding my never before touched nipple
Grabbed all over the small mound making me feel small and simple
Didn't know how it got there I felt astonished and numb
Helpless and confused and unsure and dumb
Never said yes to the things you did
Why couldn't you hear or see this inexperienced kid?
Took it where it didn't have to go

Now I'm tormented by choices I couldn't make fast enough long ago
The older me tells the younger me it's going to be ok
You could have yelled at him get the fuck away
But he took you by surprise and he didn't hear your tiny voice
They only hear curse words, yells, kicks, punches, and loud voices' choice
I blamed myself for not being strong and assertive
But without this boy's manipulation this story could have been averted
How would you like it if I grabbed your small penis?
Make you feel like a speechless small fetus
The details still hazy about all that happened
But the next incident like that with a boy I will be slapping
(Christina)

* * *

We shift the gaze of the bodies of womyn of color from the shackles of heteropatriarchy toward our re-imaginations in the celebration and affirmations of our own bodies through photography and art.

There was a picture of me and my brother, who was a big help when I was going through my down times. He also represents family in general and how supportive they have been. There was also a picture of us in sailor suits when we were very young that everyone smiles at when they see it. It's a really cute picture. It reminds me of simpler times. It reminds me of the "pretty young thing" I was and am. There was a picture of a self-portrait I drew in high school that is kind of sad looking because it shows me with my hand around my neck. It represented some of the stress I was under in school. Yet, there is strength in the picture. I was proud of my creativity. I had not been able to draw stick figures and yet I was able to do this amazing self-portrait. I was able to do what I doubted I could do. There was a picture of me and two other black women at Harvard commencement. It was one of the proudest moments of my life. The picture also represents beating the odds. We were black women with Harvard degrees. Also, we overcame the obstacles of that crazy year and the commencement was a celebration of our successes. (Christina)

The parts we chose to express love represent a very individual and subjective kind of love. For me, it shows who I love, by whom I am loved, friendship love, family love, true love, old love, new love, long-lasting love, fresh and exciting love, love for work colleagues, love for ideas, love for political concepts. It is truly all about love. At the same time we show a very objective, all-embracing kind of love: It contains songs that are sung about love, movies that are made about love, and stories that are told about love. It contains even more: our questions and critiques, our doubts and affirmations of it. And to all of that the answer is: Hell, yeah, love yourself! (Irene)

There were pictures from the trip I took to Ghana. I went with the choir from my old high school. The group performed with the Winneba Youth Choir in Ghana at Cape Coast castle. The day before we toured the castle where we were shown the slave dungeons where millions of slaves were held before they were taken away. We were told stories about the torture and I felt incredible sadness and sacredness. When the group performed, there was some sense of reconciliation. A rainbow appeared on the ocean when the two groups—one from Africa and one from the United States—sang together. It felt like we were coming back to reclaim ourselves. We sang with our brothers and sisters as if they possibly could be our brothers and sisters. It felt like a return and a symbol of overcoming. It was a reunion. A place of so much pain and suffering became a place of joy and celebration. It was a remix. Same body, different cipher and love. (Christina)

Sometimes I wonder if love will ever come. I know that sounds ungrateful. I am loved and I love my family, my friends, who are all very, very dear to me, but there is a kind of love that is still missing. That consuming love. That burning-down-in-your-stomach love. That love you feel when you know you want to stay with someone. Share your life. Have a family, eventually. Knowing that the other person just feels the same way about you. Love and be loved in return. Seems like a miracle, almost too good to be true, too unlikely to ever really happen. (Irene)

The film became and is a reminder that I needed to love myself. The Jean Grae song, "Love Song," I listened to over and over again after Tanya introduced it to us for the video. Jean Grae brings up relationship issues of a woman. But Jean Grae says it's still a love song even after relationships end. It's a love song about loving yourself. A quote from Black Artemis we used in our film stuck with me as well, "Because society does everything in its power to make a woman loathe herself, the most revolutionary thing she can do . . . is love herself." What inhibits movement? Loving myself is not only important for myself, it is important for the movement. Let's start a movement! (Christina)

The road we are traveling on in our video appeals to me for different reasons. First, I really like to drive, to be on my way, to explore and get to know new places, people, as well as ideas and concepts. When I filmed the first video, driving down from my vacation in Michigan back to campus, I did not have our video project in mind. I just loved the idea of having a video of me driving, through the country and through the city, by night. While driving I listened to the CD Tanya made for us with her favorite Hip-Hop songs, pieces, and one of them was Kanye West's "Streetlights." I ended up listening to that song a thousand times in a row, it spoke to me. Do we still have time to grow? How much time do I have? Am I getting too old for certain things? For experiments? Should I settle down, finally? What about the time I am wasting doing things that are not important? Who tells me what is important and what isn´t? How much time does it take to live? Things ain't always set in stone. There will be a lot of stops, detours, blown-up tires along the way. There is always the possibility for change of direction. I can always decide to stop, turn around, linger, and go faster. For some parts I will have company, others I will have to travel alone. I know my destination, but I'm just not there. Well, sometimes I have to admit, I do not know my destination. Or, at least, I am not sure about it. I am confused by other people, institutions, governments, world politics, local issues, social issues, financial issues, and gender issues. Talking and sharing helps a lot. In a conversation I usually can figure out where I want to be, get an idea where I would like to go, even though I know I am not there . . . yet. And probably never will be? So do I even want to be there? Where would I go if I were already there? (Irene)

It's interesting that I'm from Chicago, born and raised, but none of the pictures of Chicago were from me. (Though Chicago was in the "bodies" of the people in my photos.) I could not figure out what to take pictures of. I think I could have taken a picture of anything and told you a story about it. I noticed Irene filmed an area not too far from my house unknowingly. The community she filmed is Beverly, which is next to my community. There are many neighborhoods where the social conditions are separated by a street or a railroad track throughout the city. A house in Beverly is probably worth twice as much as one in the adjacent neighborhood. But this is all Chicago. It is one big, complex contradiction. The great thing about the video and any type of art is that it can be interpreted different ways by the receiver. It can connect us to some memories that might have been lost. It has the power to change people's lives. It allows us to imagine a better world. The video was so powerful for me personally because it was directly related to my personal experiences. The personal is political. (Christina)

A Fractured Epilogue

fractured and fragmented silences

and still i rise . . .

living.

my life continues for reasons that aren't always clear to me,

metamorphosis.

i research with people, not about people,

statistics are human beings with the tears wiped off.

where will i land?

it's like u were hiding behind a wall,

we began a partnership.

lives in infinite variety and dignity,

i don't want this burden anymore.

i don't know how to talk about this.

my healthy denial,

unfinished business.

i had to learn how to give myself permission,

sometimes there is this numbness,

detached,

fire and ice,

rebuilding walls,

our bodies are the cars our souls ride around in.

stop hitting the snooze button!

a tangled web of meaning,

the romance of knowledge as a cure,

fragmenting . . . detours . . . delays . . .

layers of information,

we all get lost.

something "too big" is going on and i render it to be elusive.

shadow places, hollow spaces

a register of ruin (?),

it is inexpressible—

life in all its pain and passion.

can our hearts possess an abundance and power in our existence?

humans struggle to live worthwhile lives in a world of inhuman catastrophe.

things collapsed, lies surfaced . . .

blown backwards . . . into a pile of debris . . .

and still i rise . . . i rise . . . i rise . . .

staggered movement,

rebuilds fractured and fragmented silences into whispers of true stories,

forging ahead on literal and figurative bridges,

catch my breath,

walk beside me in the light, take me in your arms.

the caged bird has sung,

for i now remember my song(s)

REFERENCE

Artemis, B. (2005). *Picture me rollin'*. New York: New American Library.

CHAPTER FOURTEEN

Black Girl Night Talk

Blair Ebony Smith

The Message

Here I am
woman in the flesh
And they prolly won't take me serious
It ain't my period
that be makin' me delirious
it's the world
they got me all wrong
Puttin' words in rhyme form
Hopin' they can catch on
ride wit me
take a trip down my road
if you knew how much I grow
you'd be crazy not to grow wit me
but then again everyone ain't gone vibe
I Let the pen glide
wit pride
attempting to put negative thoughts to the side
Not confined to set bars
or they definitions of a star
makin' my own definitions
And I hope you listen

The Context

Here I am again. Yet another lonely night. Nobody wants to talk about why the struggle keeps me up; they just tell me it's not healthy. Little do they know my thoughts at night keep my soul healthy. Sometimes I feel it is mind over body. Transitioning through life is not an easy task. As a twenty-two-year-old young black woman embarking on my journey toward earning a doctorate in a whole new world, I remind myself of this . . . and mostly at night.

I always gain inspiration through music. I was sitting up late listening and thinking; listening to one song on repeat. I consider myself to be a listener first and a messenger second. I gained inspiration from a track by a Rochester, New York, bred MC by the name of Hassan Mackey:

> "Elephants." *Daily Bread.* 2011
> [Chorus]
> Treat a dream like a means to an end
> speaking words from the scrolls
> verbs from the soul
> adding light to the mic through the glow
> submerged in the flow
> words from the soul (repeat)

I feel the need to express the fluidity of the word *lonely*. We focus so much on physical loneliness and often neglect the intangible. My mother told me growing up that she felt lonelier in a house full of family than she does now living by herself. Part of me is scared to go to sleep, fearing nightmares about my spiritual and intellectual, not physical, loneliness. Mackey's lines made me realize that I don't have to go to sleep to be able to dream so I write my dreams down, hoping they evolve in my uncontrollable sleep dreams.

Make your own record, and feed it to the masses. Create your own tape, vinyl, CD, mp3. Find your own medium to spread food for thought whether it be the boom box, turntable, disc ROM player, iPod. Don't be limited by my definition. Build upon my foundation for I can't carry it the whole way. That's higher learning through Hip-Hop. Rise up but don't forget the people who got you where you are, doing for you now and later, and those who look up to you. This is not just for physically lonely people but for the emotionally and spiritually lonely as well. I hope you hear me. More important, I hope you feel me and accept my loan for the lonely and "words from the soul." Read it over and over to feed your soul like a record.

Yours in the Struggle,

Sincerely,
Lonely Black Girl

CHAPTER FIFTEEN

Acting Out: A Performative Exploration of Identity, Healing, and Wholeness

Durell Callier

Prologue: OUT/Self-Benediction

I think I've heard my last and I mean last
Antihomosexuality sermon, speech, soapbox oration from in the sanctuary
    of the Lord
From in the sanctuary of the Lord!!!
No longer can I subject myself willingly or otherwise . . . to be torn down
I have tried . . . and God knows I have tried to cast out this "demon"
    called my life
These mannerisms you denounce but are battle scars of a boyhood of difference
You ask me to lie . . . to ignore the love fostered by the women in my life
These hips move as they do 'cause my momma raised me
This voice echoes a tenderness of a grandmother
These hands swapped licks with a sis, wrist limp to bend for:
    Slide baby 1–2
    Rockin' Robin Tweet tweedle dee . . . and
    Miss Mary Mack all dressed in black-black-black . . .
I have cried one too many nights
Prayed one too many prayers
Lied one too many times to you and myself

Hated who I was for far too long to allow you to poison me any longer,
I think this is where I must depart with you, my beloved brethren in the Lord
For you ask far too much from me
My life is no longer up for sale
No longer will I trade you:
Righteousness for rhetoric
Fellowship for silence
Love and affirmation for denial and dishonesty
No longer can I allow you to war against my body and spirit
I take back sanctuary, this sanctuary
Refuge and safety shall I find among the robbers and thieves the gangsters
    and prostitutes and among the others you rejected
For now on, the drug dealer shall distribute joy to this soul . . .
The prostitute's breast milk will feed this weary soul . . .
And the thugs and gangsters shall now administer my peace
Our Lord still Jesus, our love still for the Nazarene, but a love now unfettered
A love which reaches far beyond the four walls for which you erect to paint,
    remodel, renovate and decorate BUT to hide who we truly are Human…
Among the people shall my tabernacle lie . . .
With the sheep and not the wolves will I fellowship . . .
For my dignity, my life and my love for humanity and Christ is NOT, and
    I repeat, NO LONGER for sale . . .
And so may the Lord watch between me and thee while we're absent one
    from another.
'Cause I have tried, God knows I have, but I have come to love myself far
    too much to tolerate this any longer . . .
Amen.

Call to Worship: A Black Queer Boy's Journey toward Self-Recovery

The aforementioned poem speaks to years of denial, self-hate, and misery associated with not loving my sexuality. Penned after an emotionally traumatizing church service, the poem sets forth an agenda of recovery—mind, body, spirit, and participation in civic life. It is through these words and other personal writings— journal entries, poems, and plays—that I have been able to express myself wholly, freely, and begin to not only do the work of reclamation but also begin to imagine the world differently.

I believe in the power of performance. By performance, I am referring to any and all creative mediums used to credibly, vividly, and persuasively tell a story (Saldaña, 2003). Performance manifests for us bodies—bodies marked in very material ways by their race, class, gender, sexuality—forcing us to wrestle with both master and counternarratives (see Denzin, 2003). However, performance is more than a mere spectator sport in creating a dialogic of bodies—the corporeal manifestation of a lived experience on stage, juxtaposed against our own lived experiences—we are presented with an opportunity to cocreate together, and begin to reimagine and recover the world as we know it (Denzin, 2003).

Furthermore, as an emerging artist-scholar I choose to use poetry and theater as the means by which to express myself and re-present my stories as data to reflect my belief that performance allows both performers and audience to be in a place where living and life are held sacred. I walk a path made possible by the footsteps of other black, queer, and othered artists and scholars who utilized their lives and creative works as a means to educate and speak back to larger oppressive societal structures. Our work fosters healing and sustains life. Via performance we are able to cocreate a world in which we are able to explore the complexity of the simplest of human interactions while drawing our attention to larger societal structures for critique, criticism, and change.

OUT charts my personal journey of self-recovery, love, healing, and wholeness. I use the term *autoethnodrama* to describe *OUT* as an autobiographical cultural story written in play script format intended for performance (Saldaña, 2008). *OUT* exemplifies a queer politics that recognizes and encourages the fluidity and movement of people's sexual lives (Cohen, 1997). As an autoethnodrama, *OUT* explores the ways in which queer identity is performed, developed, and negotiated by the individual. *OUT* simultaneously interrogates societies rigid and fixed notions of "living out/coming out" and instead proposes understanding living "out" as a dynamic process.

Writing to Live: Methodological Approaches in Creating an Ethnodrama

OUT foregrounds my experience growing up, wrestling with and trying to reconcile my multiple identities—specifically my sexuality and spirituality—through writing. The collection of poems, journal entries, private conversations reconfigured into a coherent play started as just that: private, intimate moments of self-expression, love, and pain. The reconfiguration of those very private moments—as data—underwent several phases before finally resulting in the autoethnodrama that is *OUT*. These phases—like any other writing process—included brainstorming, gathering materials (e.g., poems, media clips), creating drafts, reworking the materials (e.g., creating dialogued text from poems, integrating media), synthesizing the individual parts into a coherent piece, and final edits.

The aesthetically blurred formatting I have chosen to use—as evidenced in my integration of multiple texts within this paper—is about the world(s) I inhabit as both an academic and artist. My coexistence in these spaces forces me to wrestle with how to truly write a performative social science text, specifically a text that would utilize a discourse that showed how the histories and performances persons live are shaped by ever-working societal forces. One way to change the world is to change how we write and perform it. My use of a blurred aesthetic is my attempt to create change and echo the wisdom of Dana Pollock (1998):

> [Performative writing] refuses an equally easy and equally false distinction between performance and text, performance and performativity, performativity and print textuality. Rather, at the brink of meaning, poised between abjection and regression, writing as doing displaces writing as meaning; writing becomes meaningful in the material, dis/continuous act of writing. Effacing itself twice over—once as meaning and reference, twice as deferral and erasure—writing becomes itself, becomes its own meanings and ends, recovering to itself the force of action. After-texts, after turning itself inside out, writing turns again only to discover the pleasure and power of turning, of making not sense or meaning per se but making writing perform. (p. 75)

OUT voices who I am and allows me to state to a larger audience and reflect to that audience: (1) the reality of my truth, (2) the reality reflection and truth(s) of a specific community consisting of other gay, lesbian, bisexual, transgendered GLBT) and queer individuals, and (3) the possibility of a differently imagined world filled with the acceptance of one's identity, the hope that lies within self-identification, and the healing and wholeness that comes from that journey.

From Autoethnography to Ethnodrama

Autoethnography as noted by Pinar (1994) allows for the re-creation and rewriting of the biographic past in order to make that past a part of the biographic present. Ethnotheater, on the other hand, employs traditional crafts and artistic techniques used in formal theater productions to create a live performance event of research participants' experiences and/or researchers' interpretations of data for an audicncc (Saldaña, 2003). As an autoethnodrama, *OUT* consists of analyzed and dramatized significant selections from journal entries, and other written artifacts, over a period of five years.

As a cohesive scripted piece, *OUT* was created through a series of various writing exercises (e.g., writing a monologue) aimed toward creating key play concepts. These writing exercises helped to reshape my poems, journal entries, and memories of conversations into monologues, juxtapose various ideas within the data, and help frame particular ideas, emotions, movements, and key concepts. Other outcomes of writing exercises used to help craft *OUT* included the usage of dialogic clashes and silence and movement were equally nourished and integral to the piece as was speaking or stillness.

OUT came into fruition in a course I was taking during the fall of 2008— Theater 418: Devising Social Issues Theater. It was during the course of that semester that I was challenged to find a topic I cared about that dealt with social issues. The final project was to be a thirty-minute play or presentation on the issue. Having already used a poem previously written as a performed monologue—an assignment prior to the final project—I decided it was best to continue with the subject matter in the poem. The poem performed initially as a monologue was titled "Audre Lorde Sho' Ain't God" and is incorporated in the script as a part of Movement II: Silent No More (see full script below). Issues addressed in the piece included voice, acceptance, and homosexuality specifically within the black church—as is my own personal upbringing and experience.

From that juncture I needed to collect enough data to write the play, which included rereading past journal entries and poems I had written, as well as writing a few new ones. Decisions had to be made in regard to what would be given precedence in the piece. I had already identified the subject to be explored—coming out as a process, seen rather as a continuum than bound by one finite moment in time and about living one's own truth. In offering this counternarrative, I proposed to allow for other GLBT voices to share in the telling of my own story. One of the ways in which this was achieved within the piece was in the moving away from the specific naming of characters; instead each is given a voice, each voice has particular characteristics, but lines are shared so as to symbolize the sharing of an experience or an idea. Not only is my personal voice spliced and permeated into four other voices that are but are not my own—by virtue of the fact that they are given different characteristics and thus become different characters—sound and media clips are also used to allow for further permeation of other voices. These characteristics give preference again to a counternarrative that highlights the dynamic process of living/"coming" out as not defined by one finite moment in time as proffered by a very white, gay male culture.

With the topic in mind, data collected—journal entries, poems, media and sound clips—as well as a clear vision for the piece, it was time to actually begin to organize and write the play. As previously mentioned a series of writing exercises became necessary to move my writings to iterations utilized by theater—namely, juxtaposition, framing, and polyvocality. The sections, which follow, will go into greater detail to define and illustrate the usage of these techniques, as well as other methodologies used in creating *OUT*.

Poetry as Method

Much of the text reconfigured in *OUT* are journal entries and poems. Therefore, I find it important to discuss the usefulness and significance of poetry within OUT. In that personal stories bring together epiphanic moments, turning-point experiences, and times of personal trouble and turmoil, these moments for me are specifically marked by poetry (Turner, 1986). In nearly each of the movements within *OUT*, there is a poem that reflects my individual conflict and attempt at resolution as related to a larger sociopolitical culture, history, and structure. Moreover this poetry acts as a way for me to reimagine the world, to name my existence and the truth of my experience in relation to larger social structures, or as Audre Lorde states, this poetry is illuminating. Lorde (1984) wrote,

> This is poetry as illumination, for it is through poetry that hope which lies in, we give name to those ideas which are—until the poem—nameless and formless, about to be birthed, but already felt. That distillation of experience from which true poetry springs births thought as dream births concept, as feeling births idea, as knowledge births (precedes) understanding. (p. 36)

My journal entries, many filled with these types of poems, serve for me as a site of knowledge production, a place in which to understand and make sense of the world. For me, this poetry allowed me to make whole my fragmented parts and to begin to reconcile personal conflicts of my sexuality with larger sociopolitical systems (e.g., church). Nestled in each piece is performance and performativity, the act of being and becoming (see Denzin, 2003; Johnson, 2006). Within these poems I was able to make sense of who I was in the moment—my being—as well as who I was becoming and to manifest me, in all of my complexities and contradictory identities.

OUT as a reorganization of my most intimate thoughts—poems, journal entries, rehashed conversations with friends and family members, and so on—thus becomes the culmination and recognition of my birthing process as described by Lorde. It is how I birthed my feelings into ideas, my knowledge(s) into an understanding, and moved beyond silence to giving voice to my lived experience. The process of finding that voice, of negotiating and renegotiating my own silences, that process however cyclical has birthed something even greater: healing.

Epilogue: Returning to the Beginning

As you read the script of *OUT*, you will notice that it is organized into movements. Movements serve as the basic overall organizational unit within *OUT*. Akin to acts, movements serve as the microcosm for the structure of my play (Castagno, 2001). However, unlike acts, which traditionally organize time and events in linear chronology so as to signal a building upon, movements signal a continuum. *OUT*, as a performance piece, in particular focuses on the fluid nature of identity. It is also important to note that the unfolding nature of, and the careful surveying of, one's life cannot be viewed as rigid, fixed moments in time but as continuous unfolding and, thus, movements of multiple identities, emotions, and the maturation of an individual over time, not specifically bound by time. Movements provide a storyline but one in which our fixed notions of a beginning, middle, and ending become interlocking reflections of the other.

Syncopation also becomes important in the way in which one would read this play and is why words and lines are spaced the way they are, to allow for an overlapping of voices at times and/or the sharing of an idea by multiple voices through the continuation and finishing of that line/idea. As readers you are meant to read with this syncopation in mind, to be able to hear multiple voices simultaneously, while grasping the unfolding nature of the story and stories told collectively at times and singularly at others. It is important to note that where words overlap, they are meant to be spoken at the same time, spacing in a particular line means that there is a pause in a particular line delivery. However there are also times where the script and delivery is delivered in a more traditional dialogue, of which lines are simply read in succession rather than together or with a particular time sensitivity. You will see both operating simultaneously within the script, which follows.

It is without further ado that I present to you *OUT*.

Movement I: The Ending is the Beginning
Audience enters
<Cue Sound: GWS 418 Clip 1: Montage (XemVanAdams and Billy Porter)>
<As clip fades, fade audience lights to black>
<Fade Stage Lights to Black>
<Cue Sound: GWS 418 Clip 2: I'm Coming Out Instrumental (Diana Ross)>
<Cue Lights: Light Show >
Enter all Characters (V4 from closet upstage center, V1 downstage right, V2 downstage left, V3 upstage left door) frolicking, skipping, clapping, doing the bump, introducing themselves, giving out high fives, lots of energy and as the music fades go into lines
<Fade Music>
<Stop Light Show>
<Cue Lights>
All voices: Are you out, what does that mean (not in sync), to various characters, even to audience members like a murmur V1 breaks the line of questioning
V1: Are you   out?
V2:   Are you   out?
V3:   Are you? (to audience)

V4: What does that mean?
V2:   Who really knows?
V3: I'm trapped in the closet (said like R. Kelley's Closet)

V4: What closet? Whose closet?

V1: Hey are you out (to V4)

V2: Uh uh, oh no he didn't

V3: Girl I know, don't he know that's private

V4: What you mean out?

V1: I mean like out? Like out of the closet out?

V4: Well if you mean have I come to an awareness of who I am, ya damn skippy, and if you mean do I feel the need to tell everyone I meet Hi my name is (state name) and I am your flaming homosexual, I vogue on weekends, wear heels for fun, and can be called upon in times of a fashion crisis than HELLZ NO that ain't me!

(V2 and V3 snap fingers and exchange a high five, stating I heard that)

V4: My sexuality is not everybody and they momma's business but I don't think I run around hiding it either.

V1: So your gay and not out?

V2: (clears throat) Scuse me, ummm sir, well I like women and men so what does that make me

V1: (with sass and attitude) Bi honey, please get with the program

V4: And I suppose she should be introducing herself as the greedy bitch, the girl you

better hide your man and yo girl from… cause if you don't watch she'll have em both?

V3: Well, scuse me sir but are you out?

V1: Yes OUT and PROUD

V3: And so what does that mean

V1: That I don't hide who I am, that unlike mister over there I have no problem introducing myself as your "flaming homosexual, who vogues on weekends, wears heels for fun AND can be called upon in times of a fashion crisis" Yes I know all of Beyonce's moves, and I do offer classes on how to keep yo man satisfied. My momma and allllllll dem know.

V4: So because you flaunt it and I don't does that mean I am any less proud, any less out, any less gay or QUEER as I'd like to call it than you?(pauses and shakes head)

(All characters move to downstage assemble horizontal line V1–V4)

V4: Well this is my   coming out story

V2:   my   coming

V3   coming

V1:   MINE (pointing to self with both hands)

V1: No great fanfare
V2:   No long soliloquies of
V3:   recanting
V4:   How I've always felt like this

V1: always been
V2, V3, V4: different
V1:   No great discovery of
V2:   hidden secrets
V4:   of love unrequited
V2: (reminiscent of schoolgirl crush, flirtatious)   crushes on
   the high school jock

V1, V2, V3: No national coming-out day for
V4:   me
V2, V3, V4:   No ritualistic
V3:   closet

V1, V2, V3: from which all
V4:   my
V2, V3, V4:   rainbow glory   sprung out   to
V1:   GLORY   OUT

V1: (loud) yell and declare
V4:   that I'm
V3: (with sass and snap fingers afterwards) here and I'm queer
V4:   But yes, it was in that space

V2: right between existence and declaration
V3:   between the spoken word
V1   and the acknowledgment

V4: of who I was
V2:   in the moment
V4:   who I loved
V3:   and enjoyed making love to

V4: somewhere between acceptance
V1:   and the rejection
V2:   of the lies

V4:   I
V3:   had learned
V4:   the limitations placed upon

Following done in steady (slow) rapid succession
V2: my
V4:   being
V1:   somehow
V2:   someway
V3:   Yes through a gradual process
V4:   Renewed daily
V2:   Through writings

Continue steady (slow) rapid succession
V3: poems
V1:   journal entries
V2:   intimate self-expression of truth
V3:   love
V2:   and affirmation

Continue steady (slow) rapid succession
V1: In everyday protest
V4:   silent
V2:   but resistant
V3:   loud but not verbose
V2:   Ever present

Continue steady (slow) rapid succession
V2: In common conversation
V4:   I broke free of the manacles which bonded me
V1:   to denial and
V3:   dishonesty

V1, V2, V3, V4: NO
V4:   This story
V3:   this life
V4:   my identity
V1:   my queerness
V2:   my understanding

Continue steady (slow) rapid succession
V2, V3, V4: my truly
V1:   living
V2, V4:   breathing
V2, V3;   loving
V1, V4:   embracing
V2:   acknowledging

Continue steady (slow) rapid succession
V1, V2, V3, V4: accepting
V1:   Never occurred in a miraculous moment
V2:   But in moments

Continue steady (slow) rapid succession
V3: Never in an instant
V4:   But through instances
V1:   have I
V3, V4:   climbed my way out
V1:   of the
                            proverbial closet

Continue steady (slow) rapid succession
V1: and found
V3:   self-emancipation
V1, V4:   liberation
V2, V3:   Have I come to know
V1, V2, V3, V4:   Freedom
<Lights fade to Black>
Cue Sound: GWS 418 Clip 3: Coming Out Stories (Trish)>
All characters leave stage

Movement II: Silent No More
<Cue Sound GWS 418 Clip 4: John Coltrane Psalm >
<Music plays throughout>
<Lights Fade Up>
V1 enters downstage right holding a bible, V4 enters downstage left
   holding bible bow at chair to pray (opposite sides)
* Prayed like a prayer in slow and steady succession rhythm can vary
   from person to person but should be consistent

V1: Now I Lay

V1, V4: me down to sleep I pray the Lord my soul to keep and if I die before I wake (V4 voice fades)

V2 enter upstage right and bow beside chair (hold cross in hand/ necklace)

V3 enter upstage left bow beside chair

V1: I pray the Lord my soul be straight

V3: Now I lay me down to sleep

V2:　　　Now I lay me down to sleep

V1:　　　　　Now I lay me down to sleep

V3: I pray the Lord my soul to keep

V2:　　I pray the Lord my soul to keep

V1:　　　　I pray the Lord my soul to keep

V3: and if I die before I wake

V2:　　and if I die before I wake

V1:　　　　and if I die before I wake

V3: I pray the Lord my soul be straight

V2:　　I pray the Lord my soul be straight

V1:　　　　I pray the Lord my soul be straight

* Repeat prayer

V4: (begin after V3 finishes) Now I lay me down to sleep

I pray the Lord… (rise from chair) Audre Lorde sho' ain't God

But I think she was right… about this one thing

Your silence to recognize me

To value my experience

To love me freely, embrace me truly, to hear me clearly

See your silence, stifled me

And disconnected me not only from humanity, but from the divine for which you professed I must come to know

See it was your silence which deafened my ears to hear the voice of your God

Blinded my eyes from seeing the face of your God

And calloused my heart from feeling the warmth of your God's love…

But perhaps it was my silence which was even more egregious than this

See it was my silence which allowed you not to Hear my Truth

Instead of speaking out, I said nothing…

Instead of forcing you to value my experience…

I like, I like a sheep followed…

And you, you unlike your God… unlike your shepherd

You, led me to the slaughter …

No grace, no mercy no salvation have I ever found at your altars, at these altars …

And with each silence of omission, commission and submission,

For each time I laughed at the effeminate choir member,

I joined you and pointed my finger and sneered at the flamboyant choir director

And for every time I condoned your outward appearances of sanctity and supposed straightness…

While you, while you Man of God fucked me raw at nite but preached damnation to me from your pulpits during the day!

For each silence inside I died…

You know, Audre Lorde she ain't neva been nobodies God…

But she sure as Hell was right…

My silence it ain't save me…v

And your silence won't save you…

And for that reason alone I refuse to be silent any longer…

For my God requires that I as in Matthew 5:16 so let my light shine… that men might see and praise my father,

Even if my light so happens to be a rainbow reflecting the full spectrum of God's love

But then again Audre she ain't God… but silence ain't saved and it ain't savin nobody

----

V1, V2, V3 end prayer where they are and say Amen in succession

V3: Amen

V2:   Amen

V1:   Amen

V4: Now I lay me down to sleep I pray the Lord my soul to keep and if I die before I wake, I pray, I pray MY Lord its ok NOT to be STRAIGHT (pause). Amen

----

V4 place bible on table beside the door and exit stage left

<Music fades down and out>

<Fade lights to black>

Movement III: Affirmation Through Community
<Cue Sound: GWS 418 Clip 5: Gay Black Men Talk (Ramon Boney)>
Characters Enter V1 Upstage Right Center, V2 Upstage Center Left,
    V3, Upstage Left,
V4 Downstage Center Right
V3 and V4 socialize throughout scene, exchange hugs in beginning
    between all three
<Fade lights up as sound fades down >
V1: My name is Ramon Boney
V4:   Thank you for the hug queer brother
V1:   and I am the host for this evenings gathering.

V1: This is actually
V4:   For the love and affirmation
V1:   one of the first opportunities I've
V4:   we exchange in our embrace

V1: had to bring together an eclectic
V4:   Thank you for the welcome queer brother
V1:   collective of gay black men who will discuss tonight
         several relevant issues as they pertain to being
V4:   With arms outstretched you say it's ok for us to be

V1: Black and Gay in America
V4: to feel this way
V2:   First of all I want to thank Raymond
V4:   Thank you for the intimacy queer brother…

V2: very much for allowing us into his home
V4:   For this moment shared between two men,
V2:   putting together this wonderful meal and
V3 move to hug V4
V3 exit stage right
V4:   For in this simple hug I am able to find and reaffirm me…
V2:   ah giving us an opportunity to do what I think
V3 move to hug V4

V4: To love and cherish this we…
V2:   is going to be the first of a very important series
V4:   And to be ever grateful for this freedom

V1: of dialogue

V1 move downstage beside V4

V4:   Thank you for the hug queer brother…

V1 and V4 hug

V1 & V4: (look at audience) No, thank you for the love…

<Lights fade to black>

Movement IV: Out Through Text: Coming out to Self, Coming out to
     Others (It Has Been a Process)

<Cue Sound: GWS 418 Clip 6: Good Morning (India Arie)>

<Fade Lights up as Sound Fades down>

V1 enters Downstage Right, V3 enters Upstage Left, V4 enters
     Downstage Left

(Characters sit back to back forming a triangle, begin with heads down
     holding journals in lap, open journal to begin)

V4: I remember the day as if it were yesterday.

V3:   Where to begin and perhaps

V4:   It was the last day of Leadershape 2004

V4: and

V3:   the beginning is less important

V4:   I hugged

V3:   Where I want this letter to end is

V4: I hugged minister Jamie Washington.

V3:   end is in

V4: He may or may not have been ordained, but he hugged me and he
     said "I know" (pause)… and told me that

V3:   in knowing that

V4: (slow deliberate grandfatherly tone)
                    "God don't make no mistakes"…

V4: I don't know if he realized then (very slowly and reminiscent)

V1:   Since here in Chambana

V4:   how much that would
                         come to mean to me (flow as usual)

V4: Every time I think of the story

V1:   I have been

V4:   I cry (even like now). (pause)

V4: The bus ride home was a lonely one, and one full of tears, I was surrounded by people who knew me, but nobody saw my tears. (pause) I wanted, (pause) oh how I wanted someone to ask me what was wrong, but what was I to say (pause). I probably would have lied, I certainly couldn't tell them, that someone had finally seen through my façade, and encouraged me. I couldn't admit to them that I was wrestling with my sexuality and my faith…I couldn't admit that I thought there was something wrong with me, that I thought what I was feeling and doing at the time was wrong. I couldn't bare my soul and say, I'm sleeping with men and I enjoy it. Couldn't dare say that I was also dating a girl and say I was a minister. I couldn't let them know how deep the hurt ran, how alone I felt, how confused and how depressed I was becoming. And so I cried alone --------------------------------

V4: I knew it then as much as I know it now I am, I was gay

V3: Where I want this letter to end is in knowing that I still love you and need you in my life

----

V1: Since here in Chambana I have been

V3:   What I can

V1:   doing all sorts of "out" things

V3: only hope for

V1:   for me at least (pause)

V3: is that you all feel the same

V4:   but I wasn't ready to admit it,

V3:   Perhaps where we begin

V1: . . . Since here in Chambana I have been doing all sorts of "out" things, for me at least. And perhaps it would be best to not describe them as "out" but liberating. I've stopped attending church… YES the suit wearing, bible toting, hand clapping, foot stomping, sure nuff Baptist bred preacher has not been to nare a service

----

Read mid-paced rapid like internal dialogue speed one line after the other

V3: Perhaps where we begin is that for the past few years

V1: the suit wearing, bible toting, hand clapping,

V3: for the past few years

V1: foot stomping, hand clapping, foot stomping, bible toting sure nuff Baptist

V3: past few years

V1: handclapping, foot stomping, Sure nuff Baptist

V3: past years, YES!

V1: I have been

V3: YES!

V1: I have been less than honest with

V3: YES

V1: you,

V3: YES

V1: myself

V3: and YES

V1: and most people I hold dear to my heart.

V4: and I don't know if I feel any better today than I did then. Thank you, Jamie Washington

From this point on slow down in pace pause 3 seconds where indicated before you begin your line

V1: (pause) and it feels good

V4: you have no idea the difference you made in my life

V3: (pause) Where to begin

V4: (pause) God don't make no mistakes

V1: and it

V4: God don't

V1: (pause) feels good

V3: to begin

V4: no mistakes

V1: feels (long pause) good

V1, V3, V4, heads down

<Lights fade to black>

Characters leave stage

Movement V: Don't Box Me In

<Cue Music: GWS 418 Clip 7: U Don't Know Me (Armand Van Helden)>

<Lights fade up as music fade down>

Enter all Characters (V1 from closet upstage center, V4 downstage right, V2 downstage left, V3 upstage left door)

All voices: I am (not in sync) V1 to each other and audience break the murmuring with:

V1: I am me?

V2:   You are you?

V3:   He is what? (to audience)

V4:   I am not a label

V2:   He is

V3, V2:   not a mothafuckin label (V2 echo the line)

V2: We are (hug closest cast member) queer

V1:   You heard

V4:   Cause we wanna be

V3: She is is

V2:   Cause we can

V4:   Just is

Move to form horizontal line after phrase

V4: I am

V2:   I am

V3:   I am

V1:   I am

V2:   Just am

V3:   My own

V1:   identity

V4: So please don't box me in (with sass)

All characters leave except V1 go to closet, remove a small box (have difficulty locating it, state oh there you are and place the box on table beside door Exit stage

<Cue Sound: GWS 418 Clip: U Don't Know Me (Armand Van Helden)>

<Lights Up Stage lights, Fade in Audience Lights as cast enter to take bow>

REFERENCES

Arie, I. (2006). Good morning. On *Testimony, Vol. 1, Life and relationship* [CD]. New York: Universal Motown.

Boney, R. V. (2007, April 25). *Gay black men talk* [Video file]. Retrieved from http://www.youtube.com/watch?v=c2wN783jBH4

Castagno, P. C. (2001). *New playwriting strategies: A language-based approach to playwriting.* New York: Routledge.

Cohen, C. (1997). Punks, bulldaggers, and welfare queens: The radical potential of queer politics? *GLQ: A Journal of Lesbian and Gay Studies, 3*, 437–485.

Coltrane, J. (1964). Psalm. On *a Love Supreme* [CD]. New York: Impulse!

Denzin, N. K. (2003). *Performance ethnography: Critical pedagogy and the politics of culture.* Thousand Oaks, CA: Sage Publications.

Goodman, K., & Simon, K. (Producers). (2006a). Hip Hop and ready to drop (Trish). In K. Goodman & K. Simon (Directors), *Coming out stories* [Vide file]. Retrieved from http://www.logoonline.com/video/misc/339370/coming-out-stories-hip-hop-ready-to-drop-part-1-of-3.jhtml?id=1604488

Goodman, K., & Simon, K. (Producers). (2006b). Actors and entertainers: Billy Porter. In K. Goodman & K. Simon (Directors), *Coming out stories* [Vide file]. Retrieved from http://www.logoonline.com/video/misc/333351/coming-out-stories-billy-porter.jhtml?id=1605073

Helden, A. V. (1999). U don't know me. On *2 Future 4 U* [CD]. Burlington, MA: Armed Records.

Johnson, E. P. (2006). The pot is brewing: Marlong Rigg's black is . . . black ain't. In E. P. Johnson & M. Henderson (Eds.), *Black queer studies: A critical anthology* (pp. 1–20). Durham, NC: Duke University Press.

Lorde, A. (1984). *Sister outsider: Essays and speeches.* Berkeley, CA: Crossing Press.

Paget, M. A. (1993). *A complex sorrow* (M. L. DeVault, Ed.). Philadelphia: Temple University Press.

Pinar, W. F. (1994). *Autobiography, politics and sexuality: Essays in curriculum theory.* New York: Peter Lang.

Pollock, D. (1998). Performing writing. In P. Phelan & J. Lane (Eds.), *The ends of performance* (pp. 73–103). New York: New York University Press.

Ross, D. (1980). I'm coming out (Instrumental). On *Diana* [CD]. Los Angeles: Classic Motown.

Saldaña, J. (2008). Second chair: An autoethnodrama. *Research Studies in Music Education, 30*, 177–191.

Saldaña, J. (2003). Dramatizing data: A primer. *Qualitative Inquiry, 9*, 218–236.

Turner, V. W. (1986). Dewey, Dilthey, and Drama: An essay in the anthropology of experience. In V. W. Turner & E. M. Burner (Eds.), *The anthropology of experience* (pp. 33–44). Urbana: University of Illinois Press.

XemVanAdams. (2008, August 16). Young, black and gay in America [part1] [Video file]. Retrieved from http://www.youtube.com/watch?v=c2wN783jBH4

CHAPTER SIXTEEN

Get It Girl Moments:
A Reflection on Dance
and Research

Grenita Hall

My life seems to be a series of moments, some dreamlike, others painfully raw and real. I'm trying like hell to get to Denzin's (2003) seventh moment.

Dance practice has provided me with a medium, a voice with which to act and interact. Moving has always been instinctive for me; visceral. My body knows how to perform and speak to an audience without indecision or complication. Growing up, and even with friends now, the informal, unstaged movement that we share and perform for one another is both communicative and celebratory in the most profound and simple ways. Historically, dance has been grounded in celebration for communities of color.

What follows is my attempt to invoke the voices and lived experiences of marginalized groups who perform such embodied practices, specifically dances of the hips and buttocks. In doing so, I seek to understand how embodied practices can be and have been labeled as either hegemonic or subversive. Historically, movements of the hips and buttocks have been both celebrated and condemned. I wish to illuminate the embodied practice, labeled here as rebellious movement, and endorse it as an empowering, unfettered mode of expression. This will be accomplished in seven moments, part autobiography and part conversation, with research literature on embodied practice and dance.

Moment One

Does my body in motion offend you? Why do you gaze at what you say you hate to watch? Is the pulse of my hips so miserable, so appalling? You are mesmerized. … can't turn away… you denounce what you don't understand, berate what you cannot define. These hips swayed at home long ago for my tribe, my children, and me. The curve of my backside, the rhythm pulse it creates… you gasp and think "stupefying." I breathe and know "emancipating." West, why do you call the poetry of my hips "subversive?" When the dun duns play, and my back bends with open arms, I feel community. When my feet connect with the earth, there is acknowledgment. Deference, pride… it is there. In what space can I shake my hips, get low and circumvolve? Where can my hips be without your gaze?

Moment Two

Mama was always pushing a politics of respectability on me. "Wear pantyhose. No decent young woman goes to church barelegged." Yes, Dorothy's girls were going to be seen as young ladies; every hard-pressed hair and Vaseline smeared inch of us. My mama's movements originated and stayed strictly in the frontal plane—movements of preparing, fixing, and giving. Never did I see her perform any of the hip-swaying, booty-popping movements I loved to do. From the moment I could catch a beat, I loved and became proficient at rolling my hips. My six-year-old self had never been in a club or juke joint, but you might wonder considering the precision and intensity I used when "shaking what my mama gave me." Dorothy didn't give that to me willingly though; she fought silently against my twirling, rolling movements while trying not to discourage me from loving dance. My mama would laugh at my hip poetics, sometimes watching intently. Her resolute refusal to dance with me, however, or proclaim "Get it girl!" like she did when I brought home a good grade pushed me to understand that her disapproval, though nonverbal, was far from silent.

My dad and his family were another story. Holidays at my aunt's house were showcase time. I would twist and sway to encouraging handclaps and yells of "Gone now, girl, where did she learn to pop like that?!" Me and my brother's funky jazz choreography and fancy footwork received many a "Watch out now!" Spades and bid whist, rum and coke, the Ohio Players, and loud laughter created this environment. Besides school, it was here that I learned to love social, Africanist dance. I made sure that my moves stayed on the safe side of sassy, never crossing over to sensual, at least in the presence of my family. What did my mom see when I performed in this way? What codes this movement of the hips and buttocks as subversive? Piedra (1997), while investigating the politics of Afrocuban rumba, coined the term *hip poetics* to open the space for consideration of the movements of the hips and buttocks as something other than illicit:

"hip poetics", a form of feminist posturing of African origin that has historically allowed women (usually of color) to negotiate a public arena where sexism and racism might otherwise render them invisible and speechless. (p. 165)

This definition of the rumba can be translated perfectly to this context of American Africanist social dance. There is a tendency upon first glance to code the shaking and twirling of the hips and buttocks as hypersexual and lascivious when, in contrast, the woman-women-girls performing may and often do consider it liberating. In many cases, it is not unusual for folks to get together after work or during the holiday and "get loose" or dance freely. These social situations, natural cultural expressions, are not limited to movements of the hips and buttocks, but can include two-stepping, juking, line dancing, and others.

There is, however, a powerful belief among many black folks that we must present ourselves in the best way possible to erase the painful stigma and stereotypes that continue to pervade the Western imagination. Unfortunately for some, this means a closing off or shutting down of various aspects of African and African American culture that may be negatively perceived. This gendered discourse labels black folks animalistic, hypersexual, ignorant, and the list continues. Sadly, I have been guilty of this as well when gazing and defining the movement practices of exotic dancers and similar performers.

Both public and private performances that celebrate the black female body need to happen over and over again to reset the current ideologies toward black women that are so ingrained in our society. Hobson (2005) asserts that we need to go back, back to where definitions and labels of sensuality began—girlhood.

We may need to recreate that circle of women—first enacted in childhood— who reaffirm that our bodies are fine, normal, capable, and beautiful. We may also need to enlarge that circle to include men, who can challenge their own objectifying gazes, and non-blacks, who can overcome the equation of blackness with deviance. (p. 111)

Disrupting these embedded definitions through mediums that begin dialogue that includes text, oral expression, art, and dance is a beginning in an attempt to present oneself in one's own way, and make the connection between knowledge, power, and truth.

Moment Three

So, we wanna teach the girls something, right? Something fresh—I know I'm dating myself! Something that will get them up and moving and talking. DB asked me to create a dance, a black girl dance, specifically to target the deliberate energy and attitude of a black girl space. Using call and response, self-proclamation, showcasing, and inclusion, each participant (one at a time) prepares to "show" her unique version of the Batty Dance. Batty Dance then becomes a vehicle for dynamic observer participation and the opportunity to display uniqueness in a supportive community environment. Although a handclap and chant initiate the movement, there are no specific moves for the Batty Dance. The Batty Dance was fashioned with inspiration from the performance piece "Batty Moves," created by Jawole Zollar in celebration of the female body. The message is clear: there will be no more apologies for the voluptuousness of my backside. No more.

I had the opportunity to work with Zollar and the Urban Bush Women during 2006 at their Summer Institute. Urban Bush Women is a performance ensemble that seeks to bring the untold and undertold stories of disenfranchised people through dance, doing so from a woman-centered perspective as members of the African diaspora community (George-Graves, 2010). Also, I had just started working with black girls in the community where we lived, and I was frustrated as to what my role with girls would be. I was positive that these girls would no doubt benefit from my judgmental gaze, copious notes, and analysis. What I failed to incorporate in my work was their voices—the intelligence and insight of children capable of making decisions regarding their place in the world. When asking for suggestions of how I could connect with the girls and get them to want to work with me, Zollar was quite insightful. She instructed me to focus on having fun with the girls and finding a commonality, not telling them that their movements are inappropriate or their music too sexual. It was with these suggestions and encouragement that I created Batty Dance.

> Ba-tty dance, ba-ba-tty dance . . .
> ba-tty dance, ba-ba-tty dance!
> my name's Grenita and here's my chance
> to show my sistas the batty dance
> break it down!

We are in the circle. We gyrate. Shake. Juke. Drop. Get low. Pop. More than just imitating the moves of our fellow homegirls, we understand them, live them. Most of us have seen women and girls like us, moving our bodies in this way to R&B, house music, or the sound of our own voices. In this space, we make the music; create our own song. In this circle, we define movement, with backs turned on those who are not participating in the circle with us. It was very important to separate ourselves from the gaze of the audience (nonparticipant observers) and define our own terms of existence and representation, which we choose to do through the celebration of our backsides. This represents a "taking back" of labels designed to debase and control black women and girls and renders such labels ineffective, creating new opportunities for self-confidence and acceptance.

It is now that we decide as a group how we will be defined, interpreted, and conveyed. Collectively, we give ourselves permission to be in awe of ourselves and each other, to praise and compliment, support and encourage. Every one present is then able to use each other's energy, compassion, and experiences as support. In this space, the lines are blurred between the volunteers and the girls; we are ALL the girls. For many of us, moving in this way for our peers who are moving in similar ways gives a vibe that says, "I see you. I see your style, your creativity. Do your thing. Shine on!"

Generational differences melt between me and the girls. We are the same, with the same energy, doubts, dreams, and fears. It is difficult at times for black girls to acknowledge each other when societal norms inundate us with so many negative and hurtful images that we swallow them as truth. Maybe to get noticed, to receive attention (positive or otherwise) we feel a need to be wilder, more flamboyant, and louder than our black female counterparts. We continue to work through that in this space. Like a mother's prayer that is constant and steadfast, what never changes in the Batty Dance is that there is room for every black girl. Whatever we bring to the space, positive and otherwise, is acknowledged and honored as our own lived experience.

Moment Four

Friday nights were the best. I couldn't date—my daddy wasn't having it, but my mom convinced him to let us go to the basketball games at the local junior college on the weekends. And we were fly . . . always with a theme, always color coordinated, and our pants/shorts/skirts were ALWAYS tight. I had the track star legs, while my girl Cola and her twin sister Kisha had glorious large butts, "ignant asses" my friend Carolyn calls them; the kind you can set a glass on. We had been dance school buddies since the first grade, performing together in everything from Disco Mickey Mouse to Prince's "U got the Look." We walked in rhythm, always ready to stop at the drop of a dime and kick some practiced choreography for onlookers. The size or roundness of your butt was key, that's for sure, but I got a pass because I knew how to *move* my butt. Paramount to a girl keeping her black card was her ability to roll, pop, and shake her backside. It was a requirement that no one questioned, seemingly self-imposed. We internalized stereotypes and used them (we thought) to our advantage, arching our back to make our butts protrude as much as possible in conjunction with the swaying of our hips. Our crew couldn't be touched. We were a combination of sassy, sensual, and *boughetto* (bourgeois and ghetto)! I'm not sure if we were willingly reduced to our backsides, or duped into believing that this attribute was of the utmost importance. Dixon-Gottschild (2003) talks of this in regard to her early years before becoming a professional dancer:

> How can I explain, or explain away, that backward but primal female desire to attract male attention… an attention that, scurrilous though it may seem from a position of critical distance, at a certain tender adolescent age seems to celebrate and affirm one's entry into the mysteries of womanhood? (p. 145)

This is the part of us that longs for acceptance and authenticity. In the black community, having big and/or round buttocks is considered a marker of belonging, just as is the ability to dance. These abilities combined made us the go-to-girls and seemed to increase our popularity.

Why are our butts, and the movement they create, always under scrutiny? Dixon-Gottschild (2003) concludes that the female butt is part of a gendered discourse with sexually charged energy surrounding the fanny in general, and the black bottom in particular, not only in dance but also in daily life. She explains that the black female buttocks represent the savage-versus-civilized binary between Africanist and Europeanist movement, informing us that the vertically aligned, erect spine is the first principle of Europeanist dance, while Africanist dance favors flexible, bent-legged postures articulated forward, backward, and sideward or in circles as well as in different rhythms. The extreme opposites of these two dance forms create a discourse of assumed hierarchy among the dominant group. By Europeanist standards, Africanist dance was interpreted as vulgar, lewd, hypersexual, primitive, and animalistic. By Africanist dance standards, Europeanist dance is seen as movement without feeling, inflexible and sterile.

Upon first view of authentic rumba, I was drawn in by the infectious drumming and dance styles that are African derived but unique in their own right. The improvisation and posturing of the participants, and the different styles associated with gender and age, are fascinating. The rumba dance style Columbia is also similar to a contemporary style of dance that began in Chicago in the early 1990s known as Footworks or Footworkin', which incorporates fast-moving foot patterns. Because of the rumba's African roots, it has been historically coded as black, dangerous, and hypersexual (Knauer, 2008). These labels have made it difficult for the art form to be passed on in history unadulterated. I identify with the history and meaning of what I have learned about the rumba; it could be my great-grandfather's story; it could be my own. Marginalized people gathered to connect with the rhythms of the drums, vibrato of the voice, and syncopation of the body. They came together to voice opinions about loss and struggle, pay homage to their ancestors, lament and celebrate life and living. Their presence is their protest; their song is their rally cry. The dance itself is multifarious; a visceral, physical response to the call of tribal beats and Spanish influences. This dance form has traveled all over the world being simulated, commodified, and commercialized by mainstream societies in North American, Europe, and even its native Cuba.

Moments Five and Six

Growing up, my only interaction with African dance was watching *Roots* and *Coming to America*. I received the majority of my dance education at a neighborhood studio run by a German family that emphasized ballet, jazz, and, later, Hip-Hop. With no historical background as to where the dances I performed originated, I was twirling and shaking simply for the love of movement and performance. It wasn't until my twenties that I participated in West African dance. Columbia College in Chicago taught a multilevel class that was open to the community. My girl Maria and I decided to take our lunch break to go check it out. We arrived shortly before 1 p.m., dressed in jazz pants and tanks. There were all types of people there, every age group and ethnicity. The instructor walked in around 1:10 p.m., greeting and hugging the regulars. He popped in a tape, apologizing for the fact that there would be no live drumming for the class that day. We warmed up to Michael Jackson's "Day and Night" and Chaka Khan's "Feel for You." It didn't seem much different from a traditional jazz class at first. Twenty minutes later, the instructor placed us in lines and started across-the-floor sequences. He softened his knees, bent at the waist, and initiated a shallow quick pelvic sway with each tap of the ball of each foot—ba-ba-ba-ba-da-ba-ba-ba-ba-da. I simply could not do it, and I was stunned. The skill I had acquired through years of lessons, staged and unstaged performance did not assist me in the least. Why could I not perform this movement? African dance is a complex art in an advanced form (Asante, 2001). I believed that because I was proficient in other Africanist movement styles, I should be able to be successful perform this one as well.

I was putting the cart before the horse. I could drop it like it was hot at the club, tootsie roll, and push it without so much as a second thought, but performing these organic, original dances required more that knowing how to rotate my pelvis. Thinking because I had African blood African dance would come naturally, and no preparation, thought, or reverence for the process of learning this art form was needed. It was then that I began to hunger to learn about the history and dynamics of West African dance and what it means to the originators, imitators, and enthusiasts of the practice. I started here, with my jazz turnout, pointed toes, and black American hips. Here is where I began.

Working with Djibril Camara and the Mara-Giri Project has been one of the most fascinating and enjoyable experiences to date. Finding non-Western forms of dance, especially West African dance, has been challenging since coming to Champaign. I found this class through my friend, as it was not listed in the course catalog. The first day of class was typical of a university dance class. All of the majors were in small clusters, stretching and conversing in standard dance vernacular. I patted my Afro, properly secured my lapa (African skirt used in performance and dance ceremony), and focused on getting every bit of knowledge I could. Djibril's energy and love for his national West African dance propelled me to attempt to master the art form, though for an African American woman with a jazz dance background, it is virtually impossible. Djibril thanked us enthusiastically for signing up for the class. He talked to us in a combination of French, Spanish, and Sou Sou, his native language. Djibril let us know that we would be learning the dance Tirreba, which is performed while villagers gather rice during harvest time. As he talked about the importance of this ritual, I could see the lack of interest and frustration of some of the dancers. One of the girls asked her friend, "Can't he just talk African to the drummer, and then the other guy can tell us what he said?" Talk African? I knew then it was going to be a long semester.

Most American dance is based on eight counts, most often taught in thirty-two count phrasing. Djibril simply begins. He moves, and you are expected to follow. He would say, "Second move" for each of the ten moves he showed us! It was hard for all of us, especially the majors, to adapt to this different way of learning. In American culture, dance is fragmented, taught, and performed. African dance, however, is reminiscent of a story or conversation that is easy and flowing. Through the weeks, we Americans became more in tune with Djibril's instruction style, which I came to enjoy. His movements were effortless, his body strong and powerful. Djibril never wanted to stop dancing. We always went past the time allotted for class, with the infectious beats of the djembe making us forget that we had places to be. Many West African dance classes end with a dance circle. The intent of forming the circle is to showcase what you have learned in class, perform for your classmates, and show honor for the skill of the drummers.

For the first four weeks, this was a major problem among the students. Most of the students were too shy to get into the circle to dance. This, of course, was unacceptable to Djibril and the drummers. Steve Di Santo, the lead drummer admonished us: "We drummers are here, playing for you. Our hands are bleeding. Please do not dishonor us by not coming into the circle." Slowly, dancers who had been trained to point, suck in, and tuck began to release and let the energy flow out of them into the atmosphere. This became the most positive aspect of the class, creating a space for connection between African and American culture, fostering new ideas about movement and its interpretation. Toward the end of the semester, we were a community, no longer separated by undergraduate, graduate, major, or nonmajor status. My desire to perfect West African technique was replaced with the ability to enjoy the process, embrace an alternative rhythm, bend and flex instead of straighten and tuck. Though many of the students would not dance this style again, we developed an appreciation for the skill and energy needed to perform West African dance.

I was late coming into the studio; the class had already begun, moving to a slow, strong beat of the djembe drum. There were no mirrors—the class faced a group of chairs where observers sat and the drummers played. I hurriedly put on my lapa, frustrated that I had brought my worn one as opposed to the newer ones

I have. There were thirty participants or more, all women, mostly black, some white. Beautiful fabrics adorned each body: colorful batik prints, silk kaftans, ankhs, and amulets, topped off with afros, locs, gelees, and pony tails. Marietou Camara, Guinean dance master and former soloist for Les Ballet Afrique, had the floor. Her pink lapa swayed powerfully while her hair, a huge afro, stood motionless. She used her hands to command us: open palm—stop and watch; one pointed finger—begin. We went through the motions, glided across the floor, used our periphery to learn and gaze at our counterparts. Suddenly the drums stopped. Marietou put her hands up. "You are woman. You are not a man. Dance like a woman."

I felt she was pleading to all of us: be in yourself, with yourself. Celebrate your female body, the roundness of your curves. Gyrate and circumvolve with purpose and pride. You are the creator of life and have those childbearing hips for a reason. We should not be ashamed. Today, Marietou encouraged us, just for an hour or so, to reject the usual messages to tuck and forget. We will not be rendered invisible today; today we will celebrate and be celebrated. From that moment forward, the energy of the class changed. Yells of "Yabo" resonated and women danced right up to the drummers, delivering powerful pelvic thrusts to the beat, syncopating the hips, arching and releasing the back in polycentric rhythms. More experienced dancers helped newcomers. One woman placed my hands on her hips so that I could "feel" the correct rhythm. I thanked her and asked her name and she replied, "Girl that's alright, you won't remember, just don't forget the hips, lol!" Somehow, because God loves me, in this class I found a familiar, safe place: "Woman, in circle, in dance, is one of the oldest forms of gathering. We gather together to share our life stories, uncover new truths, dance our bodies towards freedom, and to learn from each other's beautiful wisdom." Again, I was a welcomed woman-sister-friend.

Moment Seven

I am learning . . . to perform culture as I write it (Denzin, 2003), to experiment with movement and text, and to trust the sound of my own voice. I choose for my movements and moments to be emancipatory, and that makes them so. In everyday performance, we are speaking truth to our lived experience and inviting others to do the same. By participating in performance, I am sensitive and I know (Conquergood, 1998). I can think of no better way to enter an existing discourse about subversive or hegemonic dance practice than to dance into it, with open hearts and eyes to see those we label Other. We can all pen this continuing story. Sister-friends and brothers, of color and not, all Other in some way, together moving in different tempos to the same, pulsating, freeing djembe drum.

REFERENCES

Asante, K. (2001). Commonalities in African dance: An aesthetic foundation. In A. Dils & A. C. Albright (Eds.), *Moving history/dancing cultures: A dance history reader* (pp. 144–151). Middletown, CT: Wesleyan University Press.

Conquergood, D. (1998). Beyond the text: Toward a performative cultural politics. In S. Dailey (Ed.), *The future of performance studies: Visions and revisions* (pp. 25–36). Washington, DC: National Communication Association.

Denzin, N. (2003). *Performance ethography: Critical pedegogy and the politics of culture.* Thousand Oaks, CA: Sage.

Dixon-Gottschild, B. (2003). *The black dancing body: A geography from coon to cool.* New York: Palgrave Macmillan.

George-Graves, N. (2010). *Urban Bush Women: Twenty years of African dance theater, community engagement and working out.* Madison: University of Wisconsin Press.

Hobson, J. (2005). *Venus in the dark: Blackness and beauty in popular culture.* New York: Routledge.

Knauer, L. (2008). The politics of Afrocuban cultural expression in New York City. *Journal of Ethnic and Migration Studies, 34* (8), 1257–1281.

Piedra, J. (1997). Hip poetics. In C. Delgado & J. E. Muñoz (Eds.), *Everynight life: Culture and dance in Latin/o America* (pp. 93–140). Durham, NC: Duke University Press.

Part 4

People

We can never
forget to love.

Introduction

Identifying as a part of the generation that embraced Hip-Hop "after it lost its dignity," Sesali Bowen discusses how she came to blogging through her love of writing and humanity in "The Bad Bitch Society: Discovering Love through Writing and the New Hip-Hop." Bowen generously takes the time to break down why she and many of her peers have reclaimed words once considered epithets. More than anything, she represents for girls and women who love themselves, and it is that love that inspires bridges, new becomings, and profound truths.

Precious, the name made infamous by Sapphire's novel and the Hollywood movie, is also the name of our favorite cousin, sister-friend, and student. Representing herself, Precious McClendon offers an autobiographical narrative of her own story growing up a dark-skinned big girl in "Show Yo' Self." Giving credit to those individuals who made her feel between shame and success in her girlhood, McClendon also implicates race, class, gender, and religion as structuring beauty ideals and social norms.

In "A Conversation with Black Artemis," Christina Armstrong interviews a pioneer of Hip-Hop feminist fiction, Black Artemis, aka Sofia Quintero. Author of several amazing Hip-Hop feminist novels, Black Artemis writes stories that document urban life from the perspective of young people who are street-smart, interesting, and believable.

Have you ever talked to your mother about Hip-Hop? How about your grandmother? That is exactly what Lena Foote does in "A Mother and Daughter Talk Hip-Hop." Although Hip-Hop and all the intergenerational differences it connotes have come to represent an expected beef between young kids and their elders, Foote's piece demonstrates probably a much more common occurrence: Hip-Hop creates a multigenerational bridge.

"Summer Vacation in B'ham, Alabama, or Southern Fried Feminism," by J. Sean Callahan, is a short story about a grandmother's wisdom. The wisdom passed down from generation to generation allows us to survive. With candor and humor, Callahan teaches us a memorable lesson about enduring love and partnership.

The reader is very excited to present the work of its youngest contributor, DaYanna Crider. "I Love Music!" is an honest reflection of how an eleven-year-old feels about music and encourages us all to keep love at the center of our politics.

CHAPTER SEVENTEEN

The Bad Bitch Society: Discovering Love through Writing and the New Hip-Hop

Sesali Bowen

My decision to start a blog was one that was long overdue. I've always possessed a unique voice; a distinct way of communicating that was always recognizable and responsive. My approach to life in general has always been… different. The reality is that I have the ability to gather a following, or at least provoke a few people to say, "Amen!" What's more is that over the years, people seemed to crave to hear my thoughts. If something controversial happened at school, people wanted to know what I had to say about it. My friends would ask me for advice because they knew that it would be authentic and genuine, even if they did not agree. With the change of my facial expression, professors would halt their lecture to listen to my view on the subject matter and my classmates would sometimes stop their side conversations to do the same. In fact, it was my speech communication class, the first class I had taken completely dedicated to the articulation of my personal thoughts and opinions, that suggested I start a blog. They always anticipated my presentations and felt that my perspectives should not be limited to the thirty-three of us. It was an idea I had never considered, but it had definitely sparked my interest.

But my blog was not birthed from this suggestion alone. In response to my class's suggestion I turned to Facebook. I started to write weekly notes and tag my speech communication classmates and others I knew. As I expected, people responded very well to my ideas and rants. The comments and "Likes" started pouring in. Some people were inspired to write their own notes because of things they had read in mine. But in addition to my opinions, they were responding to something else. I always knew I could write. Writing kept me sane throughout my childhood and teenage years. I kept a daily journal, I would write poetry, and I like to think that even the letters I shared between friends at school were literary creations. But the idea that my writing style and skills contributed to the effectiveness of my presentations was a new one. "Wow, Sesali, I didn't know you could write like that" and "Very well written" were some of the accolades I was receiving from not professors or even classmates but peers who felt it deserved recognition. I decided then that it was really time for me to start owning my writing. From there, I knew I could be a great blogger.

But I knew Facebook as my outlet alone would not suffice. I wanted my blog to be a complete representation of my life and experiences. There was significance there because I felt as though I was taught how to express myself via these experiences. Life brings out a different song in all of us and I wanted my blog to be the album cover. I wanted a space broad enough to showcase all the elements that created me. I wanted to be able to talk about the strip club on one day, sex the next day, the conversation I had with my best friend about relationships the week after, followed by my theory about America's educational system, and then list the best places to get your nails done in Chicago. I wanted to be able to use words like *strag* and *socioeconomic status* in the same post. And I wanted it to not be weird at all, but instead flow like it could have come from any textbook or song lyric. I wanted people to see what a sexually liberated ghetto girl–collegiate scholar who spent a few years in the suburbs and struggled with body image her whole life looked like. I wanted people to know why I was loud and why I loved to say "Niggas ain't shit" and why I felt like reproductive justice was worth fighting for. I wanted to celebrate all of those parts of me that were so specific yet so broad that others could join in on the celebration. I wanted reading my blog to be SOLHOT, the ultimate worship to everything that is black, female, and human.

My theory on self is that all of the experiences, environments, character development, and other building blocks of the past and present, simply put, pave the way to a future self. Anything we ever were, we still are. And who we are presently will create who we become. Therefore, because the past is fixed, we are driven into action by thinking of the self we desire for the future. But that process is not always visible to others. I always desired to explain the disparity between the person I desired myself to be and the person I actually was. Being unable to do so had resulted in many misunderstandings and miscommunications in the past.

Therefore, I knew that my blog also represented a perfect opportunity to bridge the gap between the black girl I was/am to the black woman I want to be, both parts equally important and dependent on one another. Resulting, the ability to make these connections would inspire me to be a better person.

And then, in ultimate Sesali fashion, I wanted to put everyone else on, too. I wanted the girls I grew up with in Parkway Gardens to be able to relate to it. I wanted the girls from my high school to like it, and not just because everyone else does. I wanted my best friends to love it. I wanted my younger homies to believe it. I wanted the girls at my university to understand it. I wanted women to appreciate it. I wanted men to respect it. I wanted white people to pay attention to it. I wanted black people to embrace it. I wanted people to learn from it. I wanted to inspire them to learn and build from their own blocks. I wanted to send messages that reminded people that despite the uniqueness of our lives we are never alone. Despite how personally customized my blog was, I knew it was never only about me. It was about my ever-changing place in the ever-changing world.

The manifestation of all that became *The Bad Bitch Society*, a title that requires some explanation as well. I was born in 1988, just a few years too late to be considered a part of the infamous "Hip-Hop generation"... and I suffered for it. I was subsequently a part of the generation that embraced Hip-Hop after it lost its dignity, as some would say. My Hip-Hop morphed women from mothers, daughters, sisters, and lovers into objects constructed of big booties, thick thighs, small waists, long hair, and even pretty pussies. My Hip-Hop turned men into robots following each other to nowhere in particular, each one trying to shine just a little brighter than the next, and hoping their mechanical function is that of an ATM machine. I like to consider myself a part of the generation of "niggas and bitches." I know the ancestors of the civil rights generation are turning in their graves at the thought. And those from the Hip-Hop generation never forget to remind us that it was not our destiny to be deduced to objects and robots, "niggas and bitches." But here we are. In fact, the black men I care the most about are MY niggas, and my best girlfriends are without a doubt MY bitches.

I often find that the irony, complexity, and sometimes hypocrisy of my relationship to today's Hip-Hop are beyond me. But what I do understand is that it represents the voice of my generation. A voice I feel is valid despite the fact that it may be littered with profanity and messages so self-destructive that they give life itself a new meaning as we try to survive it all. I relate and identify with a generation and culture that has learned to replace man with "nigga" and woman with "bitch," to the extent that as a woman, the highest honor you can receive is that of a "bad bitch." For now, I will accept that. If being a bad bitch is how I earn respect, so be it. If being a bad bitch is the only way to open up the heart of a black man to love him, I'll do it. If being a bad bitch is the only way I can reach out to my fellow sisters and reflect our self-worth, then that is fine with me. And if being a bad bitch is the only way I can get the attention of younger generations to teach them that there we are more than "niggas and bitches," then I'll be bad as hell.

I reclaimed the coveted term *bad bitch* for myself a long time ago, after it had continuously been denied to me by others because I did not fit the part. Because I'm fat I never met the physical requirements. As a struggling college student, I definitely could not afford the title. I was not directly involved with or related to a rich or powerful man so I could not gain access via association either. Eventually I realized that none of these things really produce a "bad bitch," because I knew bad bitches that possessed none of those things as well. What all those women had in common, though, was a certain amount of confidence that produced a strong presence. They struggled but did so gracefully. I admired them wholeheartedly and wanted the same thing for myself, and just as my theory of self predicted, it started to manifest itself in my life. All of a sudden the term *bad bitch* summed up my existence perfectly and that is how *The Bad Bitch Society* came to be.

However, I felt that many members of my generation were unaware of the term's true identity and instead relied on the materialistic and aesthetic qualifications. So I knew that the first order of business was to explain and validate my position as a "bad bitch." So my first post was titled "Welcome to the Bad Bitch Society: Bad Bitch 101," and it read as follows:

> Welcome to the official blog spot of the Bad Bitch Society! I felt like it was only appropriate to kick things off by filling people in on exactly what it means to be a bad bitch. In the past, many people have numerously questioned my authority on the subject…. Hopefully this clears things up….

> When many people hear the term **bad bitch** they think of Beyoncé, Halle Berry, Nicki Minaj, even Michelle Obama. I would argue that these women are indeed bad bitches, but not for the obvious reasons most people would expect. While I would be a much badder bitch if I was exceptionally beautiful, filthy rich, a top-notch Ivy League scholar, married to a rich and powerful man, owner of Gucci bags and red bottoms, actually being a bad bitch is so much more than that.

> A bad bitch is simply a woman who feels like she is, and exudes that. Not to get it twisted, being bad isn't about walking around with your nose in the air. Instead, it's about owning (acknowledging and living up to) all the things that make you fabulous, sexy, unique, extraordinary, and BAD! It's not about being the most fashionable; it's about having and owning your own style. It's not about having a degree; it's about never

ceasing to learn. It's not even about having a great job or "gettin money" as people like to say, it's about never stopping on the path to get where you want to be in life.

See, being bad has nothing to do with perfection, nor is it a way to measure how close to perfection a woman is. In fact, being bad is about accepting the imperfections and still knowing, without a doubt, that you're still bad. Being a bad bitch is about being whole.

A bad bitch has respect for and appreciates other bad bitches. She helps bring out the bad bitch in others. A bad bitch is never afraid to show love and she is only focused on putting herself and others on, leaving no time for hate and negativity. A bad bitch doesn't stop until she gets it; "it" is WHATEVER SHE WANTS.

So to answer the question that has been posed to me so many times… Sesali, what makes you think you're a bad bitch??? I AM A BAD BITCH!

So again, welcome to the Bad Bitch Society. Go on wit yo bad self!

This post would come to be known as the bylaws of *The Bad Bitch Society* and I would find myself referencing it every now and then while writing to make sure I was holding up those standards. And every time I read it I am reminded of how I should be living my life and treating those in it.

From this point, deciding what to blog about was fairly easy. By elaborating on the diversity of the bad bitch experience I left enough flexibility for myself to pretty much talk about anything. Many of my blog topics were extensions of conversations I had with other people, events in popular culture, and general articulations of my thoughts on life and surviving it. Also, I kept into consideration popular perceptions of a bad bitch and incorporated those into the filament of the blog. Via these posts I'm able to deal with the contradictions that present themselves within my culture and existence as a young black woman. Here I can start to deal with why I prefer men with money and how I love a pair of overpriced shoes as much as the next person.

Like most bloggers, I tag my posts into categories as I write. Because my range of topics is so broad, I decided to make some of these categories permanent components of *The Bad Bitch Society* to stress that the contents are critical to a bad bitch identity. My hope was that, essentially, if someone were to study these components of my blog they would theoretically be able to teach themselves how to be a bad bitch.

- "A bad bitch would never…"—Posted tagged with this label entries contain incidents or events that go completely against the bylaws of the Bad Bitch Society.
- "Bad Bitch bylaws"—All of these posts reinforce the bylaws and provide examples of how they work practically in the real world.
- "Bad Bitch enhancement"—The contents of these posts will help you become a badder bitch.
- "Certified Bad Bitch"—I initially started these posts as a way to get readers. My ideology was that by occasionally spotlighting other bad bitches, people would be attracted to possibility being acknowledged themselves, and tune in to the blog to find ways to do so. However this component quickly evolved and became critical to the blog in a different way. It was very important to me to show others that a bad bitch comes in many different forms and deserves praise for a myriad of reasons.
- "Secret Lives of Bad Bitches"—Because bad bitches are not perfect we have quirks and issues that need to be dealt with. These posts highlight some of those issues.
- "Secrets of the Bad Bitch Society"—It should have been titled "A Bad Bitch would agree" but it was too broad and I felt the current title was more enticing.
- "Wise Words for a bad bitch"—I mentioned early that I wanted to inspire people with my blog. Any posts labeled this way are directly dedicated to that cause.

In addition to the aforementioned, there are some components that simply represent me.

- "Bad Bitch Ramblings"—These posts contain my strong opinions on issues that are relevant—sometimes. Other times they are completely random.
- "Celebrity randomness"—I am really into celebrity gossip and culture as are most of the people of my generation, so these posts contain my thoughts on what celebrities are doing and how people are responding to it.
- "Let Me See Yo Nails"—As a black girl from Chicago I identify with and understand the importance of nail culture. These posts are my tribute to that culture.

As I anticipated, people responded very well to my blog. They appreciated how I articulate my thoughts and even that I articulated them at all. I was very appreciative of the support that my blog received since it was a reflection of my personal experiences, as well as the experiences of hundreds of other black girls and women. By reading my blog people are not only validating and honoring me, but also validating and honoring themselves as well. I guess in that aspect I achieved SOLHOT, which is an accomplishment on a completely different level.

If I had to describe my blog in one word besides *bad*, I would have to use the word *love*. Everything about *The Bad Bitch Society* was rooted in love. It is documentation of my own journey toward unconditional self-love. Being absorbed in a culture in which black women are simply never good enough, it is easy to get off that track. I learned to love myself by owning my own voice and the skills that made me bad. But I'm not satisfied with that. This journey is a never-ending one that continuously drives me to improve and help others improve for the sake of all of us. This journey is about loving the good and the bad, the past for its contributions, and the future for its visions. And we can never forget to love the present for the life it represents. But the most important point is that if we do not love each other we cannot love ourselves. I love my niggas and my bitches because if I don't who will? And because I am a part of them, if I don't love them, who will love me?

CHAPTER EIGHTEEN

Show Yo' Self

Precious McClendon

I sat anticipating Tyler Perry's new movie I Can Do Bad All by Myself as the screen flooded with new movie previews. One preview in particular caught my eye. The image showed a picture of Mo'Nique chasing what one would say was a fat girl with a dark complexion, up the stairs. Her character in the movie was the girl's mother. She was yelling very bad things at her that apparently put her down. Then, she called her "Precious." I thought I was dreaming. Maybe I just imagined she referred to this young woman as Precious. I sat in denial. By the end of the preview this girl called Precious was shown running away from home and voiced a narrative of her life that included rape, abuse, rejection, and problems with her weight. The movie, I soon learned, was titled *Precious*. How could this be? A girl from New Jersey representing *my* name and *my* identity. It all felt too real. Then I realized that this moment was not only unexpected but also revolutionary.

I never expect to see images of a large, darkly hued female on the movie screen, especially not as the main character in a Hollywood film. Also, I did not expect that once I did see her, she would be a character that portrayed the very same issues I encountered in my life. However, in that theater I sat wondering whether or not other people were laughing at the imagery or her representation. Indeed, it was her representation. Claireece "Precious" Jones was being laughed at. I did not find the situation worthy of laughter or entertainment. I thought of it as something that was embarrassing to see because it exposed me. It exposed my inner thoughts and feelings. *Precious* exposed everything that I've ever stood against and resisted. It exposed the many insecurities, sexist and oppressive factors that surround me. My feelings about the movie were mixed. I was enraged because my identity had been revealed and become marketable. I was excited because the world could finally see what I go through on a day-to-day basis. I was motivated to lose some extreme weight. I was motivated to make a change.

Overall, I think I had a family structure that is not typical in American society. I grew up in Chicago, in a single-parent home, in which my father was incarcerated for most of my life. My mother is the type of woman who desires the best for herself and her child. I am the only child of my mother and one of five on my father's side. My mother has never lost hope in me. She simply encourages me to do whatever my heart desires as long as it is not detrimental to my future. My grandmother plays a big part in my life as well. My aunts are very supportive of me and encourage me to do the right thing. My three aunts, my grandmother, and my mother raised me. My mother worked in several health care facilities making a decent amount of money to support our household. Therefore, her sisters and her mom took the responsibility of helping her take care of me. It is within this family structure, no matter how much I disagreed with their lifestyles, in which I learned to be a woman.

My aunts, grandmother, and mom were all thin. Over the years, they've all put on weight and managed to live exceptionally happy lives. They would often reminisce about the times in which they were thin and had hourglass figures that complemented their independence and beauty as women. This is why it really does not surprise me when they would say things about my weight gain and how different life would be if I were thinner. Extended relatives on my mother's side were not discreet when they asked how much I weighed. Yes, it was hurtful to admit that I'd gained a significant amount of weight. At that time, however, I could not properly articulate or interpret the mindset of my relatives who would ask this question. I was ignorant to the political views and the dominant ideologies that shaped their frame of thinking. I simply excused them. The image of beauty they internalized and believed in did not include excessive weight as attractive or even appealing. I accepted their criticism as a form of love and dared not to argue against it.

My father is a supportive man. He always encouraged me to get an education although he never received his GED. He constantly told me I was beautiful, but he would also often mention that my weight was a problem. He concluded I should lose weight for health reasons. He also made comparisons between my thinner siblings and me. I know that my father loves me but often times he has a funny way of showing it. He and his wife are very in tune with one another. She is also a plus-size woman. He would often tell her that she was gaining weight and that she should work out as much as he did. These ideas of beauty followed me everywhere I went. There was no way to avoid it. I could not run. I could not avoid it. I simply found methods of resistance in every area and at different stages of my life.

There were often discourses about things within my home and in my environment in which people would always say something like "Light-skinned is in" or "It's time to bring the dark-skin brothers and sisters back on the scene." My assessment of these dialogues became not only a means of understanding but also a way to structure my life. I am a darkly hued girl and the majority of my family is as well, so I had to accept the fact that I could never be considered truly beautiful in this society. I did not have the skin color that most guys in my family as well as my neighborhood thought were beautiful. Once again, I worked against this the best way I knew how. I resisted.

Scholastic Academy was a wonderful institution for learning and building a strong foundation. It was also an entry into a more diverse and political understanding of beauty ideals. Although we wore uniforms, our physicality was visible. Everyone knew who had what body type. There was the fat kid, the stinky kid, and the smart kid. I was the fat kid and the smart kid. There were times in which I'd find myself being oppressed by the boys because of my weight. These were guys I considered my friends. They would refer to me as "Big Precious" or "Big Poppa," as in Hip-Hop rap artist The Notorious B.I.G. I accepted it simply because I felt as if I was wrong because I was fat. I accepted the ridicule because I thought that I was not beautiful. Females were also oppressive to me but they were discreet. They would not directly refer to me as or call me the fat girl, but they would exclude me from their inner circle of friends. The girls I considered out of my league were the ones that wore the latest name brands and shit to class. My mother, who earned a mediocre salary, would buy me anything if I wanted it. However, I truly didn't desire name brand clothing. I simply wanted to go to school, do as I was told, and do well as a student. This is what I did.

I became friends with people who shared the same goals of success as I did in life. I gained acceptance from my peers for being a smart girl. I was also a performer. I wrote poems about things that mattered. I wrote poems about life and things that were considerably beyond my age. I thought being smart was a way to resist the ridicule of others because of my weight. However, this was not the case. My creative talents in writing, singing, and praise dancing did not allow me to overcome the fact that I was still a big girl. I learned to deal.

In high school, while still maintaining the image of an intellectual and exceptional student, I felt that there was something missing in my life. I was plagued with the fact that I was obese. I knew that too many meals of ham hocks, fried chicken, greens, and macaroni prepared in my house were to blame. During my senior year in high school, I was denied for a job in retail because of my appearance. At that time, it did not occur to me that the store wanted to represent a certain image. I did not understand why they told me they weren't hiring and then, during the same week, hired my friend who was thin with light skin. I went back to the store to check out some things. I observed that all the black women who worked there were thin and light-skinned. The guys all had toned bodies and looked like they worked out. Could weight be a factor as to why I was denied the job? I didn't know. I simply accepted it for what it was and tried to move on.

It is also during my high school years that I'd developed a love for Beyoncé Knowles, the rhythm and blues pop singer. I aspired to be her. She had a combination of sexuality, intellect, and a humble character that make her one of the greatest performers of her time. She possesses the true ideal of beauty acceptable to most individuals—not only in the black community but in America. She grew up in a two-parent home, worked hard on her goals, and achieved her dreams. She had the full support of both parents. I had become a victim to misleading images of beauty standards. However, this did not change my views of Beyoncé and how great of singer I think she is.

There were times in which I became totally pissed off when people would say things in reference to how BLACK I'd become upon my departure to college. I knew that it was due to my exposure to sun. My pigmentation had become darker. The amount of melanin in my skin dictated my "worth" at times. It did not surprise me when my mother told me that my grandmother, on my father's side, did not accept me because of my pigmentation. It also did not surprise me when my great-aunt would call me an ink spot. The person that I am simply accepted this as normal because I accepted my abnormality or disability (so to speak) and associated it with ugliness and lack of value, although my mother and grandmother never failed to tell me that "black is beautiful." During this pivotal time, I begged to differ.

> I am not your average chick, from the size of my waist to the
> Style and the grace, silly of me, to embrace my beauty.
> Not beauty by your standards. Beauty in the sense of being,
> Comfortable with whom I'm seeing, that same reflection of me. You reject I suspect that,
>   your negativity—I reject that
> And rely on the very nature of my Intellect to see myself, as beauty in the midst of
>   adversity.
>
> —P. McClendon

College exposed me to a different reality. During my junior year, I changed my major from pre-med to Gender and Women's Studies. I really did not know what I was getting into but I knew that by this time I wanted to become a women's nurse practitioner and know more about women's issues. The courses I took explored beauty politics, representation, as well as identity. Soon I grasped the concept of femininity and the art of being a feminist. My head would often hurt when I thought about the many things I'd been taught to accept and internalize about myself just because of who or what I was according to society. My identity had been shaped by society and I managed to resist these images throughout my life, but I did not know exactly what I was doing or how to be politically correct in naming what I was dealing with on a day-to-day basis.

As a scholar, I've read several different articles about beauty standards and how they relate to our society and how they relate to my life. One article in particular really got my attention. In Shanette M. Harris's (2008) analysis of Patricia Hill Collins's research, she wrote that some African Americans have been operating under the veil of the European American gaze and have accepted their difference as negativity. Harris wrote,

> European American scrutiny and evaluation play a major role in shaping the adjustment, performance, and social relations of African Americans in [our society]. Clearly the white gaze is powerful even for those of us who are well informed of its intent…. Among African Americans who lack awareness of this phenomenon, the "gaze" can arouse feelings of shame, hypervigilance, self-criticism, social anxiety, and in general, negative and uncomfortable feelings toward the self. Obsessive concern with the self and awareness of expected behavior that arise from being observed, monitored, and evaluated can contribute to African American group devaluation and depreciation of individual members and the self. (p. 37)

This article and others allow me to better understand why African Americans can call out differences within our culture as a marker of negativity. My weight and my skin complexion have little to do with the issue at hand. It has *a lot* to do with constructions of "whiteness" and how European Americans think of African Americans. These same standards circulate through our culture and spread an epidemic of inferiority and disgrace among individual members, which, in turn, has a significant effect on how these same individuals interact with members of their race. We need to transform these frameworks and produce more active resistance.

Throughout my life, I have accomplished many things. One thing that I know for sure is that I have the ability to resist societal norms regardless of what society thinks of me. Hopefully, this has a great impact on African American individuals around me that I interact with, especially those who have this idea of difference and beauty all wrong. We must first think of ourselves not as superior but as individuals who deserve to be recognized and appreciated regardless of how we look. We must return the gaze and go back to the point in which we, as a collective group, desire to be empowered by productive forms of resistance that can and will prevail. We must think of ourselves as beautiful. We, as African Americans, must love ourselves; then we can learn to love and appreciate every bit of one another. In doing this, we can show the world that we mean business.

REFERENCE

Harris, S. M. (2008, Winter). Lifting the veil: African American images and European-American gaze: Commentary on *Black Sexual Politics* by Patricia Hill Collins. *Studies in Gender and Sexuality, 9*(1), 32–51.

CHAPTER NINETEEN

A Conversation
with Black Artemis

Christina Armstrong

I had the wonderful pleasure of being introduced to the work of Black Artemis in a Hip-Hop feminism course. We read *Picture Me Rollin'* (2005) and I had not been so excited about fictional writing in a long time. Later on in the course, Sofia Quintero, aka Black Artemis, answered questions from our class about herself and her work. I really enjoyed hearing her speak and was moved by her words and insight. I am grateful for the opportunity to have had Ms. Quintero take time out of her very busy schedule to answer questions from me and my classmates.

What writers influenced you and how?

More writers have influenced me than I can name, but I would say the greatest influences of my novels as Black Artemis have been men, especially men of color who are from New York City and frequently set their stories there. These include Abraham Rodriguez Jr. and Ernesto Quiñonez. I never had a hands-down favorite novelist until I discovered Richard Price. I am also a huge fan of young adult novelist Paul Volponi. There are countless women whose work I admire, especially feminists of color, but I suspect that coming of age with Hip-Hop in New York City—a male-dominated subculture in a very masculine city—had a profound influence on my aesthetics and sensibility. I write the kind of fiction that I want to read, and that is unapologetically feminist with lots of intelligence, edge, and texture (and I use that word deliberately instead of color.) I certainly have literary contemporaries, and I hope we are blazing a trail rather than reflecting a short-lived trend. But when I sat down to write my first novel *Explicit Content*

(2004), I had not found any work like it with female protagonists and feminist undercurrents.

What in your own experiences has influenced the writings in your books? How much of yourself do you put into the characters?

There is a little bit of me in all my characters, even the ones that are radically different from me. If a character does not possess an attribute of mine, s/he might have a characteristic that I wish I had. For the most part, however, in my work as Black Artemis, I largely do not draw from my own experiences. In other genres, I am more likely to write what I know, but when writing Hip-Hop noir, I tend to gravitate toward ideas, themes, and subjects that I would like to better understand. *Explicit Content* is about two women navigating the misogyny in the Hip-Hop music industry, an industry where I have never held a position. *Picture Me Rollin'* falls in between those two extremes. I am not like Esperanza at all, but where I live, Esperanzas surround me. I wanted to understand her because I was fascinated as to how I could grow up in the same environment as Esperanza yet have such different life outcomes. *Burn* is the Black Artemis novel that was inspired by several professional experiences as a policy wonk before becoming a novelist, and yet ironically it is probably my most imaginative work of the three.

What message do you want to send to young women? What would be your ideal world for young women?

In all my work, there are specific messages I may want to send to everyone, with an emphasis on young women. Each story has its own unique messages. However, there are messages to young women that I hope come across in everything I write. There is nothing wrong with you. No matter what is happening in your life, you are more powerful than you believe, and the first step in triumphing over your circumstances is to recognize and embrace that power. And, of course, in the words of Audre Lorde, your silence will not protect you. In my ideal world, young women do not have their opportunities and experiences socially or politically determined by their biological sex or gender identity, and their health and wellness are valued as much as that of young men. And they are safe. And all of this is not because they are young or women but because they are human.

"Because society does everything in its power to make a woman loathe herself, the most revolutionary thing she can do… is love herself." We used this quote in a film we did for class and it has a very powerful message. Where did you find the inspiration for this quote?

The only thing I can confidently say is that the inspiration probably came from multiple sources. I authored the quote, but it certainly has its roots in a broad range of feminist reading and discussion. Some of the work I was rereading while writing *Picture Me Rollin'* is mentioned in it, particularly *Sister Outsider* (1984), by Audre Lorde and *All About Love* (2000) by bell hooks. I think it's a safe bet that the convergence of those two specific works inspired that quote with a liberal dose of whatever self-help literature I might have been exposed to at the time.

You said at one point in Picture Me Rollin' *that sometimes you do the right thing at the wrong time. For instance Esperanza defends her friend who is being heckled by a customer, but it causes her to lose her job. How could someone manage their need to defend themselves and not do something that might affect their lives in a drastic way?*

Actually, the idea is that sometimes we do the wrong thing for the right reason. That is, our perceptions are based on accurate information and our intentions are honorable, but we do not handle the matter in the best way available. I have come to realize that this is a running theme in much of my novels. I can only share what I attempt to do when I am in a situation where I feel the need to defend myself. I pause to ask myself why do I feel this need to defend myself? Am I really under attack or is that just my perception? Is a counterattack in my best interest in the long run? It takes practice to strike the balance between honoring your emotions and letting them dictate your actions. When I'm successful in taking the time to detangle my perceptions, feelings, thoughts, and interests, I find I make choices that I can stand by whether or not they have the outcome I desire.

As a controversial artist, was the use of Tupac as Esperanza's mentor intentional to raise questions about the conflict between feminisms and popular Hip-Hop culture? Or, were there other reasons that he was so important to Esperanza (and you the writer)?

While I deliberately chose Tupac because of his contradictions, I did not see him as mentor character to Esperanza. My intention behind using him was threefold. One, he is very symbolic of what I believe to be the contradictory impulses in the Hip-Hop community in particular and, to a lesser extent, in Generation X. Two, I see him as a mirror character to Esperanza. In both respects, Tupac represents the revolutionary best and the mercenary worst to which Esperanza and our generation can aspire. Third, the fate he suffered serves as an omen that hangs over Esperanza throughout the novel. This is why Esperanza clings to the belief that he is still alive. If Tupac could escape the tragic consequences of his past choices, then so could she. It can be argued that Tupac fell victim to his failure to reconcile irreconcilable impulses. Among other things, *Picture Me Rollin'* asks whether it is at all possible to be revolutionary, but not gangsta? If it is, do we want to? What is the benefit, if any, to that? Those are the questions I was grappling with when I wrote it, and by the time I finished it, I had decided for myself that what separates the revolutionary from the gangsta are the values that motivates his or her actions. We all have self-interest and that in and of itself is not good or bad, it just is. However, in my opinion, the revolutionary does not separate his or her self-interest from that of the community and defines his or her self-interest beyond material needs. The gangster only cares about the community to the extent that it is in his or her material needs to care. I do believe as Esperanza comes to believe that the thug and the revolutionary are two sides of the same coin—they possess many of the same skills and talents—but what ultimately separates them is what they value and how they apply those abilities to create what they value.

Were Esperanza's pseudo flashbacks magical realism?

The short answer is no, but I see more layers in the question that I'd like to peel. This question makes me smile because when I talk about my work and that of other Latino authors writing from an urban, working-class perspective or within that setting, I will say that we are challenging narrow perceptions of what constitutes Latino literature by joking that sometimes our fiction has its *Latinadad* questioned because we are not writing immigration/migrant stories that span multiple generations and contain doses of magical realism along the way. Many of those stories are beautiful and important. That said, Latin American literature and Latino literature are not synonymous even if they have some things in common. This is not to say that there are no Latino authors who employ magical realism; just that the absence of magical realism does not make it any less Latino. Honestly, I feel that usually at the heart of questions about authenticity is an antiblack sentiment which itself is rooted in (1) a classism that equates black with urban, which in turn is coded negatively as "ghetto" (as opposed to, say, cosmopolitan) and (2) an ignorance of the fact that many Latinos are black, i.e., Afro Latino.

The scene when she speaks with Tupac is actually a fantasy of the kind of conversation she wishes she could have had with Tupac. She is both drawn to and troubled by his contradictions, especially those regarding women. This is because she sees those contradictions in herself. Therefore, the imaginary conversation with Tupac is one way Esperanza makes meaning of the misogyny she experiences and witnesses. Esperanza identifies so much with his contradictions that she envisions the discussion being at once honest, challenging, and loving. Only in her imagination has she been able to have such a conversation with a man about this.

Maite Rodriguez was a professor who related to and became a mentor to Esperanza. What do you think teachers need to know to reach their students?

I am a big proponent of meeting your students where they are in order to take them someplace better. That means several things to me. One, it means being curious as opposed to judgmental about what students like, believe, and think. Easier said than done sometimes, but you cannot deepen their understanding if your approach is to invalidate their current position. It also means using your students' likes, interests, etc., to bring them to those things that you hope will capture their imagination. For example, if I know students I am working with like street lit, I'll try to draw some connection between the novel that they're raving about with a work of literature that I would like to introduce. If the book they are reading, for example, is about a woman who is dealing with colorism, I'll say, "Well, if you like that book, you'll love *The Bluest Eye*, by Toni Morrison." Finally, it means striking a balance between making the learning environment safe for students to be able to be who they authentically are yet respectfully challenging them to reconsider their beliefs and opinions. As someone who occasionally is guilty of it, I know didacticism rarely works. By the same token, I do not believe that a learning environment that allows students to say and do anything without some accountability is conducive to learning. In such an environment, those with privilege can silence those without, and no one learns anything. Instead oppressive power dynamics are encouraged and reinforced. Not that I advocate censorship. I do, however, believe in formulating group agreements and holding each other accountable for the way our communications impact others.

Since Picture Me Rollin' *was your first novel, what do you know about the practice of writing now that you didn't know then?*

Picture Me Rollin' is actually my second novel, and for a long time I considered it my best novel. In writing it I became very aware of how powerful a story can be when I come to it with questions rather than answers. When I wrote my first novel, *Explicit Content*, I had a clear agenda as to what I wanted to write and how I wanted it to impact my readers. When writing *Picture Me Rollin'* I had not figured out where I stood myself on some of the issues I was raising. In fact, I feel that it was in writing the novel that I became clear and that clarity did not come without first complicating and grappling with what I believed when I sat down to write it. I still stand by *Explicit Content* and would never say that having an agenda automatically weakens the work. Whether or not that's a help or a hindrance depends on too many things to make such a blanket statement. That said, I do believe that *Picture Me Rollin'* is a stronger novel because, again, curiosity allows for more learning than certainty.

REFERENCES

Artemis, B. (2004). *Explicit content.* New York: NAL Trade.

Artemis, B. (2005). *Picture me rollin'.* New York: Penguin.

hooks, bell. (2000). *All about love: New visions.* New York: William Morrow & Co.

Lorde, A. (1984). *Sister outsider: Essays and speeches.* Berkeley, CA: Crossing.

CHAPTER TWENTY

A Mother and Daughter Talk Hip-Hop

Lena Foote

This may sound cheesy and cliché but my mother is my best friend. Not just because she gave birth to me but also because I appreciate the way I was raised. I was raised around different types of music, and I credit my mother with my unique tastes in music. When I think of a Hip-Hop feminist, who happens to be a mother, I think of my mom. Though she loved Hip-Hop, she was also very particular as to what kind of Hip-Hop she exposed to her daughters. My mother is a faithful Christian (saved, sanctified, and filled with the Holy Ghost) and fully human. She believes that all music is a form of expression.

My mother, Vanyette, was born in 1965. My grandmother, Anne (whom I call Mema), is from Detroit, Michigan, and was schoolmates with members from the Supremes and the Temptations. When my grandmother was still in high school, a lot of her classmates were being signed with Berry Gordy of Motown Records, and she was asked numerous times to sing backup for people like Marvin Gaye and Little Stevie Wonder. My grandfather, William, is from Uniontown, Kentucky, and moved to Gary, Indiana, in the early 1950s. He prefers the blues, country, and traditional gospel spirituals. As a result of my grandparents' union, my mother calls her musical roots "a little bit country, and a little bit rock 'n' roll"; I would also add that she is a little bit Hip-Hop soul as well.

Reflecting on my family's musical genealogy, I could not help but think about my upbringing and what I listened to when I was younger. However, when I looked at my iPod to see what Hip-Hop I had on it, I soon recognized that most of my favorite songs are from my own mother's musical Hip-Hop era. Artists including, MC Lyte, Queen Latifah, Salt-N-Pepa, and Mary J. Blige were just a few artists that my mother and I would listen to when I was a youngster.

I asked my mother if I could interview her about Hip-Hop. She was surprised because she has never been asked to do an interview before. Even though I have obviously known my mother for all of my life, she is a very interesting person and I learned a little more about her because of the interview. In fact, the interview occurred at a perfect time. When the interview took place, we were watching a VH1 special documentary about the history and significance of the famous dance show *Soul Train*.

* * *

Me: What types of music did you listen to as you were growing up?

Mom: Everything Motown, because of Mema [my name for my grandmother], soul, R&B, and disco.

Me: So Mema's upbringing and experiences had an impact on your musical tastes?

Mom: Of course.

Me: Since you are an African American, did you only listen to black artists?

Mom: Oh no… I listened to a lot of different music growing up, people like Cyndi Lauper, George Michael [WHAM!], Boy George, Randy Travis…

Me: Randy Travis, Mom?

Mom: Yes, Randy Travis… I liked country music too.

Me: Well, so we know that you loved disco, R&B, gospel, and a little bit of country music, but what did you think of Hip-Hop when it first came out?

Mom: When I first heard Sugar Hill Gang ["Rappers' Delight"], I thought it was cool because it was different.

Me: How was it so different?

Mom: Because they were talking with music… it was like poetry with rhythm and beats.

Me: But it was only men rapping, right?

Mom: Yeah, when it first came out, but then MC Lyte came out…

Me: Was she the only female rapper people knew about?

Mom: She was the only female rapper that was on the radio at that time; then there was Queen Latifah and "Ladies First."

Me: Yeah, I remember you playing that a lot when I was younger… what was it about that song that made you and other females go crazy over it?

Mom: Well, because she stood for everything our mothers taught us.

Me: What do you mean by that?

Mom: Mema always taught me to think of myself as a queen and to make sure I am treated nothing less than a queen. That song was inspiring.

Me: Now what I remember hearing is a lot of Mary J. Blige…

Mom: Yeah, that was my girl!

Me: [Laughs] Yes, Mother… I know. On a serious note though, as I think back to when we [myself and my younger sisters] were younger, you always had us in church like four days out of the week. [Mom is nodding.] However, on the way to church we would listen to "secular" music.

Mom: I feel like music is universal and I feel like I made you and your sisters aware that listening to secular music did not mean that you were going to go to hell. I believe in "good music"…

Me: …and what do you mean by that?

Mom: Whatever type of music that makes you feel good at that particular moment.

Me: Any type of music can be "good music"?

Mom: I think so… it can be gospel, it can be Hip-Hop or R&B.

Me: I remember Valery, Kiarra, and myself were talking about the music and people that we listened to whenever we were in the car and the artists that we kept talking about were [in descending order] Michael Jackson [of course, Mom was born in Gary, Indiana], Sade, Toni Braxton [when she first came out], Mary J. Blige, Sounds of Blackness, Salt-N-Pepa, George Michael, Queen Latifah, Kirk Franklin, and BeBe and CeCe Winans.

Mom: Yeah, that sounds just about right.

Me: I really appreciate that you exposed us to different types of music, not just gospel and R&B, but also jazz (WNUA 95.5 in Chicagoland area!), Hip-Hop, pop music… and even a little bit of Randy Travis.

Mom: [Laughs] That was my boy… I just did what Mema did with me and your uncle Stan, she exposed us to different types of music too.

Me: So why do you think it is important for parents to expose their children to different types of music, not just what the kids listen to?

Mom: I think children need to be well-rounded in their lives, including music. Although Hip-Hop is great and inspiring, there are many genres that inspired those rappers, from jazz to R&B, from Motown to gospel, from country to blues.

Me: So what artists do you listen to on the radio?

Mom: Well, I listen to whatever your sisters listen to in the car… Beyoncé, Alicia Keys, Mary J. Blige still, Missy Elliot, Ludacris, Snoop Dogg, T. I. ["Dead and Gone"], Kanye West, Keyshia Cole, Chrisette Michelle, and Lil' Wayne.

Me: Lil' Wayne, Mom? What do you know about Lil' Wayne?

Mom: I like some of his songs, but I don't think he is cute.

Me: [Laughing hysterically] Mom, you're hilarious.

Mom: What… those teeth, tattoos, and dreadlocks…

Me: Mom, have you ever heard of the term *Hip-Hop feminist*?

Mom: A Hip-Hop what?

Me: A Hip-Hop feminist.

Mom: No, I've heard of feminism, but I do not know what a Hip-Hop feminist is.

Me: Basically, a Hip-Hop feminist is someone (male or female) who uses elements of Hip-Hop culture in their lives to transform traditional relationships and beliefs that may be oppressive.

Mom: Say what now? You have to break that down for me.

Me: In simpler terms, someone who understands the significance of the Hip-Hop culture on the younger generation in order to become progressive in their own lives.

Mom: Oh… interesting concept.

Me: Well, by the ways that you have raised us, I think that you have a Hip-Hop feminist agenda and did not even realize it.

Mom: Thanks, sweetie.

Me: Thanks, Mom for letting me interview you.

Mom: You're welcome, baby lambchops.

* * *

When I first read "Can a Good Mother Love Hip-Hop?" by Tia Cooper (2007), in the *Homegirls Make Some Noise! Hip-Hop Feminism Anthology*, I could not help but think about my mother and how she raised us while still being a Hip-Hop fan. In the article, Cooper asks various questions concerning how to raise children in a society that is driven by Hip-Hop images, such as, "As a mother, how can I share my love of hip-hop without poisoning the fragile minds of my children? Is it possible to love hardcore hip-hop and still be a good mother?" (p. 370). I think the answer to both questions is yes. I am the result of a mother who proved that it is more than possible. My mother knew that she could raise three daughters in a society with Hip-Hop because she grew up during the golden years of Hip-Hop and she understands it.

My mother also knew that children absorb everything when they are younger, and as a result, they forever remember key moments in their younger years. For example, my sisters and I remember listening to a variety of different kinds of music. We remember my mother as someone who truly appreciates music, is very open minded, and is not hypocritical. She may not like certain songs, especially those that have lyrics that disrespect women. But she would be the first one to admit that sometimes she is a victim of the rhythm and the beat. At the same time, my mother instilled in us at a very early age a sense of confidence, self-worth, and a positive attitude about our bodies and sexuality as young black females. I remember talking to my mother about the lyrics in some popular Hip-Hop songs and asking her what they were talking about; my mother did not shy away from the topic.

I remember singing LL Cool J's "Doin' It," everywhere I went, especially in the house. At first, my mother was shocked because she could not believe what I was singing. I enjoyed singing the chorus over and over. Then she wanted to know where I heard it from. I told her from one of my cousins (who is much older than I am). I remember asking my mother what LL Cool J meant by "doin it," what exactly is he doing? This was my first and one of many conversations with my mother about the "birds and the bees," sex, and sexuality. In addition, as a result of me singing LL Cool J, she told me never to sing a song unless I knew what it meant. Or, in other words, make sure I know what I am singing about.

This is just one example of how my mother is a Hip-Hop feminist. She not only loves Hip-Hop but she also used the lyrics of songs to generate conversations with her daughters about "grown-up" things like sex and drugs. In addition, she used Hip-Hop as a way to teach us about having respect for ourselves as black women and having respect for our bodies and how to be treated. These are just a few reasons why my mother also used to blast songs like Queen Latifah's "Ladies First" and "U.N.I.T.Y." These songs not only taught us how to have respect for ourselves as young ladies, but as black women as well. My mother understood that "exposing [her] children to more self-affirming, positive, and spiritual forms of hip-hop, we can increase the variety of messages that inundate our children" (Cooper, 2007, p. 380).

As my mother stated in our interview, she did not listen to just Hip-Hop music or black artists. I remember hearing everything from Sade and jazz to BeBe and CeCe Winans and gospel, Randy Travis and country to George Michael and pop music. She made us appreciate every genre of music and not just consider the race of the artist. Within every genre of music, there is "good music"; music that makes a person feel good when they listen to a song. I listen to Sade to help me relax after a long day of studying; I listen to Michael Jackson to remember his spirit and how much I love to dance. I listen to Queen Latifah when I need to feel empowered. I listen to Mary J. Blige's "Real Love" when I need to be schooled about love. I listen to Sounds of Blackness to be inspired. I listen to Kirk Franklin and Mary Mary for encouragement to stay the course. I listen to Salt-N-Pepa and Beyoncé to feel womanly and sexy. I listen to the Temptations, the Supremes, and Marvin Gaye when I think about Mema. It is all good music to me!

REFERENCE

Cooper, T. S. (2007). Can a good mother love hip-hop? In G. Pough, E. Richardson, A. Durham, & R. Raimist (Eds.), *Homegirls make some noise!: Hip-Hip feminism anthology* (pp. 368–382).Mira Loma, CA: Parker.

CHAPTER TWENTY-ONE

Summer Vacation in B'ham, Alabama, or Southern Fried Feminism

J. Sean Callahan

I sat at the kitchen table and watched my grandmother and my aunts make pigs-in-the-blanket with cocktail sausages and canned biscuits. "I don't see why nobody in the wurld would evah wantta eat can biscuits." That sentence, like my grandfather, came out of nowhere. The women at the table responded with ninja-like reflexes, first one aunt, then the other.

"Nobody feel like making biscuits from scratch all-tha-time. You can't tell the difference no way."

"You can too tell the difference. I can tell the difference," he snorted.

* * *

Summer vacation in B'ham, Alabama, circa 1984. You know it's early when you're up before the sun in the summer. One of the ways we used to pass time during our two-week vacations was to ride out to the cane fields with our grandfather. The only drawback was getting up and out of bed at dark thirty in the morning. But there were two advantages. One was getting to chew on sugar cane straight out the ground. The other advantage was being able to eat my grandmama's homemade biscuits, hot and fresh, from the oven. My granddaddy always wanted fresh biscuits with his breakfast, so, for as long as I can remember, she would wake before he did ('round dark fifteen, I imagine) to make him breakfast before he left for work. I remember wondering if she ever got tired of getting up every day and making biscuits.

One morning I woke up and sat in the kitchen with her while she made breakfast. That's when it happened. All in one motion, I watched her pull a roll of canned biscuits from the Frigidaire, open the can, and muffle the pop of the pressurized air.

"Oooooo, you know granddaddy don't like canned biscuits," I whispered. She placed the preformed raw biscuit dough on the pan, put the shiny blue paper in the garbage, looked toward me and said, "Baby,… n' you just don't tell ev'rythang."

It's about quarter before the cock crows and I'm eating scrambled eggs, cheese grits, bacon, and hot (canned) biscuits with my granddaddy. He can't tell the difference.

CHAPTER TWENTY-TWO

I Love Music!

DaYanna Crider

I love music. Music makes me feel comfortable with myself because of the beats and the words. The beats make me want to dance. I memorize and tap the beats on the walls, on the door, and on my computer desk. When I think about the beats I hear… boom, boom, ta-ta, ta-ta, ta-ta.

I listen to the words for comfort… (singing) "no I'm not lucky; I'm blessed; yes." And… "the lovers; the dreamers; and me; la-la, la-la." The words make me feel beautiful inside. I love love songs. One of my favorite songs is "You See Right Through Me" (clean version). When I'm going through, the words open me up. The words make me feel confident… like "go; go; go; motivation." I love music.

Part 5

SOLHOT

I wish to live.

Introduction

Part 5 is written and edited by a collective of people engaged in the work of doing Hip-Hop using critical pedagogy as influenced by theory, practice, performance, and politics in Saving Our Lives, Hear Our Truths (SOLHOT). The pieces are meant to teach and be an example of a practical application of Hip-Hop feminism in general and a specific application as it relates to organizing and organizing for black girls. It discusses the lessons (both intellectual and personal) and the impact SOLHOT has had on the women (homegirls) of SOLHOT. Also part 5 is about the complexities in the making and creating of SOLHOT.

Born out of Ruth Nicole Brown's vision for a space that centered and celebrated black girlhood, absent of victim narratives and cultural deficit theory, for many SOLHOT is a utopia. However, a utopia that celebrates black girls in a global, national, local, political, and social space that validates racism, heteropatriarchy, and capitalism is on its best day amazing and on its worst day arduous.

Part 5 begins with Kristen Smith's "In the Words of Others We Find Ourselves." Smith comes to her calling to become part anthropologist, part storyteller, part researcher by her experience in a nontraditional university course where she reads the works of Zora Neale Hurston and participates in SOLHOT. She writes, "SOLHOT creates a community of girls and their allies, a community that strives to have all feel loved, safe, and celebrated for who they are and the place they hold." She ends noting that Zora Neale Hurston and SOLHOT have given her "a template to produce scholarship that leads to social action for purpose and to represent the truths and essence of people" like her.

(Young Adult) Organizing," Sheri Lewis discusses the intergenera-
ns in organizing, particularly the intergenerational tensions that arise
p organizing and in SOLHOT organizing. She addresses that while
 (three) generations collectively suffer from the same social issues—
, gender, and sexual inequalities—it is necessary for each generation to
in ways that are meaningful to their respective historical moments.
er aptly titled essay, Jessica Robinson asks, "Can We Be for Black Girls and
 Their Sexuality?" Formulated as a soundtrack and in conversation with
s feminist theories, in her essay Robinson lists six critical areas of concern
 discussing and thinking about the health and well-being of black girls and
r sexuality.

"Check-In," by Porshe Garner, gives readers a glimpse into how black girls
lize Hip-Hop by telling their story with a black girl flow in the SOLHOT
tual, Check-In. Using the concept of *flow storytelling* to define the ways black
girls make sense of Hip-Hop in their everyday lives, the significance of this study
demonstrates that black girls are not only consumers but also active participants
in the Hip-Hop movement.

In "On being in the Service of Someone Else's Shine," Taylor-Imani Linear
addresses the importance of black girls and women in SOLHOT (and in general)
to honor their individual callings and talents for the betterment of the collective.

"To the Visionary," by Desiree McMillion, is a letter penned to Ruth Nicole
Brown thanking her for her work in creating SOLHOT and the legacy she has
created in Champaign-Urbana and to girls' studies in doing so. McMillion also
discusses the personal impact SOLHOT has had on her own life.

Closing with "Portrait of a Black Girl: Seeing Is NOT Believing," Claudine
"Candy" Taaffe discusses her role as researcher as both a black woman researcher
and a black girl participant by using visual ethnography to document the narratives of black girls.

CHAPTER TWENTY-THREE

In the Words of Others
We Find Ourselves

Kristen Smith

Prologue: The Makings of a Researcher

This three-act play is a composition of the makings of Zora Neale Hurston (1891–1960), her legacy, and lessons to researchers who "poke and pry with a purpose" (Hurston, 2010, p. 143). on behalf of issues concerning the black community.

Introduction

Zora Neale Hurston's character exemplified candor, defiance, innovation, and creativity. Researchers who examine Hurston's work are able to follow a path less traveled to expressed and genuine respect for those she examined. For the past several months I have immersed myself in literature by and about Zora Neale Hurston. Interestingly enough, through close examination of her words, I uncovered my identity as a researcher.

Daily, as I enter the University of Illinois at Champaign-Urbana campus I question my mental, physical, and spiritual accord within the university. Due to lack of sufficient and imaginative research and courses regarding the present conditions of black people and, more specifically, black women I often find myself questioning the findings of research data. As I read scientific- and sociological-based research from major contributors in the field, I often feel a sense of vulnerability as the basic daily experiences of my life are scrutinized, deconstructed, and formulated into concepts describing my condition and fate, as decided by the tainted eyes of researchers.

Sitting with Zora Neale Hurston and her research methods and practices has allowed me to express the agility and essence of black people and bring them to the focal point of my research and scholarship with an interpreted eye of clarity. Premised from the words of Zora Neale Hurston and those whose words she captured I have uncovered the makings of being a researcher and what elements have contributed to the ethos of my research.

My Expedition

On Mondays from 3 p.m. to 5 p.m., like clockwork I enter a sacred space in which all academic courses and stuffy professors are obliterated from my mind. The pressure and chains of being first generation, being the spokesperson for the entire black race, and being feminine and sexy for all gaping eyes who stare with envy or curiosity are broken. At three o'clock, I enter a safe haven in which my soul is restored beyond measure. At three o'clock, transformation begins, all haters become lovers, all stress becomes blessings, and all oppression is merely motivation. I converse with brothers and sisters who are intrinsically linked and bonded with one another in an armed resistance against the struggle. From 3 p.m. to 5 p.m. I become liberated in a class that centers on education, art, and politics—a class where I met Zora!

Act I: The Makings of a Researcher

As I reflect on my life I would never have thought of being/becoming a researcher. For so long oppression caused a doubt of uncertainty and pessimism regarding my present and future fate within society. Stereotypically and statistically I was never meant to read, write, or attend college, especially not for the benefit and purpose of the conditions of those who, like me, based on societal norms, are not supposed to make it. Growing up in a low-income neighborhood that fostered a love for Tupac over Shakespeare, p-poppin over the tango, and hot cheese and chips over filet mignon are not seen as factors that speak to the makings of a scholar or researcher within the academy. I never thought the preferences that my family and friends considered as an integral part of our daily lives could ever be documented as research or scholarship. Yet, as a young child I remember writing creative stories that elaborated the basic elements of my community. From card games, to sneaking into my older sister's house parties, being involved in petty crimes, fights, and scoping out the interactions of local drug addicts and drug dealers were depicted throughout my stories because these were the components of my life. Prior to being introduced to Zora Neale Hurston I simply bypassed this part of my life as merely insignificant. However, writing these stories, searching them out, and watching them unfold with a keen eye were factors and an early indication of my intentions of being a researcher.

As a young child Zora also became absorbed in stories that were reflective of her surroundings. "Zora learned what would become the primary language of her own literature, the vital force of her life as a storyteller. She learned this language—these phrases and stories and nuances—by heart. Which is to say she learned them irrevocably—not as memorized information to be recounted by rote, but as an essential part of who she was, and who she was to become" (Boyd, 2003, p. 39). Like Zora, I would soon learn that my/our surroundings, which helped to build our distinct characters, are worthy of being brought to the center stage of politics, arts, and research.

For some time I felt as though my enrollment in college slowly disconnected me from my friends, family, and community in Louisiana. Yet, it is in college where I was able to assess an understanding and lexicon of structural, economic, and psychological factors that later helped to focus my inquiry concerning black communities. These pertinent issues that inhibited my mobility as a youth—inadequate education, inequitable access to healthcare, and an ever-present discriminatory criminal justice system—were lacking in the realm of scholarship. My temporary dislocation from my community allowed me to take a look in from an outsider perspective while bound in a genuine love and concern for those within the/my community itself. Valerie Boyd, author of Zora Neale Hurston's biography *Wrapped in Rainbows* (2003), notes Hurston's similar transition. She writes, "Zora had draped black folk culture around her like a magnificent shawl. But it was fitting her 'like a tight chemise,' as Hurston observed, 'I couldn't see it for wearing it. It was only when I was off in college, away from my native surroundings, that I could see myself like somebody else and stand off and look at my garment'" (p. 115). This ability to examine myself and others outside the confines of my environment allows me to view our social conditions under a different lens.

Act II: Reflective Research
There will always be obstacles that researchers endure in their determination to adequately reflect the actions and attitudes of those they become immersed. Zora "occasionally, though, wrote personal notes to herself. One day, when she was beginning to wonder if she'd ever finish the book—and if she'd ever be published again—Zora wrote herself a note of stern upliftment: 'you are alive, aren't you? Well, so long as you have no grave you are covered by the sky. No limit to your possibilities. The distance to heaven is the same everywhere'" (Boyd, 2003, p. 427). No longer shall I be silenced along with the millions of people of color whose stories and experiences are buried under multitudes of paperwork that has been rejected as not being suitable to be studied or celebrated. Zora's relentless journey to immerse and find herself among the words and actions of others allowed her to

centralize black people and their true genuine state within the twentieth century. It is up to future researchers like me to follow suit. Often she grappled with the ability to decentralize authority as a researcher yet her impulse was "not to isolate (her)self, but to lose the self in the art and wisdom of the group" (Boyd, p. 427).

During my junior year in college I was introduced to Saving Our Lives, Hear Our Truths (SOLHOT). SOLHOT is based in the local community near the University of Illinois and focuses on using arts-based projects to reflect on what it means to be a black girl and black woman in general, but specifically, what it meant to be black and female in central Illinois and to provide opportunities to improve both ourselves and the local community. SOLHOT in this sense is a living, breathing research site. It is a reflexive-reciprocal teaching-learning praxis. While what is described sounds beautiful, being reflexive, reciprocating, and quieting yourself to listen to someone else's truth is a difficult task. In order for the volunteers to become better at teaching, learning, and being reflexive in SOLHOT, a class was organized to brainstorm several ways to minimize the errors we encounter in the field. At the conclusion of one of our many discussions, a male volunteer, the only male in SOLHOT, posed a question essential to the focus of centering Zora Neale Hurston's work and that of SOLHOT's. He asked, "How can we recognize something that we don't even see in ourselves?" What happens if the person who is to depict the story from those living the story captures an aspect that the person does not recognize? Is it than an accurate portrayal or merely misrepresentation at the interpreter's expense? It is important for both researcher and those being researched to unequivocally agree on a story's depiction to obtain accuracy in character or representation in order to portray a full and coherent composition respecting the lives and those living them. In the black community, the misrepresentation of black people via research is not only historical but also occurs in contemporary scholarship, often at the expense of policy, laws, and de facto realities that have real consequences and propagates structural inequalities. It is highly essential that we not replicate this vicious crime of misrepresentation, which murders one's character and detains one's ability to audaciously speak for herself.

Act III: Poke & Pry.

The main questions researchers grapple with is what are the purpose and goals of your research, and what is your motivation for the focus of your research? As an impending researcher, I believe the most important research is one that steps beyond the confinements of academic circles and classrooms, but that is derived and steeped in community circles. Zora emphasizes that "research is formalized curiosity. It is poking and prying with a purpose" (Hurston, 2010, p. 143). Zora reaffirms that research serves a mutual relationship, curing the curiosity of the researcher while creating a center stage for these communities her research examined. Zora was preeminent for her era, believing that, despite pervasive Jim Crow laws, black people deserved center stage in not only scholarship but also in the arts. Zora "was starting to feel that 'the flaming glory' of black life should not be buried in scientific journals. This material—particularly the music—belonged onstage, where it could be exposed to a wider audience and presented in the context of black folk life" (Boyd, 2003, p. 226).

The representation of black people in the arts—and art that displays the everyday experiences of black girls and women—is still lacking, yet the work of Zora has not gone in vain. SOLHOT utilizes a similar research template to Zora Neale Hurston. SOLHOT participants, through the process of being together, come to reveal the many hurtful ways they have been categorized, their involvement in programs within the juvenile justice system, as well as the social problems they face, from police brutality to physical violence at the hands of the law, among peers or loved ones. SOLHOT creates a community of girls and their allies, a community that strives to have all feel loved, safe, and celebrated for who they are and the place they hold.

In my future endeavors I wish to re-create the scope of research in order to portray the lives of ordinary individuals who play hand games, eat sour pickles over piano lessons, or spend afternoons at the country club's recreation center, which may not be accessible in their communities but nonetheless essential to their well-being. These components of black culture are worthy of the focus of academic scholarship. Each day is another battle to not only be seen and heard but also understood. Every day is a constant struggle to find not only a voice for myself within the academy but also one to represent for others who have been silenced and deemed not worthy of academic scholarship or research.

Zora fought endlessly for the people, practices, actions, and beliefs of those in her community in order to represent a part of herself and their lives, an endless battle she fought throughout her publishing years. Publishers denied her work often and relentlessly deemed her scholarship either ahead of her time or not aligned with mainstream research. We have the ability, like Zora, to take ourselves and the girls' everyday lives and bring them to the center of attention and shout, WE ARE HERE!

Zora reaffirmed search for reality, rather than concede to wishful illusions. Often researchers are inclined to settle for the demands of the academy and for what is deemed as scholarly and noteworthy scholarship. To hear truths is one thing, it's another to represent it. Many critics opposed Zora, yet she stood firm in her work. In declaring my intent to do research in this way, I am sure I will face antagonism even within my own and respective communities. Yet as long as I am reflective of those I encounter and those whose truths I am trying to tell then that is more important. My college years have ingrained in me to remember that despite my bank account or future status, Zora "had long ago cast her lot with the folk; in fact, she *was* the folk. And whatever educational, economic, or political gains she'd made over the years had not fundamentally changed that" (Boyd, 2003, p. 283). The ability to stay grounded and not be swayed by monetary and dominant conventional forms of what publishers and tenure committees consider academic truly defines the passion and genuine characteristics of a researcher.

Afterword

The legacy Zora Neale Hurston left as a researcher, anthropologist, novelist, playwright, columnist, educator, and speaker characterizes her relentless nature and drive to travel throughout the country and the Caribbean to bring a voice to communities that were not examined accurately or understood previously. Hurston was scrutinized within her community and also by greater society, yet she remained defiant in her conquest to collect, record, and express these stories, not based solely through a scientific or sociologist lens but also as an artful expression. Zora Neale Hurston taught researchers that there are different ways to navigate their research in their efforts to poke and pry for a specific purpose. Zora Neale Hurston gives a template to produce scholarship that leads to social action for purpose; to represent the truths and essence of people like me. Zora trusted her heart and stayed true to those who meant the most to her, the ordinary person in which both her heart and soul came into contact. Each encounter in some way contributed to the Zora's character and her approach to research. Her research and research methods are like a fossil, leaving traces of those she encountered and sharing their lives with us in the present as well as her fervor for research and anthropology. Zora stated, "I know nothing is destructible; things merely change forms. When the consciousness we know as life ceases, I know that I shall still be part and parcel of the world" (Boyd, 2003, p. 433). Will your part and parcel leave a legacy that is representative of the people in which it will forever change the scope of research? The work of research, particularly done in this way, is revolutionary.

REFERENCES

Boyd, V. (2003). *Wrapped in rainbows: The life of Zora Neale Hurston*. New York: Scribner.

Hurston, Z.N. *Dust tracks on a road: An autobiography*. New York: Harper Perennial.

CHAPTER TWENTY-FOUR

Youth (Young Adult) Organizing

Sheri Lewis

Introduction

I speak about youth organizing as a young adult embarking on social change through an organization called Saving Our Lives, Hear Our Truths (SOLHOT). SOLHOT promotes advocacy, produces knowledge, and builds leadership skills in black girls and women while organizing to alter the relations of power. I am a lead organizer in SOLHOT and the group I supervise meets at a local middle school in Champaign, Illinois. We meet every Friday from 3 p.m. to 5 p.m. and engage in activities, discussions, and body movement. Prior to our Friday meeting, once a week the volunteers (Homegirls) meet to organize the space by creating a curriculum, reflecting on issues brought up by the girls, and facilitating discussion topics. The SOLHOT space (group) is very significant for the young women who engage in promotion of social change in that it challenges all members to use their skills and talents to create a safe, educational, and spiritual environment for one another. As an organizer for this program it has been a remarkable experience for me due to the opportunities I have gained to build relationships, create visual arts for the body and soul, engage in dialogue, share stories, exchange knowledge, challenge and be challenged by youth.

Our Own Spaces

Youth organizing is a tool that enables youth to create their own theories, implement them through practice, and execute strategies for social change. In the space of SOLHOT, I use Ruth Nicole Brown's perspective of using Hip-Hop feminist pedagogies within black girl spaces to assist me in my analysis of Hip-Hop and youth organizing. Youth culture has been effective at communicating messages that promote social justice. Similar to ethnic groups that share similar cultural values, young people see the world as a place of possibilities and challenge the adult world to acknowledge its contradictions. In order for youth organizing to make a significant impact there needs to be spaces that are facilitated for and by youth. Such spaces allow for youth to dialogue about what issues affect them. For example, youth may want to address poverty, unequal educational policies, or voter registration. Once the issues are addressed organizing takes place. Although youth organizing—to most—is an excellent tool for leadership development, there seems to be an assumption that all organizing looks the same and should follow a particular model.

While social organizing in America has its own long history, regardless of race, conversations about black social organizing in the present almost always discuss the organizing of the civil rights movement of the twentieth century as a leading example for proper and powerful examples of youth organizing. However, even during that time, youth had various ways and means of organizing for social change. Peniel E. Joseph uses the example of the different organizing strategies used in the civil rights movement versus the slightly later black power movement. He writes, "The Black Power movement focused on increasing political power through conferences, community organizing, independent schools and the strategic use of electoral politics… and symbols associated with advocacy and self-defense" where the civil rights movement took action through "sit-ins, protests, marches, beating, and boycotting" (2006, p. 3). Joseph also argues that the Black Panther Party movement was blamed for the downfall of the civil rights movement instead of recognizing the power movement "as an alternative to ineffectiveness of Civil Rights" (p. 3).

Hip-Hop activists of the late 1970s to early 1990s created social change differently than the civil rights movement and black power movement. While youth of the earlier Hip-Hop generation benefited from the policy changes from the civil rights movement and programs developed by the black power movement, the new Hip-Hop generation mobilized through music. Hip-Hop became a culture that emphasized agency through fashion, beat boxing, slang, break dancing, turntables and disc jockeying. Hip-Hop music analyzed and discussed the challenges of poverty, violence, and racism, the problems persisted and remained. Youth during this era created avenues and culturally relevant approaches in order to challenge the status quo and organizing evolved as time progressed and the state of America transformed.

Not only were the styles of organizing within Hip-Hop challenged, the issues also were questioned. Within black culture, Hip-Hop and its utility continues to be an ongoing debate, however, it has been a tool for gaining support for youth, community involvement, and encouraging critical dialogue about the state of black culture. This is demonstrated by a few organizations and campaigns such as VOTE or DIE, Hip Hop Caucus, Hip-Hop Summit, SOLHOT, and other youth organizations. These organizations stand to create change and promote civic engagement for youth of color. Though this may appear to look great for funding purposes, the process of organizing is often ignored.

The ways in which youth organize around issues is often dictated in the sense that organizing must follow prior organizing models or past organizing developments. Within Hip-Hop, some may argue that organizing fails without massive movements, production, speeches, and educational forums. However, youth organizing is performed daily by young people in different ways. For example, gathering a group of school children together to create a safe space after school is organizing. Facilitating private dialogue within that space is organizing. Advocacy is organizing. These require collective effort to discuss issues in order to challenge the status quo, which in turn creates social change. So while it may be argued that writing a song about poverty, having a discussion about sexual health, or encouraging middle school children to create their own spaces is not political or organizing may stand corrected. As society becomes more progressive due to change in economy and leadership, media-organizing style will look different from how it appeared in the 1960s and 1970s. Being that Hip-Hop has become an influential culture it has also been used to encourage youth to actively participate in social change. Youth are able to relate to the Hip-Hop culture, therefore, it is important for one to recognize Hip-Hop's impact on organizing.

There is no one way to organize. In working with SOLHOT, with an array of age groups and generations, I found that the more experienced organizers had trouble agreeing with the youth's ways of organizing. The earlier generation of organizers felt that only production of knowledge, stories, and forums was the "right" way to organize. Moreover, the issues youth were affected by were not deemed as "political." There seemed to be this idea that only marching or holding rallies is organizing or that issues about racial and gendered inequalities are more relevant issues. This does not apply to all youth organizers. Organizing for one's self, whether it is for self-love, saving Hip-Hop culture, abortion access, or dialoging about nontraditional ideologies about religion, identity, or relationships political organizing. Even the ways in which youth choose to organize are valid, whether it is through discussion groups, writing, dancing, advocacy—it is all political.

Although Hip-Hop began in the late 1960s, the generations have evolved. The lyrics have changed in music, fashion is different, and social issues are targeted in various ways. At many forums early Hip-Hop activists and musicians claim that Hip-Hop is dead or not political. Kimala Price writes,

> The issue may not be whether young people are interested in politics. It may be an issue that we're not looking in the right places nor recognizing certain activities as political. Perhaps we are blinded by our own opinions of what political engagement entails that we fail to see that the world is changing right before our eyes and those older understanding are not as resonant as they once were. (2007, p. 393)

Hip-Hop's generations suffer from the same social issues—race, class, and gender inequalities. Since Hip-Hop is known to target youth and channel aggression for a more positive cause it is important for the early Hip-Hop activists-scholars-musicians not to degrade, criticize, ridicule, or belittle contemporary youth's ways of organizing or dealing with issues. This holds especially true for the current generation whose artists and musical talent are different. Though there may be more sexually explicit lyrics and images in Hip-Hop, it is still a culture that youth today are a part. Although music labels are more capital driven and centered (meaning money is more prominent than political messages), the collective effort for youth to come together through the mist of capitalism is a form of organizing. The state of society creates different interests for youth to organize around. For instance early Hip-Hop activists organized for the legitimacy of Hip-Hop as a political tool for resistance. Now that Hip-Hop has evolved from a political tool to entertainment it is still a culture that intertwines political engagement with entertainment as a form of resistance and understanding issues. If Hip-Hop is most prevalent and relatable to youth, then why not use it as a tool? Youths can negotiate their active participation in social inequality as well organize for them.

Sometimes the ways in which entertainment is presented and represented becomes the focal point instead of how youth organizing can combine all positive and negative representations (or not) and make an impact on their community. Many Hip-Hop feminists have talked about these contradictions. In SOLHOT the young girls express their understanding of what it means to be a girl in Hip-Hop videos versus in their community.

The generational tension assumes that there needs to be mentorship. Although support from an earlier generation is helpful, that is all that is needed: support. This support includes listening, patience, and understanding. We as youth organizers need to make it work for us as earlier organizers made it work for them. It is time for organizers to begin to challenge their notions of organizing and support each other. Youth organizers need to create their own spaces without dependence on more experienced organizers. We often wait to be told what to do. If we wait then how fast can we act on urgent issues? It is our job to define ourselves for ourselves.

Hip-Hop has influenced youth of today in different magnitudes, yet it should not be assumed that youth do not understand or want to understand what it means to be liberated and informed activists and, most important, loved. Youth organizing is also about a collective struggle. In this collective struggle youth organizers need to create their own stories and teachings that will enhance their skills in creating social change for young adults. Youth can be accountable for their actions as well as working through them. The state of society is contingent upon the participation of our youth. We have the people power to create and it is our time to shine and to take on social change with innovative tactics and using our skills.

REFERENCES

Joseph, P. E. (2006). *The Black Power movement: Rethinking the civil rights–Black Power era*. New York: Routledge.

Price, K. (2007). Hip-Hop feminism at the political crossroads: Organizing for reproductive justice and beyond. In G. D. Pough, E. Richardson, A. Durham, & R. Raimist (Eds.), *Home girls make some noise!: Hip-Hop feminism anthology* (pp. 399–401). Mira Loma, CA: Parker.

CHAPTER TWENTY-FIVE

Can We Be for Black Girls and against Their Sexuality? A Soundtrack

Jessica Robinson

Track 1: Intro. Composer: J. Robinson (contains samples of P. Collins)

Black girls can have agency and control over their bodies if we would just believe that they are capable of doing so. Webster's dictionary defines *agency* as "the capacity, condition, or state of acting or of exerting power." *Agency* is defined by Patricia Hill Collins in *Black Feminist Thought* (2008) as "black women's self-definitions" and furthermore is claimed as "essential" for black women (p. 131). Therefore, if we use that definition to define *agency*, I am stating that I want us to know the worth and brilliance of black girls to control their own existence because it is essential. Historically, black female persons have been viewed as either undersexualized with caricatures, such as the mammy, or oversexualized with stereotypes such as jezebel. We also see these same stereotypes being played throughout (current) mainstream culture. Through movies, music, and other forms of media, we see the constant ownership of black girls' bodies by other people and systems as apparent. Similarly, some rhetoric around sexuality education, family structure, and expectations suggest that black girls cannot own and be responsible for their own bodies. However, if we are truly invested in black girls and their well-being, then we must believe that they can have power and agency over their own bodies, decisions, and health.

Track 2: Education and Motivation. Composer: J. Robinson

The current debate on sexuality education is whether to have a comprehensive education curriculum or to have an abstinence-only curriculum. This is for young people of school age. The abstinence-only curriculum consists of educating young people on how sex is not only wrong but hazardous if not married to a person of the opposite sex. This curriculum is filled with exaggerations and misinformation to scare students into believing that sex will ruin their lives if not married. This particular curriculum also puts focus on traditional family structure, gender stereotypes, and devalues LGBTQ issues. Meanwhile, it shames parent structures not resembling opposite sex two-parent homes, people already engaged in sexual activity, and constructs members of the LGBTQ community as invalid. Abstinence-only sex education uses marriage as the key to sex. Meanwhile, this assumes that people are interested in marriage in the first place and that everyone can get married legally. It ignores the fact that some people are not invested in making marriage their particular choice. It also gives no education about sex after people are married, if they are interested in waiting until marriage. I would argue that we do need sexuality education. However, a comprehensive sex education curriculum would be more appropriate for addressing a broader and more inclusive set of issues. Comprehensive sex education first and foremost focuses on the proven fact that abstinence is the only 100% way to prevent pregnancy and the transmission of sexually transmitted diseases. However, this comprehensive approach recognizes that abstinence may not be an option for some people. The curriculum focuses on education and resources, such as teaching how to prevent diseases and unwanted pregnancies and where to access these resources, and avoids steering students into believing certain rhetoric. We know that there are young people having sex. We also know that there are high sexually transmitted infection (STI) rates in our country. But what we also know is that these same people who are contracting diseases are being taught abstinence-only sex education due to the federal funding for it. If young people are having sex, we have to equip them with the tools to make their own decisions and make them safely.

Track 3: The Talk: No Place Like Home. Composer: J. Robinson (contains samples from D. C. Hine and P. H. Collins)

We must first and foremost be able to talk about sexuality in the home. This includes experiences, emotions, and behavior. We have to reject the "culture of dissemblance" advanced by Darlene Clark Hine (1989). Hine defines the culture of dissemblance as "behavior and attitudes of black women that created the appearance of openness and disclosure but actually shielded the truth of their inner lives and selves from their oppressors" (p. 912). Hine uses this concept as a way to discuss how black women and girls talk and do not talk about their experiences related to sex. She specifically pays attention to sexual assault and rape. These topics of sexual exploitation and abuse invade our lives as black women and girls. From a historical standpoint, black girls (and women) were raped during slavery as a way to produce more slaves and for the pleasure of their oppressors: slave masters. Consequently, since "Black women as a class emerged from slavery as collective rape victims, they were encouraged to keep quiet in order to refute the thesis of their wanton sexuality" (Collins, 2008, p. 223). Therefore, we have been taught that because of the actions of others we cannot express our disdain for sexual abuse and we also cannot enjoy being sexual, for these actions have caused our oppressors to label us as barbaric. We want to preserve our identification as woman in the eyes of the society we live in. We want to be able to be equal to our white counterparts who are viewed as pure and sacred. So we teach our daughters to be quiet and to keep sounds and conversation of sex and sexuality silent. We must be able to talk about body, sex, and sexuality in the home. People in the home are the first resource for education. We cannot rely on a system to educate our daughters. We must create the space in our homes to talk about (1) what our sexual organs are, (2) what do they do, (3) continue conversation about what that means for our daughters, and (4) give resources to normalize this very natural thing. We have to teach our daughters in the home first to not be ashamed of their bodies. We have to teach them to not feel embarrassed about being a sexual being. Moreover, we cannot teach our daughters to be silent about abuse. Abuse is a crime. Point. Blank. Period. Furthermore, abuse is a crime of power. The abuser is usually attempting to assert his or her power onto their victim during an attack. Therefore, we have to give our daughters tools to understand their own power. We have to give our daughters the power to know and feel comfortable with identifying sexual assault as exactly what it is and having the opportunity to feel control over their bodies. This does not mean that if we do not disclose abuse we are, in a way, powerless. By no means does not disclosing take power away. However, the ability to identify sexual abuse as a crime against the body and a crime of power is indeed a powerful tool. This gives us agency to know that abuse is not normal. It gives us the power to know that our bodies are for us, not for the objectification of others. It is imperative that we give our girls this power. In the case of sexual abuse, we must give them the power to know that it is not normal and their attempted abusers or abusers are at fault. In the case of consensual sex and sexuality, we must give them power to know that they make the decisions and that their sexuality is contingent upon their decision and no one else.

Track 4: Trust. Composer: J. Robinson
(contains samples from CDC and A. Lorde)

We must trust our black girls to make these decisions and to have control over their own being. The Centers for Disease Control and Prevention (CDC) states that 1 in 4 young people in the United States has had an STI (2008). Of those cases, 50% were women of color (CDC). We are infected and affected. In order to decrease our numbers and still give us agency over our own bodies and sexuality, it is necessary to make sure we have the tools to make safe choices. We have to teach our girls to love themselves to say when and under what circumstances they want to have sex—if they even decide to. We should not decide it for them. We have to educate them on why making this type of decision is vital to their survival. Audre Lorde says in her poem "Litany for Survival" (1995, p. 255) that "for those of us who cannot indulge the passing dreams of choice… it is better to speak remembering we were never meant to survive." We live in a world that does not believe that we are capable of making decisions about our own bodies and minds. We are given instructions on how to make everyone else happy with the exception of ourselves. The rhetoric around waiting until marriage is to save something for your husband so that you are still pure for him. We are never taught that our bodies are more than law-carrying, baby-making burdens. We have to believe that we have agency over our bodies. That agency can consist of waiting until marriage because that is a personal decision. That agency can consist of being involved with someone of the same sex. That agency can be to choose to parent in different ways including but not limited to in a single household, without being married, or with a person of the same sex. On a smaller level agency can be to just understand your body and know how it works and love what you have. We are taught that our vaginas are dirty for us but, in turn, "ok" for other people's consumption. We have to love our bodies just as much if not more than everyone else thinks they do.

Track 5: Unspoken Rules. Composer: J. Robinson

We are taught not only by school and home, we are also taught by society. This goes for everyone living in American society. Unfortunately, black girls live in a society that was not meant for their survival. America is a white, patriarchal society. Consequently, black girls are not beneficiaries of the privilege that manifests from this institution. Since we are not privileged by society, black girls become imprisoned by the thoughts and actions that manifest as mainstream culture. In relation to sexual expression, it is not only black girls who suffer but most certainly they suffer in a different way. In 2009, Miley Cyrus, a very popular pop artist and actress, appeared at the Teen Choice Awards with a stripper pole as a prop. This display was ruled as fun and partylike by many. My question is how would KeKe Palmer, a popular young black television actress and singer, be seen if she indeed performed with a stripper pole? My view is that in a society that views white women as the pure and untainted standard, Miley Cyrus can be on a stripper pole on national television because it is seen as her being playful. It is seen as her stepping into a place we just know she would never be in real life. It is her adding a prop to her dance routine plain and simple. Now for KeKe Palmer, she would not get away with such behavior marked as playfulness. If Palmer performed a routine on a pole during one of her performances or on her television show, the visual would not be viewed the same. Keke Palmer comes from a history and present of women and girls who look like her being labeled as jezebel for such acts. If KeKe Palmer was to perform in that way, it would be viewed as racy, sexual, and, moreover, customary. Stripping and sex work is not a playful idea in black women's lives from the view of the mainstream. Palmer would just be fitting into the mold of the rest of her "sistas" if she was to perform in that manner. We have unspoken rules placed on our bodies and minds as black girls that disable us from expressing ourselves freely if we do not want to be classified as hoes and sluts.

We were not meant to survive because we have restrictions placed on us that will not allow us to live freely without labels. Shackles on our minds and bodies are ways we are controlled by others. Sexuality is a natural aspect of being human. I would argue that sexuality is as important as spirituality, emotions, physical well-being, and mental well-being. If someone threatens your physical well-being, it's illegal. If someone causes you mental distress, you want them away from you. So what about your sexual well-being? What if you have so many restrictions placed on you that you don't even know what sexuality is? Unfortunately, this is the reality of the lives of black girls who are continuously critiqued and controlled by society. We have to put as much effort into giving our girls control over their bodies as we put into them having control of their minds. The critical part is giving them the power to decide what control is, what it looks like, and how they want to make it happen. We must continue to fight for our freedom.

Track 6: From Now on Every Word of This Song Is Going to Be about You. Composer: J. Robinson

In all, sexuality education is imperative for our young people. Moreover, the type of sexuality education matters because the material affects black women and girls in a tremendous way. We need to be in support of the self-agency of black girls, especially as it relates to sexuality and bodies. If we do not believe that black girls can make their own decisions if given the proper tools, such as education and resources, then we cannot say that we are invested in them. We cannot say that we are invested in them because we are not invested in their mental, emotional, and physical growth. We can talk about self-love, self-respect, and pride all we want but if we continue to feed into the ideas of the oppressor—that our bodies are only machines, birth canals, and muses for other people—then we are indeed rejecting the love, respect, and pride that we deserve. Sexuality is a part of life. We need to give our girls back that part of their lives in a positive way. They deserve it. We cannot continue the quiet talk of sex, including conversations surrounding assault and rape. We cannot continue to only tell our girls to "not bring no babies in here." We have to make the conversation holistic. We have to include talk of agency. We have to include talk of protection. We have to include talk of abstinence. We have to include talk about girls. Talk about boys. Talk about who we are and where we have been. We should not be afraid to share our stories with our daughters. They need it. We need it. Together, we need school, home, and society to give us our sexuality back. We must work toward making sure black girls can own their own images and bodies and that includes their sexuality in all of its forms.

Thank You: What?... and It Don't Stop

This album is the definition of artistic freedom. I was able to express how and why I love my body and the ability to love myself through that body. We all want to feel love. We all want to know what it is. I hope that I have found it in writing and feeling what I feel is the ultimate love of self: agency. I wanna give a shout out to the creator, my family, my loved ones, Dr. RNB, SOLHOT, G. Alcaraz, Hip-Hop feminists, brothers, hoochies, lovers-haters, and all in between, and finally, music. Within these people and things, I find ability to be my own agent for love and change of self and the world. I will survive. We will survive.

REFERENCES

Centers for Disease Control and Prevention. (2008). http://www.cdc.gov/

Collins, P. H. (2008). *Black feminist thought: Knowledge, consciousness and the politics of empowerment*. New York: Routledge.

Hines, D. C. (1989). Rape and the inner lives of black women in the Middle West. *Signs, 14*(4), 912–920.

Lorde, A. (1995). Litany of survival. In *The black unicorn: Poems* (p. 255). New York: Norton.

CHAPTER TWENTY-SIX

Check-In

Porshe Garner

Red spotlight up on center stage. Voice delivers lines at free will.
I wish to live because life has within it
that which is LOVE that which is good, that which is BEAUTIFUL.
Therefore, since I have known all these things, I have found them REASON ENOUGH
And I…
Wish…
To…
LIVE.
So what happens when the hope to live is taken or threatened?
By a photo?
Person?
Video?
Word or song?
You see I was just showing love to boys *who don't wanna be loved who don't wanna be loved*
But then again I guess Weee should have known better because Weezy F. Baby did tell us "yeah these bitches I swear I care about EVERYTHING BUT these bitches"
Momma's telling me everything, but not enough.
So I will figure life out on my own with the help of friends who know half-truths and others who know half of that.
In the end I thought it was never supposed to be for sale and that love was what I was giving and getting.

And

I

Check-In

Scene ends. Stage goes completely dark

The performance piece above is a combination of black women's and girls' voices, both young and old. It is their truth about life, liberty, and the pursuit of happiness, their pursuit of love. The purpose of this paper is to expound more on the ways in which black girls use poetry, writing, and dance to tell their truths and stories. These ideas are significant because the most popular and commonsense narrative focuses on how Hip-Hop has ruined this generation of black girls. However, in this paper I demonstrate how black girls use Hip-Hop as storytelling specifically as it relates to SOLHOT. This automatically shifts our assumptions about black girls as victims to thinking through the ways they actively use and contribute to Hip-Hop's cultural and creative expression.

I believe that black girls themselves hold the most significant answers about Hip-Hop and the influence it has on their lives. It is through the simple and indirect conversations that black girls hold among themselves and during Check-In that I am able to better understand how they interpret and read the images presented to them through Hip-Hop. Therefore, I have made every attempt to present girls' responses in their own words. More than just what they say, I attempt to give the reader a glimpse into how black girls utilize Hip-Hop by telling their story with a black girl flow. Because of what and how black girls responded in this study, I came up with the concept of *flow storytelling* to define the ways they make sense of Hip-Hop in their everyday lives. For certain, the significance of this study demonstrates that black girls are more than consumers but also active participants in the Hip-Hop movement.

What Is SOLHOT?

Savving Our Lives, Hearing Our Truths (SOLHOT) is very hard to define because of how revolutionary it is. SOLHOT is a space where black girls are able to define and know what is and is not SOLHOT. A space has been created for girls to define who they are and who they want to be without the definition already provided for them by society. In SOLHOT societal labels are resisted; rather we call each other by our names—those that our family gave us and the names we call ourselves. On any given day the space can change and be constructed differently by the girls. Today the girls may want to be known as the African Queen, rocking an afro, but tomorrow they may show up as the African Queen with a weave wrap. Today they may think that Tupac is revolutionary, but tomorrow Lil Wayne may get the revolutionary vote. All of this is SOLHOT and that's okay! The interesting and most compelling take-away message from the SOLHOT space is that the lil' homies are able to define and know what is and is not SOLHOT. Perhaps it is easier to create a list of what SOLHOT isn't, but SOLHOT is not a program, it is not a space that seeks to silence the voices of black girls, nor is it a space to teach black girls how to be "girls."

A Ritual: Check-In

"Check-in" is a welcoming ritual that occurs at the beginning of every SOLHOT and was initiated by Sheri K. Lewis in 2007. Check-In allows lil' homies[1] and homegirls[2] to provide a personal narrative of what took place since the last time the group met. Responses gained by way of Check-In often range from the particulars of a day or weekend, relationships issues, parental issues to simply "I don't know." The process of Check-In resembles free styling in a cipher: narratives are built off of other narratives; there is a call and response type of structure to it. Hip-Hop lyricists often refer to *the cipher* as a conceptual space in which heightened consciousness exits. "The cipher is a privileged outlaw space" (Perry, 2004, p. 107). Those inside the cipher are central, so it casts an insider rather than outsider consciousness. The best way to describe the term, one popularized by the Five Percent Nation, is that it indicates a mystical and transcendent yet human state, that it creates a vibe amid community, as well as enacts a spirit of artistic production or intellectual-spiritual discursive moments (Perry, p. 107). Gwendolyn Pough goes on to explain cipher in terms of Hip-Hop as "a place where people gather to create knowledge and exchange information" (2004, p. 41). Pough goes on to state,

> The cipher is both a space that Black woman create for themselves and a space in which they question themselves about what it means to be a Black and woman in the larger U.S. public sphere. Black women have historically found ways to make their voices heard and to claim a space for themselves in the public sphere. (p. 42)

Pough's definition and explanation are very relevant to Check-In and how it operates in SOLHOT. Check-In as cipher allows the girls to exchange information about themselves and to create and re-create knowledge. Ciphered knowledge is raw, unscripted, and uncut. Furthermore, black girls are known to "bring wreck" in SOLHOT cipher defined by Pough as "reshaping the public's gaze in such a way as to be recognized as human beings—as functioning and worthwhile

---

1 *Lil homies* is a term developed by the girls ages eleven to thirteen as an act of naming themselves for the purpose of SOLHOT and their participation. In SOLHOT we respect the thoughts and ideas of the lil' homies as they are the reason for SOLHOT.

2 *Homegirls* are adults who take an interest in black girls through the SOLHOT program. Typically, homegirls are University of Illinois at Champaign-Urbana undergraduate and graduate students. *Homegirl* is a term of endearment that was created as a way to define the volunteers as more than just traditional volunteers but as a part of the SOLHOT group.

members of society—and not to be shut out of or pushed away from the public sphere" (p. 17). It is through the simple and indirect conversations that girls hold among themselves and during Check-In that I am able to better understand how black girls interpret and read the images presented to them through Hip-Hop.

Black Women, Girls, and Hip-Hop

Discussions of Hip-Hop often leave out the opinions and complexity of women and girls who are consumers. While women have always been a part of Hip-Hop, their roles and images have progressively changed. During the pioneer stages women were involved as break dancers and eventually took on the more visible role of emcees and rappers; however, more recently women in Hip-Hop have become commodity driven in that sex and sexuality has become their sole image. While in the early 1990s Queen Latifah was vocalizing U.N.I.T.Y., more present-day music and women artists have come to rely solely on their bodies as a means to an ends (Kelly, 1998; Smith-Shomade, 2002). Men continue to exploit the female body but it seems as though women have also become comfortable with this message. While Hip-Hop did not create exploitation of women, it can endorse and accelerate it. Aisha Durham (2007, p. 306) defines Hip-Hop feminism,

> Hip-Hop feminism addresses women's positions on Hip-Hop and its relationship to women. Aisha Durham (2007) defines Hip-Hop feminism as socio-cultural, intellectual and political movement grounded in the situated knowledge of women of color from the Post–Civil Rights generation who recognize culture as a pivotal site for political intervention to challenge, resist and mobilize collectives to dismantle systems of exploitation (p. 306).

What is the relationship between Hip-Hop and black girls? The way in which black girls are excluded from the conversation regarding Hip-Hop would suggest that there is only a top-down relationship, where Hip-Hop only (negatively) influences black girls. However, I argue that there is and should be a bidirectional relationship between Hip-Hop and black girls. Black girls as consumers and creators of Hip-Hop are often ignored and misunderstood. Critics often complain that black girls are too heavily influenced by the messages conveyed through commercial Hip-Hop music. Girls are being taught that they should shake half-naked to get the attention from men and boys, but this is not the case for every girl who lives Hip-Hop. In fact, I would argue that while girls listen for content, it is the catchy hooks, verses, and beats that have them sold. So what then happens when youth, particularly black girls, listen to the music and enjoy the icons and messages they hear?

I argue that nothing happens to the girls who listen to the music that is popular among their age group. Black girls think about Hip-Hop in complicated ways other than positive and negative evaluations; however, it is always assumed that black girls will be harmed or influenced by the lyrics they hear. For example, rap artist Gucci Mane's "Imma Dog" (2009) is a very popular but degrading song. In the lyrics he refers to himself as a dog, how he plans to treat the woman that he intends to have sex with like a dog by feeding her like a dog and passing her to his friends or his "dawgs." This song has a rhythmic tone and melodic beat. The bass is heavy and gets the crowd at any party jumping. Black girls and women alike go into a dance that only they know and understand complete with the lyrics and attitude. Yes, the lyrics talk of the misogynistic ways men use women for physical gratification, but in the moment when one is listening and "jamming" to this song, or one similar to it, the context or ramifications behind the song are not being thought about or considered. When forced to think about and consider the true meaning behind the song, even I can admit that the lyrics are distasteful and degrading; however, I can be found enjoying the song just like the girls that I work with. Does this make us "bad" or does this discredit the research I do for black girls? The answer is no! Joan Morgan in her text *When Chickenheads Come Home to Roost* (1999) raises a similar question as she describes her coming into her own feminism. She states, "And how come no one ever admits that part of the reason women love Hip-Hop—as sexist as it is—is 'cuz all that in-yo-face testosterone makes our nipples hard?" (p. 58) While Morgan later situates her answer in relation to the differences that exist in feminism, I think that her question and response are valid and support my argument. Morgan answers that women who enjoy Hip-Hop music are not any less of a woman, but the real debate should be one that addresses the fact that women are often times seen as victims and not simply women. Morgan had the desire to explore the complexities of being a black woman, including those who love patriarchal Hip-Hop culture.

Joan Morgan (1999) also writes what she describes as a gray area in Hip-Hop where contrary women artists, such as Lil' Kim and Queen Latifah, exist as being the "truth" (p. 62). That truth is that black women and girls are complex and take on different roles but all are equally important, even in Hip-Hop. Consequently, there is no singular cut-out pattern of a real black woman or girl. Women can participate in the movement of Hip-Hop without being the victim or a "passive dupe" (Brown, 2009). Whatever role black girls decide to take on, whether it is similar to a Queen Latifah or Lil Kim, their opinions and ideas are still very much valid in all spaces. Black women and girls do not just consume Hip-Hop they also do Hip-Hop in their everyday lives and the stories that they tell.

Artist Gucci Mane has another popular song titled "I Think I Love Her" (2009) that can be used as a rebuttal for women and show how women in the industry are capable of doing Hip-Hop. The lyrics discuss how a woman, Susie, makes Gucci believe that she loves him; however, her love and allegiance to him are ploys to access money and power, ploys she uses with him as well as other men.

Prior to Susie's part in the song, Gucci Mane refers to Susie as a bitch and liar. The hook comes when Gucci Mane states, "I think I love her," and Susie gives a resounding, "Nigga you don't love me." When this song comes on in social settings women sing loud and boldly, even replacing Susie's name with their own. Susie's verses and chorus tell Gucci—and men in general—that while they may believe they have the last laugh, it is critical to realize that women are potentially playing them. While the most important message is not that women should join men in retaliation, but that women should not be taken for granted or thought of as believing the conditions that men present them. Now the flaw in this particular argument is that in the song Susie is really cocaine. So it is not that Susie is the female that Gucci can trust, Susie is Gucci's profit and moneymaker. Susie has access to all the spaces of "ballas and hustlers" because she is what they are distributing. This double meaning and alternative interpretation can be referred to as polysemic interpretation.

Polysemic interpretation states that there are multiple meanings that exist for a text and can be interpreted differently for different audiences (Flynn, 2009). Polysemetry is seen by some scholars as a tool used by the "oppressors"; however, those who are meant to be oppressed resist the dominant meanings and draw on meanings that fit their needs and desires (Flynn). Now rewind back to the social scene and women are still singing this song with conviction despite the real meaning of the song. These women have resisted the intended message of the song and created their own, one that empowers and elevates them. Moreover, Gucci Mane's song, and the reaction it gets from women, shows that women love Hip-Hop but really want to hear and find their voice within Hip-Hop.

Check-In provides black girls who participate in SOLHOT the space to hear their voices in Hip-Hop through the stories they tell about their lived experiences. It is Hip-Hop that is embodied when black girls correct someone who mispronounces their name by stating, "Get it right, get it tight," as retold in Ruth Nicole Brown's book *Black Girlhood Celebration* (2009). Additionally, Hip-Hop is embodied when black girls create fictitious stories as a resistance to stereotypes others may have of them.

Analysis: Let Them Check In...

Check-In allows black girls to find and express their voices through the movement of Hip-Hop. Kyra Gaunt wrote, "Male folklorists and cultural anthropologies have had a tendency to write about black verbal conflict, or dueling, as a male preoccupation... girls share in this tradition regularly through their daily performances of hand clapping games, cheers, and double dutch" (2006, p. 132). "Check-In" fits within Gaunt's framework of black girls' daily embodied musical practices. Therefore, the following introduces girls' stories as told by them of their lived experiences. Stacey, Jordan, and Brittany (pseudonyms are participants of SOLHOT whose ages range from twelve to thirteen. These three lil' homies decided to Check-In and this is analysis of what they had to say.

Stacey and Jordan
Stacey: Well, for two weeks I was incarcerated in JDC with a whole bunch of fat people with braids. You gone eat your cornbread? Naw, for real I wasn't going to say that um,
Jordan: (interrupts Stacey) I was going to say I got incarcerated for arson.
Stacey: Deadly! Deadly arson! I was lighting trees on fire and I was throwing… well, really this isn't arson, I was throwing the rocks in people's windows.
Jordan: I was going to say that we—me and friends—brought some Hennessey and then we put a match inside the bottle to see what it was going to do. Was it going to blow up? And then we accidentally sat one [bottle of Hennessey with lit match in it] too close to my friend's house and then it like, it like burned the curtains off the wall.
Stacey: and then I was going to go along with the story and see how many mean faces she was going to do until we said naw, we was just playing.

The example vignette above also depicts the ways in which black girls are able to resist the opinions that others may have of them. However, black girls do not immediately react in this way. They are watchful and then they determine how they will proceed in resistance. The example vignette came as a response to emotions felt by two particular girls throughout the sessions of SOLHOT when in the presence of a homegirl volunteer. With a vigilant eye they were aware of the body language and facial expressions of that homegirl. Consequently, being the lyricists that they are, they developed a story to get a reaction from her as stated toward the end of the example. As black girls, they resisted the stereotypes of how they are supposed to be and act and developed a very creative story to debunk these stereotypes and show that they are literarily inclined.

Given the current state of the educational system and its failure to meet the need of students of color, some scholars would find it hard to believe that African American girls are able express themselves in such a way. It is through this assumption that black girls learn to negotiate within these spaces. They are aware of story structure, providing not only an introduction but also including a climax and resolution to the story. In Check-In this story line is delivered in the form of Hip-Hop. Hip-Hop as an art is about captivating the audience with metaphors while telling a story about lived experiences, or simply as entertainment. The girls introduced their story above with something far-fetched like being incarcerated, but they go on to support it with even more details that could potentially happen. While the girls provided this story for pure entertainment, it could possibly be the lived experience of some black girls. In some respect the authors of the story are able to transpose lived experiences and fiction to reflect the life stories of black girls across the spectrum, much like authors such as Sapphire. Sapphire, in her text *Precious*, compiles various realities of black girls into one master story to inform the audience of the struggles black girls face and their resiliency.

Additionally, Stacey and Jordan knew, given past experience with this particular volunteer, that they would be judged and assumed to be very reckless—the most popular portrayal of black girls. It is very interesting to see how the story builds but more interesting to see how the girls determine when to end their story and how to use it in a beneficial way.

Brittany
I'm here because my mom and my dad used to fight all the time and my mom used to get the crap smacked out of her sometime and he just beat her and she started to fight back.

Black girls like Brittany have stories to tell. With Brittany's proclamation during Check-In, we are able to see her story and see its resolution. While it is thought that children should not be exposed to certain situations, such as abuse, black girls are able to persevere and state, "I am here!!!" This statement alone holds the most power in the vignette above. I am here can be the beginning clause, ending clause, or complete sentence to a statement. For a black girl to say, "I am here" means that despite all the adversity, trials, and stereotypes she still chooses to be present, seen, and heard. I am reminded of the statement "I am here… and what?!" Again the spirit of Hip-Hop resonates through these three words that could come as a challenge to an opponent. Much like in the other vignettes this vignette calls on an audience to no longer disappear black girls but challenges these authorities by making them hear and understand their stories.

Again this vignette invokes the ideals of resistance much like the resistance Nina Simone (1991) talks about in her biography *I Put a Spell on You*. Her resistance was discussed throughout the text and came through her music. As a classically trained musician, when playing in certain venues, she demanded the crowd's undivided attention while playing. She resisted the disrespect of her craft and demanded respect for her music. Similarly black girls demand respect for themselves within spaces by using their literary and verbal skills. Additionally, Nina showed her resistance through her revolutionary work "Mississippi Goddam." Nina Simone had been going through life just existing until she realized how unfair and unjust the world was for her people. It was at that moment that Nina came to life and started her revolution. I believe black girls also possess the power of the revolution; it just may take an experience like Brittany's to realize it or a simple grooming of their talent.

Furthermore, Check-In can be seen as a forum that evokes accountability. When coming to Check-In you are to come with your honest self, like Brittany. Brittany felt comfortable telling the truth because no one would judge her and she trusted the people that were in the space. Other participants come to SOLHOT with the same expectations. It is in this same manner I believe others are able to excel and receive encouragement when they are not doing well. It is Check-In that causes all participants to feel obligated to tell the truth so there will not be a need for fabrication. In SOLHOT there is no need to lie because they know they all enter the space at the same level, being able and willing to learn from one another. Check-In celebrates black girls in their entirety. We praise one another when we do well and encourage each other when we are not at our greatest potential. Through these ideals it only makes sense that participants say, "SOLHOT saved my life." Because SOLHOT holds each other accountable, the space is a life-saver. It prevents some from making decisions that could be life altering and encourages others to keep up the good work.

Methodology

I used an ethnographic interview approach in order to collect data. Ethnography is a common practice among the social sciences and works through participation in the subjects' lives. Ethnographers work to convince the reader through authenticity, plausibility, and criticality (Golden-Biddle & Locke, 1993). Consequently, I spent twenty-seven hours in the field and each session of SOLHOT had approximately seventeen participants.

The context in which I studied African American girlhood, and worked with black girl participants in this study, was Saving Our Lives, Hearing Our Truths (SOLHOT). In SOLHOT participants included black girls and young women living in Champaign-Urbana ranging from eleven to forty-two years in age. Workshops and weeklong groups were hosted over the course of two months and took place at a local public nonprofit institution. I created (or cofacilitated) several prompts, which allowed participants to speak freely on the subject of Hip-Hop and black girlhood. These prompts included "Contemporary Clark and Clark Doll Study," "What's the Script," and "I Am Not My Hair or Am I."

Discussion

Based on the results of my study, grounded in the voices of black girls, I developed the concept *flow storytelling*. Flow storytelling explains black girls' usage of Hip-Hop to create and tell their own story or narrative in any way they so choose. Flow storytelling is black girls' way of informing us, as the listeners, of the information they deem crucial. Similar to Hip-Hop, black girls are able to rock the mic with lyrical metaphors through the stories they tell or evoke emotions through dramatic dance and performances. Whatever it is, black girls stay true to themselves and express the issues that are important to their communities and lives. It is through flow storytelling that black girls not only tell it how it is but they also renounce judgment because, after all, it is their story and space. Not only is Asia's Check-In from the introduction an example of flow storytelling, but also the comments of Stacey, Jordan, and Brittany reflect that spaces like Check-In need to exist for black girls to be participants in Hip-Hop.

As previously stated, black girls do not just consume Hip-Hop they "do Hip-Hop" in how they tell stories, evaluate images, and create new images in their own words. The example given in the introduction is how black girls tell their own stories in ways in which everyone can contribute. While the "Check-In" was initially one person's, others were able to chime in with their advice. It is through ways such as Check-In that black girls do Hip-Hop by being able to grab the audience in ways only they know. Black girls tell their own stories and give their own opinions in this way and are not censored; they simple tell it how it is.

REFERENCES

Brown, R. N. (2009). *Black girlhood celebration: Toward a Hip-Hop feminist pedagogy*. New York: Peter Lang.

Clark, K. B., & Clark, M. P. (1939). The development of consciousness of self and the emergence of racial identification in Negro preschool children. *Journal of Social Psychology, 10*(4), 591–599.

Clark, K. B., & Clark, M. P. (1950). Emotional factors in racial identification and preference in Negro children. *Journal of Negro Education, 19*(3), 341–350.

Collins, P. H. (2000). *Black feminist thought: Knowledge, consciousness, and the politics of empowerment*. New York: Routledge.

Durham, A. (2007). Using [living Hip Hop feminism]: Redefining an answer (to) rap. In G. D. Pough, R. Raimist, A. Durham, & E. Richardson (Eds.), *Home girls make some noise! Hip Hop feminism anthology* (pp. 304-312). Mira Loma, CA: Parker.

Flynn, K. (2009, October 15). Interpreting lecture. Black women and popular Culture across the African Diaspora. African American Studies 380. University of Illinois at Champaign-Urbana.

Gaunt, K. (2006). *The Games Black Girls Play: Learning the Ropes from Double Dutch to Hip-Hop*. New York: New York University Press.

Golden-Biddle, K., & Locke, K. (1993). Appealing work: An investigation of how ethnographic texts convince. *Organization Science, 4*(4), 595–616.

Hunter, M. (2005). *Race, gender, and the politics of skin tone*. New York: Routledge Taylor & Francis.

Kelley, R. D. G. (1998). Playing for keeps. In W. Lubiano (Ed.), *The house that race built* (pp. 195–231). New York: Vintage.

Ladner, J. A. (1972). *Tomorrow's tomorrow: The black woman*. Garden City, NY: Anchor.

Masko, A. L. (2005). "I think about it all the time": A 12-year-old girl's internal crisis with racism and the effects on her mental health. *Urban Review, 37*(4), 329–350.

Morgan, J. (1999). *When chickenheads come home to roost: My life as a Hip-Hop feminist.* New York: Simon & Schuster.

Omi, M., & Winant, H. (1994). Racial formation. *Racial formation in the United States from the 1960s to the 1990s* (2nd ed., pp. 53–67). New York: Routledge.

Perry, I. (2004). *Prophets of the hood: Politics and poetics in Hip Hop.* Durham, NC: Duke University Press.

Pough, G. (2004). *Check it while I wreck it: Black womanhood, Hip-Hop culture, and the public sphere.* Boston: Northeastern University Press.

Rose, T. (1999). Flow, layering and rupture in post-industrial New York. In G. D. Caponi (Ed.), *Signifyin(g), sanctifyin', & slam dunking* (pp. 191–221). Amherst: University of Massachusetts Press.

Scott, K. A. (2005). African-American girls' virtual selves. Penn GSE *Perspectives on Urban Education Journal, 3*(9), 12-28.

Shorter-Gooden, K., & Washington, N. C. (1996). Young, black, and female: The challenge of weaving an identity. *Journal of Adolescence, 19*(5), 465.

Simone, N., & Cleary, S. (1993/1991). *I put a spell on you: The autobiography of Nina Simone.* New York: Da Capo.

Smith-Shomade, B. (2002). "I got your bitch": Colored women, music videos and punnany commodity. In B. Smith-Shomade (Ed.), *Shaded lives: African American women and television* (pp. 69–109). New Brunswick, NJ: Rutgers University Press.

Stephens, D. P., & Phillips, L. D. (2003). Freaks, gold diggers, divas, and dykes: The sociohistorical development of adolescent African American women's sexual scripts. *Sexuality & Culture, 7*(1), 3.

Stokes, C. E. (2007). Representin' in cyberspace: Sexual scripts, self-definition, and Hip Hop culture in black American adolescent girls' home pages. *Culture, Health & Sexuality, 9*(2), 169–184.

Strack, R. W., Magill, C., & McDonagh, K. (2004). Engaging youth through photovoice. *Health Promotion Practice, 5*(1), 49–58.

Wyatt, G. E. (1997). *Stolen women: Reclaiming our sexuality, taking back our lives.* New York: J. Wiley.

CHAPTER TWENTY-SEVEN

On Being in the Service of Someone Else's Shine

Taylor-Imani Linear

Recognizing Your Shine Is…
The affirmation of your gift.
The spiritual connection that you make with yourself in order to reach
    and understand
your contribution to this space.
Sometimes daunting.
Perhaps unacknowledged
or left untouched.
Recognizing your Shine is
a revelation.
A decree.
An implication.
A right.
Mandatory behavior here.

The quote "In the service of someone else's shine," spoken by one of the veterans of realizing her shine, Claudine "Candy" Taaffe, was the realest thing that I had ever heard. As a prominent figure, both in and out of SOLHOT, her words checked the piercing eyes of the girls sitting around the circle in room 170 on September 28, 2009. While sitting in a dimly lit room due to the sun's setting, we, the girls, were captivated. As a spectator and listener, both of and in the circle, I was in awe. At that moment, I received confirmation that I was operating within the space that I needed to, in order to affect and be affected by change. It was then that I realized my spirit of servitude and humility was exactly what was due in the space. In order to continue to be a part of SOLHOT and be an active participant within SOLHOT, benefiting from the transaction of love, I needed to pay homage.

I sat and pondered about what humility means to me. What did it look like for me in relation to other people? What about what that looked like in relation to the other black girls around the circle? What about those girls who were not physically in the circle? What about those who were physically in the circle but were not mentally and spiritually in the circle? How was I supposed to honor them? I realized this honoring was integral and imperative to my existence in the space whether physically, mentally or spiritually.

I had a revelation. This honor and appreciation of someone else's shine was of upmost importance. It's like this: Everyone attached to SOLHOT has to have the understanding that you can only learn about yourself and others when you are willing to walk for someone else, or serve them, with all of your heart. Many people, including some of the girls in the circle, were and are offended when the subject of servitude is brought up, due to the individualistic and egotistical ideologies that outward settings impose upon us on a regular basis.

In short, a transformation needs to happen. Upon walking through the door of room 170 or the library at the middle school, an unveiling must happen. The second our feet hit the floor on the other side of the door, we shed the world's perception of who we are, their negative notions of what we represent, their antilove tactics and understandings. This is absolutely pertinent for the space that we are trying to create. However, what happens sometimes is that we forget how ingrained the world's ideas are in us, and we forget to shed those layers that are imposed upon us.

As a result, WE answer questions from the perspective of the outer world, which hurts each other…. WE aren't REALLY listening, thus creating pain, which is the way of the world…. WE place ourselves at the center of focus, which in turn erases someone, silences them, dehumanizes them. This type of operation, not pure or straight from OUR hearts, is dangerous. It is dangerous because it is not who we truly are on the inside. It is NOT who we were born to be, but instead who we have been raised to be. This notion is dangerous because if left unnoticed will be the destruction of our space, and inevitably our TRUE SELVES.... I make such a strong claim because it is that SERIOUS and important in the furthered love and respect for each other and ourselves. If there are no true selves of the black girls of the WORLD, or if those true selves do not have a space to be seen, heard, listened to, accepted, loved, spoken to, praised, honored, related to, and connected to, WHO WILL EVER KNOW TO THINK ABOUT US? Who will ever feel a heavy yearn to cater to and acknowledge all that a black girl is or has to offer? How will we conserve our lives and our truths? These pressing questions only further stress how important it is for those who have the spirit of black girls in their hearts to continue to nurture their love and appreciation of who WE are. It's pertinent for the black girls that do not know they have shine, or do not know how to maximize their shine. It is equally important for those aware of their shine to transfer and manifest such shine legacy.

In order to do this, you must first realize that "Humility IS EVERYTHING" (Taaffe, 2009). I would propose that if you have nothing else, understanding that you are forever to be indebted to someone else's shine, or in the "service of someone else's shine," presents the ability to ALWAYS have the right heart for this work... the work of saving black girls and saving yourself in the process. Instead of wondering whether or not your love was that love that "never made it to always" (Garner, 2009), you will receive confirmation that your love will carry for generations and generations and generations (Hansberry, 1969, p. 116). It will be that love for sure that has always been intended for always, even in its conception. It will be that love that is felt for always and transferred to those who do not know about such a phenomenon. Such a fluid and pure transfer of love and power will forever be ingrained into the lived experiences of black girls if we share. So, loving is living, and living is helping other girls to realize that they too want to live. Lorraine Hansberry said it best as she conceptualized the love for those outside of herself,

> I wish to live because life has within it that which is good, that which is beautiful and that which is love. Therefore, since I have known all of these things, I have found them to be reason enough and—I wish to live. Moreover, because this is so, I wish others to live for generations and generations and generations. (p. 100).

This mind-set has to be the central focus of our work and our lives in order for any type of positive relationship to conjure itself. Candy spoke exactly what needed to be said and heard that day. I thank her and pay homage to her for that.

It is my hope and prayer that all of us who intend on doing this work have this truth engrained in our hearts, not by the world because that is impossible, but by sheer impulse and concern for the space.

By the pull of the girls from their text messages.

By the feeling that the girls get from seeing us every Friday
whether we are late or on time.
By the loss of words when asked to describe what SOLHOT is.
By the joyful frustration of doing the work,
actually getting in the trenches.
By the thought that WE may not be here in years, or the next moment for that matter.

And by our own will to continue to live and fight for combating who they think we are VS. who WE say we are.

Being in service of someone else's shine should equate with joy of your own personal accomplishments. And further, it becomes our own accomplishments, because WE are US, anyway, right? Perhaps that is what it is supposed to be? Such a merger provides a platform for learning and humility to interact and transfer over time from one girl to the next. Just as love and power are fluid, or should be in our space, so should humility. It is SOLHOT that creates a space of respect, servitude, and adoration for the free expression of black girls. Humility is the gas or energy that fuels the power to be fluid in our space. In order for us to expect others to understand that "WE ARE HERE!," we must internalize and dwell in a place or state of mind contingent on deeply understanding that everyone is equally allowed to be present fully. We must be able to humbly accept their shine honorably.

Honoring Her Shine Is…
The affirmation of her gift.
The spiritual connection that you make with her in order to
   reach and understand
your contribution to this space.
Sometimes rough.
Perhaps unknown
or left untouched.
Recognizing her Shine is
a revelation.
A decree.
An implication.
A right.
Mandatory behavior here.

REFERENCES

Garner, P. (2009). Love that never made it to always. Educational Policy Studies: Advanced Graduate Seminar. University of Illinois.

Hansberry, L. (1969). *To be young, gifted, and black*. New York: Penguin.

Taaffe, C. (2009). In service of someone else's shine. Educational Policy Studies: Advanced Graduate Seminar. University of Illinois.

CHAPTER TWENTY-EIGHT

To the Visionary

Desiree McMillion

> SOLHOT is for all of us who… are less than celebrated on a daily basis, yet are committed to dropping our bags, spitting our rhymes, and healing our hurts.
> —Dr. Ruth Nicole Brown

Dear Dr. Brown,

By and large, praise shows that it can be an effective, positive, motivating force for those being praised as well as those giving praise. Research shows one should be extremely specific in the praise they are giving, therefore, I am and have been *specific* in praising you, Ruth Nicole Brown, the visionary of Saving Our Lives Hear Our Truths.

I am most positive you will be remembered for your work; especially within our community Champaign-Urbana, as well as other communities in which you have visited and will contact in the near future. God has created YOU, a human being equipped with so many talents; talents such as an academic scholar, writer, performer, intellectual, mentor, instructor, researcher, mother, professor, organizer, inventor, journalist, producer, friend, inspirational speaker, and an artist. In the words of the powerful soulful singer and song writer Erykah Badu, you are very "serious about your shit!"

Is it safe to say, when you created Saving Our Lives, Hear Our Truths— SOLHOT— you were not sure in which direction it would go, success or failure?

Well it appears to be a big success, one of your biggest hits, might I add; damn woman, you are an artist-scholar and you are doing it. For those of you reading this and are not aware of what SOLHOT is or isn't all about, SOLHOT is about black girlhood celebration and so much more. I would like to engage in further conversation regarding SOLHOT and what SOLHOT is all about, but I think introducing the readers, to Nikki B's book would be a better option.

In your book *Black Girlhood Celebration: Towards a Hip-Hop Feminist Pedagogy*, you discuss the importance of celebrating black girlhood and experiences. You present the challenges of providing a place or space for the girls to have a voice and to be heard. This speaks volumes for the reasons *Black Girlhood Celebration* is necessary.

One area in your book reminds me particularly of myself (back when); my voice is very dictatorial and I was always told to be quiet. In SOLHOT, we have a rule for grown folk: *You cannot tell the girls to be quiet.* This requires us to become comfortable with black girls' voices—whether we are loud or silent. Dr. Brown, you have always told us in class and in your writings, "It is not about black girls coming to voice. It is about listening to and loving black girls' unique articulation of voice and silence."

Nikki B, you have also introduced us black girls to so many African American women writers on whose shoulders we stand. Inspirational readings such as *To Be Young Gifted and Black* (1969), by Lorraine Hansberry; *The Fire Next Time* (1963), by James Baldwin; *Soldier* (2001), by June Jordan; *I Put a Spell on You— The Autobiography of Nina Simone* (1992); *Pedagogies of Crossing* (2005), by M. Jacqui Alexander; "The Lesson" in *Gorilla, My Love* (1992) and "On the Issue of Roles" in *The Black Woman: An Anthology* (2005), by Toni Cade Bambara; The Girlfriend's Train," by Nikky Finney in *The World Is Round* (2003); "A Litany for Survival," by Audre Lorde in *The Collected Poems of Audre Lorde* (1997); "Speaking for Ourselves: Feminisms in the African Diaspora" by Beverly Guy-Sheftall in *Decolonizing the Academy: African Diaspora Studies*, (2003); "On Our Own Terms: Ten Years of Radical Community Building With Sista II Sista,*"* by Nicole Burrowes, Morgan Cousins, Paula X. Rojas, and Ije Ude in *The Revolution Will Not Be Funded: Beyond the Non-Profit Industrial Complex* (2009); *This Bridge Called My Back: Writings by Radical Women of Color* (2002), by Cherrie L. Moraga and Gloria Anzaldúa; *Decolonizing the Academy: African Diaspora Studies* (2003), by Carole Boyce Davies; *Playing with Fire: Feminist Thought and Activism through Seven Lives in India* (2006), by Sangtin Writers and Richa Nagar; *Color of Violence: The Incite! Anthology* (2006) and *The Revolution Will Not Be Funded beyond the Non-Profit Industrial Complex* (2007), by Incite! Women of Color against Violence; to name a few. You encouraged us to read and analyze exemplary works, primarily by black women writers, to better understand how our writing may serve the communities of which we are a part and have a deep love for. As you stated this is methodology and with a library of such writings, how can we **not** want to live in the skin we are in? Again, I thank you.

Lorraine Hansberry states it best in her own words in her writings. In *To Be Young Gifted and Black*, she states: "I wish to live because life has within it that which is good, that which is beautiful, and that which is love. Therefore, since I have known all of these things, I have found them to be reason enough and—I wish to live. Moreover, because this is so, I wish others to live for generations and generations and generations and generations" (p. 100). You have encouraged us to live and to represent in a powerful way, "us," yes, black girls. You have proven to us time and time again, we can be black, angry, loving, bitter, emotively funny, intelligent, strong, spiritual, and, most of all, defiantly proud of ourselves, our heritage, us, black girls, black women.

You have stated time and time again, we should celebrate ourselves; we are finally becoming to know something profound about ourselves and who we are. Let's not hide behind the academy anymore—stand up and show who we really are and what we stand for. In your work you have laid the foundation of truth and set direction for a workable language, yes we are the revolution.

What I know for sure after being accompanied by your teaching, conversations, training, girlhood personality, and being educated under your direction, I am in the right place at this very moment. I am assured through your actions, your words, your grace, that I have a gift, I am special, I have a voice, and I should be heard. As mentioned in your book *Black Girlhood Celebration: Toward a Hip-Hop Feminist Pedagogy*: "black girls are more than what others have defined us to be." You have given me a valuable lesson, one in which I would translate into these words,

> Never undersell the importance of my own thoughts and ideas, allow myself to be used in a positive way in order to help shape a young black girl's life. I was once a loud young black girl, now I am a loud older black girl, who loves herself and the space she is in. I define me.

Your many accomplishments lead me to believe you have a calling and the Almighty God is not finished with you yet. Don't give up on your dreams Dr. Brown. Keep encouraging others to follow and share your goals and see this powerful thing we call "SOLHOT" to complete fruition. We can make it GLOBAL, I want to view this on a larger scale; yeah, so LARGE, we need to call in armored trucks to carry us. LUV 4 U AND ALL U DO 4 US, US BLACK GIRLS, BLACK WOMEN. CELEBRATION all around us!

Love, Desiree

REFERENCE

Brown, N. R. (2009). *Black girlhood celebration: Toward a Hip-Hop feminist pedagogy.* New York: Peter Lang.

CHAPTER TWENTY-NINE

Portrait of a Black Girl: Seeing Is NOT Believing

Claudine Taaffe

Introduction: Invitation to Inhale

During my engagement with the act of research, I have felt pressure to extract meaning, produce knowledge, share insight, and, all the while, remain sane. The pressure manifests a circular process as I find myself involved in an endless search of "that" book that will answer the questions roaming my mind concerning my life's work. I more often than not pass on article after article that fails to serve as testimony to my lived experiences of working with young women of color, while simultaneously trying to write about those experiences in such a way that does not impair the intense nature of what I learn about the lives of black girls. In the spirit of Audre Lorde (1984), at the risk of having what I speak be misunderstood or bruised, I suppose my doctoral process is an attempt to write that book of which I search. Also recognizing the complexity involved in that task, Alice Walker (1983) echoes,

> In my own work I write not only what I want to read—understanding fully and indelibly that if I don't do it no one else is so vitally interested, or capable of doing it to my satisfaction—I write all the things I should have been able to read. (p. 13)

Until the time I can aptly identify this research journey for those not knowledgeable of or invested in the lives of black girls, I will consider the direction of my mission in the space of educational research to be a visual, liberating, black girl–centered political project.

Saving Our Lives, Hear Our Truths (SOLHOT) creates the space for the experiences of middle school–aged black girls to be legitimized and documented, a vehicle for their voices to be heard without judgment, and a tool to reclaim the traditions of black women's activism and self-determination via visual ethnography. In this paper, I position myself as a part of SOLHOT as a research site and, more important, as a site of praxis where I conduct research in both of my roles of black woman researcher and black girl participant. Included in this paper is a discussion of the points of entry of an emerging SOLHOT approach to using visual ethnography, specifically photovoice, in the work of documenting the narratives of black girls. I intend to reflect upon the ways that qualitative inquiry has influenced how I think about my work with black girls; and I argue that although qualitative inquiry has allowed me an entry into a space of meaningful conversations with black girls by way of visual ethnography, it is also that same space with black girls that has forced me to reimagine my thinking about the endless possibilities for black girls to become producers of knowledge in their use of visual ethnography. I will offer a preliminary discussion about how visual ethnographic methods are transformed when being engaged by black girls and women involved in community-based, liberatory work.

The long-term goal of documenting this examination of my work with black girls is to produce a name for the unique and creative ways that we [black girls and black women] make visual ethnography work for us in the telling of our stories within the academy without needing to subscribe to the deficit-based ways that work with black girls in educational research can typically be attended to. Given that the examination of black girls utilizing visual research strategies is potentially breaking new methodological ground within qualitative inquiry and is ongoing, I am presenting this information with an intention of "writing to know." I am using my poetic voice interspersed within a traditional academic tone to help guide the reader in the understanding of the ways of working with black girls and photography being presented in this paper. I do this in agreement with Richardson (2000) who says that since "writing is a vital element of the research process, the more creative the writing, the more possibility to discover new aspects of our topic and our relationship to it" (p. 923). In taking this liberty, I realize that I am admitting to the engagement of poetry as "a risky business" (Cahnmann, 2003), and that is a risk I am willing to take. I think in poetic verse as it allows me to see best what I know, what I need to know, and what I might be able to share. Cahnmann concurs when she says, "Writing poetry and poetically inspired field notes allowed me to be honest with the limitations and assumptions in my own understanding in ways that might never have been questioned otherwise" (p. 34). My hope is that the intention of my work comes across to the reader so that the incredible insight that black girls have to offer to the world of qualitative educational research can be realized. I remain steadfast in my commitment to Ruth Behar's (1996) assertion that "when you write vulnerably, others respond vulnerably. A different set of problems and predicaments arise that would never surface in response to more detached writing" (p. 16).

Self-Snapshot: A Brown Girl's Testimony

Within academic spaces, I am an Afro-Latina activist-scholar hungry for opportunities to challenge and reimagine status-quo theoretical frameworks while simultaneously manifesting spaces of praxis, as called for by Paulo Freire (1970) who suggests that educational praxis should combine both action and reflection as part of the educational process. I believe in the power of young people and the courage of the most marginalized among us. I believe in attempting to speak all of the languages one needs to speak in order to connect with others in a genuine spirit of humanity. I believe contradictions show us where we hurt as well as from where we can learn how to love and be free. I believe that contradictions existing within educational research can either bind our hands with a tie of status quo participation as researchers or free us to slide our pens into engagement with writing styles not normally considered trustworthy but nevertheless proof that we were there.

I also believe that Saving Our Lives, Hear Our Truths is a verb, an adjective, a noun, a call to action, and an experience that surpasses every binary ever created about black girls and women. In SOLHOT we are always negotiating back and forth between being black girls and being black women depending on the moment at hand. When you truly "get it" about SOLHOT, you keep coming back in whatever ways you know how. And because there is no space in SOLHOT to lean back and serve only as a witness, when someone doesn't "get it" about SOLHOT, the girls will let them know— all the while still offering their love to black women freely.

In SOLHOT, when the girls dance I dance, too—well, sometimes. I was afraid to dance. I didn't want to. But I kept coming back because I wanted to be there—right there, being free with girls. So, I began taking photos of us dancing. The girls came to know me as Candy, "the girl with the camera." It was just that simple. I am not a professionally trained photographer. The only "literature" I engage with concerning photography is that my father has lived his life taking pictures and that's how he met my mother. On my own, I never considered my photos to be that complex or evidence of some gift or piece of art. It was only when I began to see the girls taking photos themselves that I came to believe in the power of photography and how incredible a talent the girls manifest when the camera is in their hands.

SOLHOT participant. (2009). *From me to you.* **Urbana, Illinois**

I am beyond humbled by what black girls have taught me about surviving and thriving and in the ways they have taught me. They have shown me how to keep love at the center of the survival of self when others who are not interested in your life story stack the odds against you. In giving themselves the permission to be free, they have also given me the permission to be free. In having no fear to grab hold of a camera, they have strengthened my courage to document in words what we do and how we do it. They have taught me a language through which to connect not only with them but to also reconnect with my father.

Only in my work with the girls have I come to understand how important it is to own this gift of photography, recognize its potential to disrupt paradigms and binaries, trust in it, and share it freely. Since this recognition, I find my photography of and with black girls to be about finding freedom, to serve as our way to let the world know we are here and we are looking at you looking at us. When asked about the choices I make when I take photographs in SOLHOT my answer is always very simple and short—I take photos of black girls and women as my way of saying, "I see you and I believe in your beauty, your brilliance, and your right to be here in all the ways you know how." I have come to realize that when black girls take photos, it is their way of contributing to the production of knowledge concerning the real questions that should be asked of black girls. In many ways, they become the creator of the methodology and no longer the object of it.

Taking photos in SOLHOT has been my way to dance, to be loud, to sing, to be beautiful, to be bold, to be courageous, and to be right here. It is my hope that through our collective photography the girls can see the reflections of just how incredibly beautiful and strong they are. I will be forever grateful for their permission to have me and a camera share in their world. They have given me a gift that is truly beyond measure!

SOLHOT: A Space of Freedom Dreams

SOLHOT participant. (2010). *We see you see us.* Urbana, Illinois

SOLHOT is an arts-based, afterschool program for black girls dedicated to creating a space for them to speak the stories of their lives out loud through text, photography, dance, and performance. The program typically operates out of a public middle school on a weekly basis in the afternoon. In the program, black girls from the community work in partnership with mostly college-aged female students in an engagement of an activity-based curriculum centered in themes that the girls deem most important.

In SOLHOT there is an explicit move away from the traditional mentoring type of programs available for young women of color. Rather than university students assuming the role of mentor to the girls, the goal is to create a space whereby both the girls and women feel loved, safe, and supported for who they are in SOLHOT, as well as the other communities of which they are a part. It is within those traditional mentoring programs that barriers are constructed that prevent the acknowledgment of black girls as legitimate producers of knowledge—a knowledge that plays a special part in the reclaiming of traditional black women's activism and an activism committed to the work of articulating the ways in which race, gender, and class intersect and, at times, keep us invisible.

SOLHOT participants. (2008). *Invisible Black Girls.* Urbana, Illinois

In contrast to the mentoring model, the women in SOLHOT are not presumed to know everything and the girls in SOLHOT are not presumed to know nothing. In the space of SOLHOT, our ways of being in the world are articulated, interrogated, and reimagined collectively.

For the women involved in SOLHOT, there is specific attention placed on facilitating a process of understanding what it means to be a black girl living under particular societal forces. To that end, in every session, there is priority placed on having discussions that move in the direction of topics that the young women deem the most relevant and important to them in that moment. In those interactions, the women in SOLHOT are afforded an opportunity to learn and understand what it means to be a black girl living in a predominantly white and conservative community. In those same interactions, the girls are exposed to dynamic discussions with black women about the ways in which our experiences intersect, regardless of the differences in age and life position.

In SOLHOT, on a weekly basis black girls and women work together during the afterschool hours getting to know each other and themselves, valuing where we come from and affirming who we are in this present moment. We exchange stories about what it means to be a daughter, a friend, a cousin, a mother, and a student— all the while remaining whole as black girls becoming black women and as black women re-remembering what it means to be a black girl. Once a week each girl is given a disposable camera to take images (both of people and symbols) that represent home, love, beauty, community, and what it looks like to be a black girl growing up. We also work with digital cameras and document those people, places, and things about school that bring us joy, pain, or need to be changed. We come together each week to discuss the photos we have taken and write about them using poetry, prose, and song. Along with documenting what we see going on around us, we have very honest conversations about how we would like things to change for the better. We discuss the changes we are willing to make as students and make suggestions about how people in decision-making positions can do things differently. Our photos and our words show the outside world what we believe in and embody what we would like to change so that the lives of black girls can be better understood and honored.

In SOLHOT our space is sacred. We live in it. We allow ourselves the vulnerability to feel our feelings inside of it. We love each other and we give each other attitude. We always tell the truth. We don't apologize. We question the rules and we ask the right questions. The womanhood of SOLHOT women is not dependent on the girls being "good" and the girlhood of SOLHOT girls is not dependent on the women being "all-knowing" adults. In our space, the learning and teaching is bidirectional— at all times we are teaching and learning with each other and creating new pedagogies, methodologies, and research findings. We love taking photos and understand more than most that we are documenting the ways in which we observe the world observing us. We are confident in sharing our narratives unapologetically with the world and if there is but one thing we are sure of, we are sure that in every space in which we stand at any given moment is the space in which we are the most proud of being a black girl! Inherent to the space of SOLHOT is a call for imagining a new world, for creating freedom dreams while also recognizing the caution spoken by activist-scholar Andrea Smith (2005),

> From our position of growing up in a patriarchal, colonial, and white supremacist world, we cannot fully imagine how a world that is not based on structures of oppression might operate. Nevertheless, we can be part of a collective, creative process that can bring us closer to a society not based on domination. (p. 191)

In that spirit, I continue to believe that the ability to imagine is freeing, necessary, and needs to be considered a political project when spaces with black girls are engaged as revolutionary movement work.

Just Because: Poetry Is a Better Tour Guide

It is reflexivity that Laurel Richardson (1997) urges researchers to take seriously when she states, "Reflexivity, I believe, will help us shape 'better' ethnographies and better lives for ourselves and those who teach us about their lives" (p. 107). I must continually affirm for myself that I can only make sense of the tensions embedded within my role in the research process as long as I, and those I work with, can be touched to the core of our beings so that we actually bleed out our truths rather than have our lived lives of contradictions suffocate us. I negotiate with myself on a daily basis that I will continue my work of being a servant-leader in the process of social change and scholarship by performing my commitment to my belief that only by being vulnerable in telling and sharing our stories, and reflecting on those stories, can we identify and, hopefully, resist and transcend the constructions that keep us suffocated in our own truth. And in that resistance and transcendence, by freeing ourselves, we can move closer to actually experiencing liberation as individuals who are a part of a larger collective that the academy must remain accountable to.

There are frozen moments that create space in-between my nagging doubts about my research with black girls. In those moments, I breathe deeply and write a spoken-word piece, what authors of qualitative methods call "poetic texts" that illustrates my frustration, confusion, anger, and obvious resistance to accepting my place in the world of research, young people, social change, and writing. These poetic texts are my stories through which I hope to convey my understanding (analysis) of the stories black girls share with me. And although my stories invite the reader to simply bear witness to an actual moment in time within SOLHOT, the stories themselves should also be considered an extraordinary disruption to the binary of static and fluid. The performance of these stories allows for the collective creation of meaning and identity. As argued by Gloria Anzaldúa (1999),

> My stories are "acts" encapsulated in time, "enacted" every time they are spoken aloud or read silently. I like to think of them as performances and not as inert and "dead" objects (as the aesthetics of Western culture think of art works). Instead, the work has an identity; it is a "who" or a "what" and contains the presences of persons, that is, incarnations of gods or ancestors or natural or cosmic powers. The work manifests the same needs as a person, it needs to be "fed," *la tengo que bañar y vestir.*[1] (p. 89)

It is my intention to use text and images to make the stories about black girls live beyond the researcher moments that I am afforded and privileged to be a part of. More often than not, the inscription of spoken word on my tongue is the only language supporting the lens through which I experience research within the academy. I have come to embrace the use of poetic text to assist me in speaking out

---

1 "It has to be fed and clothed."

loud, creating sense of boundaries in my lived experience that are never straight, and at the end of the day, these methods help me survive. Laurel Richardson (1997) argues, "Lived experience is lived in a body, and poetic representation can touch us where we live, in our bodies" (p. 143). Poetry creates a space for me to engage my fears as well as provide a comfortable point of entry into political and academic conversations about research, youth work, and social change. Still, despite the small comfort I experience in using poetry as my point of entry, I also acknowledge the vulnerability inherent in the risk. I hang on to the words of Ruth Behar (1996) when she argues, "Writing vulnerably takes as much skill, nuance, and willingness to follow through on all the ramifications of a complicated idea as does writing invulnerably and distantly" (p. 13). In the midst of my inner dialogue concerning qualitative inquiry, visual ethnography, and working with black girls, the following text manifested itself carefully and with trepidation:

qualitative inquiry
      allows me to know you by
      your name
      and not a number

ethnography
      invites me into your daily

documentary photography
      assists in the re-remembering
      of my moments with you

photovoice
      shifts the camera from my hand
      to yours

BUT
solhot takes all that
      to a cliff
squashing all binaries into
the red dirt of the black women
who did all this
before

she sayin' for real this time,

just because!

ain't no issues to be documented here
for policy makers to ignore
       beneath a mask of examination

i AM the issue
       me
my name
my blackness
my hair
my hips
my words
my breasts
and the pitch of my voice

your interview
       still felt
       like an investigated hug

your documented photo
       caught my bad side

and the voice captured
       in photo captions
       was not HOW i said, WHAT i said

SO
the time has come
to name names
to give life
to this method and rhyme

this black girl's life story
       is about to rock another
           methodological moment

stay tuned.
—Taaffe, 2010

Qualitative Inquiry: Seeing Black Girls

When I begin to imagine engaging revolutionary practices with young people, particularly with young women of color, I find myself giving more thought to the possibilities that exist within out-of-school programs rather than within American classrooms. While public education in America is typically characterized as a site for academic achievement and citizenship development, classrooms in the United States have also served as sites of oppression and resistance for young people from marginalized communities. Although students spend less time in out-of-school programs as compared to the classroom, afterschool programs offer young people more opportunities for exercising their criticality, creativity, and self-expression. Activist-scholars Ginwright, Noguera, and Cammarota (2006) describe the process best:

> We suggest a Freirian perspective of young people, one that posits their capacity to produce knowledge to transform their world. In this regard, youth should be recognized as subjects of a knowledge production that underpins their agency for personal and social transformation. (p. xix)

Given the absence in out-of-school programs of the standards-based curricula that exists in schools, young people are less constrained in their innate ability to produce knowledge that is not only meaningful to them but also of importance in reimaging the methodological approaches currently used in conducting research typically upon the backs of youth. Out-of-school programs that are developed with the goals of liberation, self-expression, and testimony in mind also provide opportunities for young people to position themselves within a sociopolitical, real-world context.

> *qualitative inquiry*
> *allows me to know you by*
> *your name*
> *and not a number*
> —Taaffe, 2010

Qualitative inquiry remains an often-utilized methodology in working with young people and other marginalized groups, yet it often remains nested in debates concerning validity and its potential for offering scientific basis for truth. Qualitative inquiry finds its tradition in anthropology and sociology. In working with members of marginalized groups, a more specific method to benefit educational research with youth is critical qualitative methodology. It's important that the methods engaged in using qualitative methodology are methods whose logic is embedded in the overall methodology. The more traditional characteristics of qualitative research are that the research has a natural setting, it is descriptive, the researcher is more concerned with process as opposed to outcomes, and overall meaning is of great concern to those involved in the research process (Bogdan & Biklen, 2003). The use of qualitative inquiry allows the researcher to have a more intimate relationship within the setting of the research site and the research participants.

In traditional research projects with young people, some tales take center stage, while other stories remain to exist on what seem to be the margins. Those stories situated at center stage, more often than not, become considered "the norm" and other stories that might differ are considered a "departure from the norm." Thereupon, standards often arise based on this norm, and individual tales that differ, or depart from that norm, are devalued and subordinated (Delgado-Bernal, 2002). In the field of research concerning black girls, what creates the story at the center is more often than not the story of white, middle-class girls. As a consequence, the behaviors of black girls are compared to standards created for white girls. The product of this kind of thinking is that behaviors of black girls are then labeled as deficient, thereby divorcing the choices of black girls from the structural issues of racism, sexism, patriarchy, and heterosexism at play in their lives. It is imperative that researchers truly practice the values of a diverse society by insisting on the inclusion of black girl narratives in the literature about girlhood, those stories concerning the process by which black girls come to know, perform, and interrogate their reality. Of the stories that exist within research, a story most becomes alive when told to another person. While the personal narratives lifted up in this space of praxis offer a description of the lens through which black girls' view and attempt to understand the different worlds they inhabit, they also provide researchers an opportunity to deconstruct the deficit model used to define and structure black girlhood. However, I caution that these voices should not be considered the absolute measure by which scholars and practitioners should think about all African American young women. Their stories are just a mere portion of the complex existence that black girls (and women) perform and deconstruct in a society entrenched in a patriarchal, capitalistic, heterosexist, and racist legacy.

What positions SOLHOT as unique is the creation of a space for the engagement of methods that allow for black girls to tell the stories of their own lives through print and visual images. As a researcher I am given the responsibility of documenting those stories and carrying their messages inside the walls of the academy. At the center of a research project is often a story. At the core of my research project are photographs that exist within a tradition of visual ethnography yet demanding the construction of new ways to be seen and considered valid evidence of how black girls investigate their own lived lives.

ethnography
invites me into your daily

documentary photography
assists in the re-remembering
of my moments with you
—Taaffe, 2010

The use of visual methods has historically played a position within the field of qualitative inquiry, although the intentions for its use have been varied. Overall, there are ordinarily two intentions behind the use of visual methods in qualitative inquiry. One, with regard to the creation of images by the researcher for the purpose of documentation, and two, the collection of images for the purpose of analysis (Banks, 2007). These two uses are not separate from each other and often work in conjunction in a researcher's attempt at extracting meaning from the population they are engaging. In either case, photos are often used to derive meaning whether that meaning results from the use of photographs in interviews (called photo elicitation) (Banks, 2007) or the creation of images for participants to better elaborate on their lived lives. And although through the use of photographs for the purpose of documentation, for example, there still exist issues of interpretation given that although photographs may capture a moment in time, it is a moment in time that occurred within a particular context, ideological moment, and/ or include participants who bring to the photo (however invisible it might be) their own distinct narratives. John Collier Jr. remains a pioneer in the usage of photography in anthropological research and credited with being concerned with the vitality of the groups he was engaging with despite the oppressive conditions under which they existed (Pink, 2007).

The use of photography for the investigation of social phenomenon dates back to the 1930s (Banks, 2007), and as early as photography has been used in social science research, there has been, and continues to be, issues concerning representation (the factors apparent—or not—in their decision of what to photograph), the negative impact on the researcher-participant relationship in taking photos in a voyeuristic manner and of the multiple interpretations that can exist surrounding one photo, for example, which counts as valid? This issue can be further exasperated in the use of photography with young people particularly if the research design may be one in which deficit-based assumptions exist of the youth involved in the project. If a researcher enters a space already consciously or unconsciously having negative ideas concerning the potential of the youth involved to construct critical opinions of the world in which they inhabit, then that same researcher would attach no worthwhile meaning to photographs taken, created, or given text to by the youth.

your interview
still felt
like an investigated hug

your documented photo
caught my bad side

and the voice captured
in captions
was not how i said, what i said
—Taaffe, 2010

With the rise in the use of digital cameras (and disposable cameras as well), the field of qualitative research saw the emergence of the photovoice method for visual ethnography. As defined by Wang and Burris (1997), photovoice is:

a process by which people can identify, represent, and enhance their community through a specific photographic technique. It entrusts the cameras to the hands of people to enable them to act as recorders, and potential catalysts for change in their own communities. (p. 369)

Photovoice allows for research participants to acquire an enormous amount of agency in being the creators of the images and not the subjects. Normally, the use of photovoice is based upon three main goals: (1) to enable people to record and reflect their community's strengths and concerns, (2) to promote critical dialogue and knowledge about important community issues through large and small group discussion of photographs, and (3) to reach policymakers (Wang & Burris, p. 370).

Photovoice serves as an appropriate site of entry for working with black girls as the method allows for the girls to determine what about their lived lives will be examined and the ways in which the images are discussed. A disruption that working with black girls in SOLHOT offers to the space of photovoice is that before the goal of reaching policymakers concerning the issues of the environment in which black girls live, the first priority is placed on how the girls themselves are viewed. Whereas, photovoice is typically engaged as a tool of civic engagement—a method for empowering youth to become more invested in the issues of the community in which they live—in SOLHOT we are focused first on the way we see you seeing us.

As with any research method, potentials and limitations of the method itself exist. In working with youth populations, working with visual images requires attention to issues of consent, funding (as digital cameras remain expensive to buy in bulk), and boundaries of space (the inability of young people to take digital cameras home with them). However, some issues of funding can be attended to with limited purchases of disposable cameras that the youth can take home (in which the creation of more spaces to photograph is created). Also, the potential for a rise in youth engagement with the method results as well from the rise in use by them of camera phones.

The engagement of visual methods by black girls and women remains a field rich of liberatory potential, thereby freeing their narratives from the grips of deficit-based research. In many ways, photographs taken by a black girl is her way of talking back with a potential for being heard above her so-called loudness.

> so the time has come
> to name names
> to give life
> to this method and rhyme
>
> this black girl's life story
> is about to rock another methodological moment
> —Taaffe, 2010

REFERENCES

Anzaldúa, G. (1999). *Borderlands: The new mestiza=La frontera* (2nd ed.). San Francisco: Aunt Lute.

Banks, M. (2007). *Using visual data in qualitative research.* Los Angeles: Sage.

Behar, R. (1996). *The vulnerable observer: Anthropology that breaks your heart.* Boston: Beacon.

Bogdan, R. C., & Biklen, S. K. (2003). *Qualitative research for education: An introduction to theory and methods.* Boston: Allyn & Bacon.

Cahnmann, M. (2003). The craft, practice, and possibility of poetry in educational research. *Educational Researcher, 32*(3), 29–36.

Delgado-Bernal, D. (2002). Critical race theory, Latino critical theory, and critical race-gendered epistemologies: Recognizing students of color as holders and creators of knowledge. *Qualitative Inquiry, 8*(1), 105–126.

Freire, P. (1970). *Pedagogy of the oppressed.* New York: Herder & Herder.

Ginwright, S., Noguera, P., & Cammarota, J. (Eds.). (2006). *Beyond resistance: Youth activism and community change.* New York: Routledge.

Lorde, A. (1984). *Sister outsider.* Trumansburg, NY: Crossing.

Pink, S. (2007). *Doing visual ethnography: Images, media and representation in research.* London: Sage.

Richardson, L. (2000). Writing: A method of inquiry. In N. Denzin & Y. S. Lincoln (Eds.), *Handbook of qualitative research* (2nd ed., pp. 923–948). London: Sage.

Richardson, L. (1997). *Fields of play (constructing an academic life).* New Brunswick, NJ: Rutgers University Press.

Smith, A. (2005). *Conquest: Sexual violence and American Indian genocide.* Cambridge, MA: South End.

Walker, A. (1983). *In search of our mothers' gardens.* New York: Harcourt Brace Jovanovich.

Wang, C., & Burris, M. A. (1997). Photovoice: Concept, methodology, and use for Participatory Needs Assessment. *Health Education & Behavior, 24*(3), 369–387.

CONTRIBUTORS

Christina Armstrong is a daughter and granddaughter of educators. She received her master's degree in Educational Policy and Management from Harvard University. As a reflection of her desire to see healthier people and communities, she is invested in love, justice, and the arts.

Sesali Bowen is a writer, trainer, and advocate for black girls everywhere. A Chicago native, she has combined her firsthand experience as an "around the way girl" with a black feminist reproductive justice framework to inform, share, and build knowledge about black girls. She is currently finishing her bachelor's in Women's and Gender Studies at DePaul University and facilitating a black girl–centered program at a school on Chicago's South Side, where she currently resides.

Ruth Nicole Brown is Assistant Professor of Gender and Women's Studies and Education Policy, Organization and Leadership at the University of Illinois Urbana-Champaign. Her first book, *Black Girlhood Celebration: Toward a Hip-hop Feminist Pedagogy* (Peter Lang, 2008), demonstrated how liberal assumptive frameworks of culture and society have contradictory implications for the type and quality of value assigned to black girlhood. She is an artist-scholar whose public scholarship aims to articulate imaginative narratives and alternative visions that make for a better world.

J. Sean Callahan is a teaching assistant and a doctoral candidate in the Department of Educational Psychology at the University of Georgia Athens. His research interests include Hip-Hop, conjure-ritual theory, and designing culturally responsive curriculum for culturally diverse gifted learners.

Durell Maurice Callier is a doctoral student in the Department of Education Policy, Organization and Leadership at the University of Illinois Urbana-Champaign. His current research interests include understanding the ways in which performance can be utilized pedagogically and as a political-organizing tool. An artist-scholar, Durell actively seeks to create scholarship that is deeply personal, politically spiritual, intrinsically accountable, and ultimately artistic!

Christina Carney is a doctoral student in the Ethnic Studies Department at the University of California at San Diego. She received her BA in Interdisciplinary Studies at the University of Illinois with a minor in African-American Studies and Gender & Women's Studies. Her dissertation examines queer space and the political discourses involved in its formation and construction.

DaYanna Crider is an eleven-year-old from Rantoul, Illinois.

Sheri Davis-Faulkner is a doctoral candidate in American Studies at Emory University. As a Critical Race Feminist scholar, her work explores body narratives in popular media and resistance pedagogies in literature. Camp Carrot Seed is a part of her field research for her dissertation.

Lena Foote is a graduate of the University of Illinois Urbana-Champaign and was a Ronald E. McNair scholar. She majored in Media and Communication Studies.

Porshe Garner is a doctoral student at the University of Illinois Urbana-Champaign in the Department of Education Policy, Organizational Leadership. She received her Bachelor's of Science in Psychology from the University of Illinois. Currently her research focuses on black girl's usage and interpretation of Hip-Hop to tell stories about their lives.

Grenita Hall is a mother, partner, daughter, dancer, artist, and doctoral candidate in the Department of Kinesiology at the University of Illinois Urbana-Champaign with an emphasis on Cultural, Pedagogical, and Interpretive Kinesiology. Her research interests include black secular dance, performance studies, and gender.

Dominique C. Hill is a poet, dancer, scholar, and doctoral student at the University of Illinois Urbana-Champaign in the Department of Education Policy, Organization and Leadership. She embodies a passion to dismantle binaries and create more fluid spaces for understanding black women and girls. She utilizes dance and poetry to challenge identity norms, historical tropes, and narrow conceptions of black femininity, education, and the body.

Zenzele Isoke is Assistant Professor of Gender, Women, and Sexuality Studies at the University of Minnesota. Her first book, *Urban Black Women and the Politics of Resistance* (Palgrave-Macmillan Press, 2012), examines both the practical and discursive roles that black women activists play in Hip-Hop politics, Black LGBTQ politics, and other contemporary social movements in Newark, New Jersey. Her second book project is tentatively titled, *Unheard Voices at the Bottom of Empire* and examines African Arab women and Hip-Hop culture in Dubai, UAE.

Adilia E. E. James is a PhD candidate at the University of Chicago in the Department of Sociology. She received her MA in Educational Policy Studies from the University of Illinois. Her research interests include gender and sexuality theories, family studies, and labor and employment.

Tanya Kozlowski is a doctoral student in the Department of Education Policy, Organization and Leadership at the University of Illinois Urbana-Champaign. A Chicana lesbian scholar, activist, poet, partner, and teacher, her research interests include identity formations, women of color feminisms, and education.

Chamara Jewel Kwakye is a daughter, writer, story listener, storyteller, autoethnographer, performer, and currently a Chancellor's Postdoctoral Fellow at the University of Illinois in the Department of African American Studies. Her research interests include life histories of black women and historic and contemporary educational policy. Through her research, she emphasizes the relationships among race, gender, sexuality, the African diaspora, and education by asking not only how these things reframe African American & Women's Studies but also what insights Women's Studies and African American Studies might bring to transnational and educational critique in particular.

Shaunita Levison is a doctoral candidate in the Department of Education Policy, Organization and Leadership at the University of Illinois Urbana-Champaign.

Sheri K. Lewis is a native of Chicago's South Side and is pursuing her doctoral degree in the Department of Education Policy, Organization and Leadership at the University of Illinois Urbana-Champaign. Her dissertation will focus on black girlhood as practiced in Saving Our Lives Hear Our Truths (SOLHOT). She has lobbied in Washington, D.C., for reproductive rights. She is passionate about black girlhood, reproductive justice, and pedagogies of love.

Taylor-Imani A. Linear is a master's student at the University of Illinois Urbana-Champaign in the Department of Education Policy, Organization and Leadership. She is a native of south suburban Chicago. Her research interests include black youth culture and history.

Precious McClendon is a graduate of the University of Illinois Urbana-Champaign and majored in Gender & Women's Studies. She is a Hip-Hop feminist playwright and is currently living and working in Chicago, Illinois.

Desiree "Dee" McMillion, EdM, is a doctoral student at the University of Illinois Urbana-Champaign in Education Policy, Organization and Leadership. Her research interests include black mother–daughter relationships, performance, and community-based education.

Porsha Olayiwola is a graduate of the University of Illinois. She is a poet extraordinaire, currently living in Boston, Massachusetts.

Jessica L. Robinson is a lover and fighter from the Midwest. Her current research interests include cultural politics, reproductive justice, girls' studies, and community organizing. She is currently a reproductive justice community worker and master's student of sociology at DePaul University in Chicago, Illinois.

Blair Ebony Smith is a doctoral student in the Department of Cultural Foundations of Education at Syracuse University and blog writer for the Student Hip-Hop Organization at the College of William and Mary. As a graduate scholar, she is interested in the intersections of Hip-Hop culture, identity, schooling, and social justice.

Kristen Chanel Smith is a doctoral student in the Department of Education Policy, Organization and Leadership at the University of Illinois Urbana-Champaign. She is originally from Baton Rouge, Louisiana, and has worked with the Congressional Black Caucus Foundation.

Claudine "Candy" Taaffe is a doctoral student at the University of Illinois Urbana-Champaign in the Department of Education Policy, Organization and Leadership. Her research interests include visual methodology, youth organizing, and African American girlhood. Her dissertation is a two-year long visual ethnography of middle school–aged African American girls, who use photography to speak back to the deficit-fueled images of them in schools and popular culture.

Darlene Vinicky is a graduate of the University of Illinois Urbana-Champaign. She enjoys learning about gender and sexuality and is very interested in food justice.

Loy A. Webb obtained her BA in Political Science from the University of Illinois and is currently a JD candidate at the John Marshall Law School. Her favorite quote is "Until the lion gets her own historian, the tale of the hunt will be told by the hunter, not the hunted." Her role as a playwright is to be a lion historian and tell the untold stories of black women.

Irene Zavarsky, PhD, is a self-employed trainer and theater pedagogue in Vienna, Austria. A political scientist by training, her research foci include film, media, and representations.

Critical Pedagogical Perspectives

Greg S. Goodman, *General Editor*

Educational Psychology: Critical Pedagogical Perspectives is a series of relevant and dynamic works by scholars and practitioners of critical pedagogy, critical constructivism, and educational psychology. Reflecting a multitude of social, political, and intellectual developments prompted by the mentor Paulo Freire, books in the series enliven the educator's process with theory and practice that promote personal agency, social justice, and academic achievement. Often countering the dominant discourse with provocative and yet practical alternatives, *Educational Psychology: Critical Pedagogical Perspectives* speaks to educators on the forefront of social change and those who champion social justice.

For further information about the series and submitting manuscripts, please contact:

Dr. Greg S. Goodman
Department of Education
Clarion University
Clarion, Pennsylvania
ggoodman@clarion.edu

To order other books in this series, please contact our Customer Service Department at:

(800) 770-LANG (within the U.S.)
(212) 647-7706 (outside the U.S.)
(212) 647-7707 FAX

Or browse online by series at:

www.peterlang.com